1992

Queens, Empresses, Grand Duchesses and Regents

Also by Olga S. Opfell

The Lady Laureates:
Women Who Have Won the Nobel Prize
(Scarecrow Press, 1978; 1986)

The King James Bible Translators
(McFarland, 1982)

Queens, Empresses, Grand Duchesses and Regents

Women Rulers of Europe, A.D. 1328–1989

Olga S. Opfell

McFarland & Company, Inc., Publishers
Jefferson, North Carolina, and London

British Library Cataloguing-in-Publication data available

Library of Congress Cataloguing-in-Publication Data

Opfell, Olga S.
 Queens, empresses, grand duchesses and regents.

 Bibliography: p. 261.
 Includes index.
 1. Europe—Empresses—Biography. 2. Europe—Queens—
Biography. 3. Europe—Princes and princesses—Biogra-
phy. 4. Regents—Europe—Biography. I. Title.
D107.064 1989   920.72′094 [B]   88-43484

ISBN 0-89950-385-3 (lib. bdg. : 50# alk. paper)

Printed in the United States of America.

McFarland & Company, Inc., Publishers
 Box 611, Jefferson, North Carolina 28640

In memory of Johanne,
who took great pleasure
in queens

Contents

Contents

Foreword

In the long gallery of queens and empresses, most acquired their titles because they married kings or emperors. But several, thanks to inheritance or an occasional coup d'etat, were or are actual sitting monarchs, famous and obscure. History is also filled with the figures of women regents, so appointed when kings died and left underage heirs. Many of these queen consorts, however, were manipulated by ministers of state and advisers.

Five regents have been included here because they wielded real power. Four were the mothers of kings or queens; a fifth, unmarried, was the half sister as well as the sister of boy co-czars. The medieval Margrethe proved the strongest of all. Queen consort in Norway, the mother of a short-lived king of Denmark and Norway, she was regent in both countries, and later, by conquest, "sovereign lady" of Sweden. Although she was never crowned Queen of Denmark, her 20th century counterpart chose to call herself Margrethe II.

This book is offered as a guide to the main events in 39 royal lives, the achievements and failures, and the women's impacts on their times. It seemed fitting to begin with the 14th century, which heralded the modern era and boasted five women sovereigns. The 15th century had five, the 16th century six, the 17th century three, the 18th century eight, and the 19th century five. The 20th century has had seven, including two grand duchesses.

Over the years, as the chapters will show, their roles have moved from autocrats to constitutional monarchs without the power to make policy or law. Yet, as Robert K. Massie says, modern queens, like modern kings, have "risen above the hurly-burly of daily politics and ascended into the shimmering sphere of symbolism and national spirit." Royalists still believe—in Cecil Beaton's words—that "the presence of the purple is indispensable as the insignia of the nation."

All the kingdoms, empires, and grand duchies represented here are European. (To be sure, colonial possessions extended worldwide, and Russia laid claim to Asian territories.) Some of the geographical names, however, have disappeared from modern maps. Livonia bordered on the Baltic in parts of what are now Latvia, Lithuania, and Estonia. Courland (Kurland) was

situated in the present western Latvia, touching on the Baltic and the Gulf of
Riga. Holstein-Gottorp was a "patchwork" duchy in northern Germany and
southern Denmark. The Kingdom of Navarre in 1328, the date of Juana II's accession, and until 1512, when Ferdinand of Aragon conquered it and sent the
d'Albret dynasty fleeing, occupied the present Spanish province of Navarre
and a smaller region on the northern approaches to the pass of Roncevalles,
now part of the French department of Pyrenées-Atlantique. In 1530 that region
(Basse Navarre or Tierra de Allién Puertos or Ultrapuertos) was returned to
the d'Albrets, making two kingdoms; Spanish Navarre, as a Castilian vice-
royalty, kept its own laws and privileges. When a d'Albret heir became King
Henri IV of France in 1689, his tiny kingdom passed to the French crown.

At the cost of strict consistency, native spellings have been followed except
in cases where the anglicized versions of names are all too familiar. Thus,
Giovanna and Juana are used in preference to Joan or Joanna, João instead
of John, but Ferdinand and Isabella for Fernando and Isabel (hence the 19th
century Isabella II), Elizabeth for the Russian Elizaveta, Catherine for
Ekaterina, Charles XII for Karl XII. Because the Holy Roman Emperor Charles
V was known by various names and numerals in the countries he ruled, it
seemed preferable to stay with plain Charles.

Titles have been anglicized—e.g., the Duke of Alençon rather than duc
d'Alençon. Further it should be noted that although Isabella was queen regnant in Castile, she was queen consort in Aragon. Ferdinand however, was co-
sovereign in Castile. Their daughter Juana inherited only the throne of Castile. Maria Theresa was the Holy Roman Empress consort, but she ruled over
Austria as archduchess and over Hungary and Bohemia as queen. Also, the
titles of English women rulers have changed from Mary I, Queen of England
and Ireland, to Elizabeth II, Queen of Great Britain and Northern Ireland.

Because of the difference in the Julian (old style) and Gregorian (new style)
calendars, dates in reference books vary by ten days. Where known with certainty, the new style has been followed. Thus Elizabeth Petrovna's death is
reported as occurring in early January 1762, rather than in late December 1761,
as given in some sources. Reigns have ended with death or abdication. Since
the two mad queens, Juana of Castile and Maria I of Portugal, never abdicated,
they were technically queens regnant until they died. (A similar situation ex-
isted with King George III of Great Britain.)

The material derives from encyclopedias, area guides, travel books, general
histories, information packets from embassies and consulates, *Burke's Royal
Families of the World, Facts on File*, and the books listed in the bibliography.
Travel in England, Austria, Germany, and Denmark also made possible the
gathering of certain facts.

I am indebted to various reference librarians, history professors, and
museum and institute directors in the United States and Europe, who kindly
responded to my inquiries. But above all I owe gratitude to my husband, John

B. Opfell, for his constant help, advice, and encouragement; to Ruth Loring for reviewing the manuscript and making critical suggestions; and to Edward Hee, Asger Munksgaard, Jenny Erickson, and Ole Rabendorf for providing valuable information.

Olga S. Opfell
Torrance, California

Juana II
Queen of Navarre, 1328–1349

A granddaughter of Juana I, the first Queen of Navarre in her own right, Juana II was thoroughly French by heritage and inclination. Altogether she spent only six years in her small kingdom that straddled the Pyrenees. Basse Navarre, on the other side of the mountains, had been an integral part of the Kingdom of Navarre since the 10th century.

Navarre had been ruled by Frenchmen since 1234, when Thibaud, Count of Champagne, had assumed the crown bequeathed to him by his uncle, Sancho VII, and taken the name of Teobaldo I. The marriage of Teobaldo's granddaughter Juana I to Philip IV (the Fair) in 1294 began a succession of French kings in Navarre, for Philip assumed co-sovereignty with his wife. When Juana I died in 1305, their eldest son Louis inherited her property and styled himself King Luis of Navarre and Count Palatine of Champagne and Brie.

Juana II received the name Jeanne at her birth in 1310 to Louis and his wife, Marguerite of Burgundy. During her earliest childhood, her parents lived at the French court. There tragedy struck in 1314 when Philip, convinced that the purity of the Capetian monarchy was at stake, angrily ordered the arrest of his three daughters-in-law: Marguerite, Louis's wife; Blanche, wife of Charles, Count of La Marche; and Jeanne, wife of Philip, Count of Poitiers. Marguerite and Blanche were accused of committing adultery with two gentlemen-in-waiting, the brothers Philip and Gautier d'Aulnay; Jeanne of Poitiers was charged with knowing about the affairs but failing to reveal them. Court gossip had it that the first reports of the trysts may have come from Philip the Fair's own daughter, Isabelle, wife of Edward II of England.

As the two knights were put to death, Marguerite and Blanche were placed in solitary confinement in the Chateau Gaillard, Richard the Lionhearted's impregnable fortress. Fortunately for Philip of Poitiers, the *Parlement* proclaimed his wife's innocence, and she went free.

Shortly afterward, King Philip IV died in a hunting accident and was succeeded by Jeanne's father, Louis. Since his wife sat in prison, convicted of adultery, their daughter's legitimacy came into question. In the hope of producing a son, Louis decided to marry the beautiful Clemence, daughter of the King of Hungary. Not wishing to go through long, complicated negotiations with the church for dissolution of his marriage, he chose a quick way out, ordering Marguerite smothered between two mattresses. (His sister-in-law Blanche enjoyed a better fate. After some years she left prison and took the veil at the Abbey of Maubuisson.) So Louis obtained his Hungarian bride. But in the summer of 1316, after only 18 months on the French throne, where he had earned the sobriquet "the Stubborn," he died of pneumonia following a taxing game of indoor tennis and overindulgence in iced wine. The son Clemence bore him posthumously died five days after birth.

Since her mother's disgrace, Jeanne had lived with her grandmother, Duchess Anne of Burgundy, and her uncle, Duke Eude IV of Burgundy. Many saw the little girl as rightful heiress to the crowns of France and Navarre and the counties of Champagne and Brie.

Immediately upon her father's death, her uncle Philip of Poitiers assumed the regency and assembled a council of barons, which approved his accession after considering part of a centuries-old set of laws of the Salian Franks. The original Salic law said nothing about the inheritance of kingdoms, simply that Salic land could not be inherited by a woman. But the barons gave the law a special interpretation: "Lilies do not spin wool. France is too noble a kingdom to be entrusted to a woman." From this time the Salic law came to mean that a woman could not inherit royal authority.

Secure in his power, Philip V was crowned at Rheims, along with his wife. But the angry barons of Champagne were not prepared to see Jeanne lose Champagne, Brie, and Navarre as well as the French crown. They staged a feudal revolt, which the new king quickly put down. Nonetheless, Philip V made some concessions to them and then married his daughter to Jeanne's uncle, Duke Eude; Jeanne was granted a rich dowry and promised to her cousin, Philip of Evreux. (In the Middle Ages princesses were often betrothed in early childhood. The pledge was given solemn character by a "marriage of the future ceremony" in church when the boy and girl, hands linked, were blessed. Consummation of the marriage usually took place when the bride reached 14.)

Not to be outdone in making concessions, Jeanne's advisers encouraged her to renounce her rights to Champagne and Brie in return for an annual rent and a generous cash payment. Her rights to Navarre she would not surrender. Philip, however, considered he held them already, but during his brief, six-year reign he never visited the country. On his death, Jeanne's second uncle took the French throne as Charles IV and declared himself King of Navarre.

At this stage Jeanne's supporters reclaimed Champagne and Brie for her and refused to relinquish those fiefs until another agreement could be worked out, raising the annual rent and cash payment considerably. (Jeanne made her final renunciation of the counties in 1335.) In Navarre meanwhile, the Cortes,

6

Jeanne de France, fille de Louis x.

elle n'a pas été reconnue Reine de Navarre.

Juana II, Queen of Navarre. Courtesy Bibliothèque Nationale, Paris.

resenting Charles, refused to send a delegation to Toulouse to observe his swearing in. Nonetheless, Charles the Bald, as the Pamplonese derisively called him, considered himself king there.

When this last Capetian king died in 1328 without male issue, the barons again brought forward the Salic law, refusing to consider Jeanne, now a beautiful young matron of 17. Among the claimants to the throne were two nephews of Philip the Fair, the sons of his brother and half brother. The first was Philip of Valois, the second Philip of Evreux, Jeanne's husband. Favor fell on Philip of Valois, who took the French throne as Philip VI.

Pointing out that Navarre did not observe the Salic law, the Cortes indignantly rejected him as ruler, demanding the daughter of the late King Luis instead. That same year it acclaimed Jeanne as Juana II, Queen of Navarre.

She and Philip of Evreux came to Pamplona to uphold the *fueros*, the compilation of Navarrese rights and privileges. The Cortes now permitted Philip (Felipe) to be crowned with his wife, but made both of them promise to step down once their heir reached age 21. The new king and queen succeeded to a limited monarchy with the nobility as the most visible class. The clergy also exerted considerable power, and Juana and Philip found it prudent to maintain good relations with the Bishop of Pamplona.

Before the end of the 13th century, a *fuero general* had been set down for the country. To update it, Philip of Evreux supported a complete revision, but he succeeded only in adding some modest amendments, a few dealing with the activities and lending practices of Jews and Muslims. Since generally Navarre had been tolerant of its minority groups, Juana and Philip were aghast when early in their reign a wave of anti–Semitism broke out. It owed more to resentment against Jewish moneylenders than to any other cause. Hastily the young rulers moved against the rebellion and ordered its leaders punished.

Because Philip of Evreux held great fiefs in Normandy, he and Juana stayed in Navarre for only five years, returning to France and leaving their kingdom to a succession of able governors. At Evreux they reared eight children: three sons – Charles, Philip, and Louis, and five daughters – Inez, Jeanne (1), Jeanne (2), Maria, and Blanche, who later wed Philip VI.

Because of an efficient tax collection system in Navarre, Juana and Philip lived well. In addition, the nobles and clergy, exempt from taxation, made private donations to the sovereigns for war and weddings.

Soon war was on the horizon. The conflict would be known in history as the Hundred Years War. In 1329, as Duke of Aquitaine, Edward III of England had paid homage to Philip VI, but 11 years later he claimed the French throne as his rightful inheritance from his mother, Isabelle, who reputedly had accused her sisters-in-law of adultery years before. Edward's design on the throne was mostly an excuse to legitimize a dispute over the Flemish wool trade, French support of the Scots against the English, and Channel raiding of English shipping and ports. Skirmishing had begun in 1337.

As the war between the French and English began with a series of disjointed campaigns, Philip of Evreux gave what help he could to his cousin, Philip VI. While her husband was absent, Juana administered their French domains of Evreux, Angoulême, and Longueville. Royal governors still ruled Navarre.

Before long, Alfonso XI of Castile asked the King of Navarre for help in fighting the Muslims and retiring them from Andalusia; Philip of Evreux collected money and troops and marched to Algeciras, where his soldiers performed valiantly. But at Jerez de la Frontera he fell ill and died in 1343. Since the heir, Charles, was only 11, Juana continued as the absentee ruler of Navarre.

In 1346 Edward III invaded France from Cotentin in Normandy, close to Juana's home, and devastated the countryside along the way. As the French hurried to check his advance, Edward was forced to stop and do battle at Crecy. Here the English longbows proved so effective that the French lost 15,000–20,000 men. In sharp contrast, the English suffered fewer than 50 casualties.

The following year the Black Death, or bubonic plague, began to devastate Europe. Juana II died as it raged on in 1349, but she was not a plague victim.

Her political significance was slight because of her largely absentee role. Yet history remembers her because her special case gave a new and portentous twist to the Salic law.

Giovanna I
Queen of Naples, 1343–1381

The much-married Giovanna has been called "the most complicated heiress of the 14th century." Her champions describe her as a martyr, her detractors as a conspirator in assassination, but all agree that the tragic consequences of her first marriage made for a tumultuous reign. For most of her life she struggled to keep her throne.

When Giovanna was born in 1327, a member of the illustrious House of Anjou, her father, Charles, Duke of Calabria, served as the authoritarian Lord Protector of Florence, a position he owed to his father, King Robert of Naples. He was, however, so unpopular that the Florentines expelled him; within a year of his daughter's birth, he died of fever. A few months later, his widow, Marie de Valois, had a second daughter, Maria.

Upon Marie's death three years later, her two small daughters were installed as their grandfather's wards at Castel Nuovo, overlooking the Bay of Naples. Robert's kingdom, a papal fief, covered the lower half of Italy, south of Rome, including the principalities of Taranto and Durazzo. It also encompassed the French duchy of Provence with the city of Avignon, where the popes had resided since 1309.

In spite of continuing wars with Aragon over Sicily, King Robert, dubbed "the Wise," lived in elegance with his second wife, Queen Sancia, freely indulging his taste for the arts and acting as generous patron to painters, sculptors, and goldsmiths from Tuscany and France. An aging Giotto stayed in the royal household from 1329 to 1333, as had Simone Martini some years before. In 1333, heeding papal advice, Robert pressed for the marriage of six-year-old Giovanna to his brother's grandson, Andrew, younger son of Charles Robert, who sat on the Hungarian throne. The agreement with the Hungarians stipulated that on Robert's death his crown should go to Andrew. The backward boy of seven came from Buda to Naples for a resplendent "marriage of the future" ceremony and settled down at court with a large Hungarian entourage that immediately antagonized the Neapolitans.

Showing signs of great beauty, Giovanna was strictly raised and carefully educated. Her Sicilian nurse, Philippa, had been wet nurse to the Duke of Calabria. In time the young princess participated happily in the banquets and balls, tournaments and regattas of her grandfather's chivalric court.

Andrew, who had come under the influence of a swaggering tutor, Friar Robert, grew indolent and too fond of food and drink. The Neapolitans at court continued to scorn him and his Hungarian followers.

Robert, a "royal Solomon," had established a rich library, partly devoted to Muslim literature. In 1341 the poet Petrarch turned up at Castel Nuovo to see the famous collection and to seek royal favor, which Robert readily granted. Another user of the royal library was the young Boccaccio. Basking in the "happy, peaceful, generous, and magnificent city," he had fallen in love with Robert's natural daughter, Marie d'Aquino, a nobleman's dazzling wife, whom he celebrated as Fiametta, or Little Flame.

King Robert died in 1343. Breaking his promise to the Hungarians in Buda, he had dictated a will that made Giovanna his heiress and overlooked Andrew. By an earlier agreement he had left the hand of his granddaughter Maria in marriage to Louis, Andrew's elder brother, who had ascended the Hungarian throne in 1342.

Since the young queen had not yet reached her majority, a regency council began to govern. In protest Friar Robert encouraged the arrogant Hungarians to swarm over the court, making Giovanna and the Dowager Queen Sancia virtual state prisoners. The newly crowned Pope Clement VI, asserting his right to govern Naples, dispatched Petrarch to Castel Nuovo as his emissary. Giovanna was so pleased with the poet-prelate that she appointed him her temporary domestic chaplain and consulted him on the "Parliament of Love" she had set up to arbitrate lovers' quarrels. Her own marriage had been disappointingly consummated.

By this time the widows of two of King Robert's brothers, who lived at subsidiary courts, were busy in the marriage mill. The Princess of Taranto presented her handsome son Louis as a more suitable husband for Giovanna than Andrew. But the queen demurred although she neither loved nor respected Andrew. Likewise, the Duchess of Durazzo pushed for the marriage of her son Charles to the queen's sister, Maria, whom King Robert had promised to Louis of Hungary. Soon after, Maria was abducted from the palace and secretly married to Charles.

Amid these events the pope appointed a legate to govern Naples, and the young queen received the investiture of the crown during a ceremony at which Andrew stood as a spectator. Soon a papal bull called for a dual coronation of queen and consort, but it made clear that Andrew had no claim on the throne. Plans were laid for a lavish rite in September 1345.

In August a pregnant Giovanna went with her husband to their summer residence at Aversa while the court hunted in the neighborhood. There, under mysterious circumstances, several noblemen strangled Andrew and threw his body into the garden. The tragedy at Aversa plunged Naples into anarchy. Some knights suspected of the murder fled to their castles; other persons were caught and tortured, among them Giovanna's old nurse Philippa and her granddaughter. Rumors implicating the queen in Andrew's murder were first whispered, then shouted. Even her brother-in-law, the Duke of Durazzo, accused her. Later, however, he returned to her banner. At the end of the year, overwhelmed by an atmosphere of hate and suspicion, Giovanna gave birth to a son whom she named Charles Robert for his Hungarian grandfather.

Preeminent among advisers she had inherited from her grandfather stood Nicholas Acciajuoli, a close friend of the Princess of Taranto, whose son Louis, well known for his military exploits, was considered one of Andrew's chief assailants. Acciajuoli counseled his sovereign to accept Louis. Deeply in love, Giovanna married him in 1347.

The news about his brother had infuriated Louis of Hungary. When he learned of Giovanna's remarriage, he swore revenge, marched his army from Hungary, and before long hammered at the gates of Naples.

The disheartened queen found she had little support. Leaving her young son in a papal guardian's care, she sailed for France to seek protection from Pope Clement VI. Arriving in Aix, however, she was detained by Provençal nobles, who believed reports spread by Hungarian emissaries that she intended to sell her domains in Provence for enough money to carry on her war against the Hungarians. The Provençals confined the queen as a state prisoner but treated her with courtesy and respect.

Hoping to pacify Louis and prevent vengeance, Giovanna had ordered the gates of every town in her kingdom thrown open and had told her subjects to offer no resistance. But her plan did not work. Louis moved his army to Aversa, where he took many prisoners and ordered the execution of the Duke of Durazzo, whom he suspected of Andrew's murder. When he entered Naples as a conqueror, he held more inquisitions, and Giovanna's sister, the widowed Duchess of Durazzo, fled with her children. In the days that followed, Louis sent Giovanna's son off to Hungary, where he died shortly upon arrival.

Distant relatives obtained Giovanna's release from the castle in Aix, where she had been held for two months, and she made a triumphal entry into Avignon. She had decided to plead her innocence before a Consistory Court in the papal palace. There her husband joined her. The beauty defended herself so eloquently in Latin that the court declared her innocent of Andrew's murder. The pope awarded her the Golden Rose, a highly valued decoration. Then, acclaimed by cheering crowds, she and Louis of Taranto were led around the walls of Avignon as the Count and Countess of Provence.

Soon the Great Plague suspended most activities in Avignon. It claimed among its victims seven cardinals and Laura de Sade, the love of Petrarch's life. The plague, which inspired Boccaccio's *Decameron*, also frightened Louis of Hungary out of Naples.

When news of Giovanna's acquittal reached the Neapolitans, they united in calling for her return and restoration to the throne. Secret messages went to Avignon, promising that they would rally to her side if she could supply money and muster men to arms.

After several unsuccessful attempts to reach a peaceful settlement with Louis, Giovanna sold her diamonds for a sum far less than she had expected. She offered Avignon and the surrounding countryside to Clement for 80,000 gold florins, one-fourth of the papacy's annual expenditures. Simultaneously she asked him to give Louis of Taranto the title of King of Naples. She herself had never been crowned.

Soon after the couple returned home, their daughter, Francesca, was born. A year later, Giovanna again became a mother; this baby, Catherine, died in infancy.

With suave skill Acciajuoli had helped the queen's cause at Avignon, and now she made him Grand Seneschal. Fortunately for her, Louis of Taranto enjoyed fighting her battles; Louis of Hungary had returned to the attack in 1350. One of his most audacious soldiers, answering directly to his lieutenant, Conrad Wolf, was Duke Werner of Urslingen, captain of a mercenary band called the Great Company. Soon Louis of Taranto brought Werner over to his wife's side and with his help captured some of the castles and garrisons held by the Hungarians.

After being taken prisoner, Werner reattached himself to Wolf, who accepted a papal suggestion to deliver up the towns of Aversa and Capua for 120,000 florins and return to Germany. But within a year the Hungarian forces besieged Aversa, and once more Louis entered Naples.

Following the capitulation of Aversa, Giovanna and Louis of Taranto went to Gaeta by sea, hoping to retreat to Provençe. But their fears proved premature. In Naples the Hungarian troops found the people so militant that they pulled back to Aulia. With their removal, the pope decided it was time to make peace. Louis of Hungary proposed a truce but demanded another trial for Giovanna before the pope and cardinals. Again they pronounced her innocent of Andrew's murder. But she refused to accept a treaty draft which excluded her husband from the Neapolitan throne. Finally the pope gave way to her firmness and granted Louis of Taranto his royal title.

Giovanna loved pomp and glitter and spent money lavishly for the coronation in the spring of 1352. Midway through the festivities little Francesca suddenly died of convulsions. Within two years the young queen had lost all three of her children.

No sooner had Louis of Hungary disappeared than a new challenge arose. Sicilians had rebelled against an oppressive regency and Giovanna, remembering that the island had once belonged to the House of Anjou, agreed to help them. With Louis she hurried to Messina. Just as their expedition seemed to be going well, they were forced to leave because a civil war had broken out in Naples between Louis of Durazzo, brother of Giovanna's murdered brother-in-law, and her husband's eldest brother, Robert of Taranto. With help from the crown, Robert was victorious.

When Louis of Durazzo died in 1360, Giovanna, showing her usual generosity, agreed to educate his eldest son, Charles, whom she afterwards adopted. At the time Charles came to Castel Nuovo, the queen also adopted her sister Maria's daughter, Margaret.

With the ending of the civil war, the court entered its most frivolous period under the lively queen. Increasingly her enemies berated the luxury of her table, her magnificent dress, and the constant round of often lustful entertainments. Critics also complained that she ran her life largely on impulse. Ignoring them, her husband took to the high style with abandon, seeking every pleasure and becoming flagrantly unfaithful. Worn out by his excesses, Louis of Taranto died of fever in 1362.

During her second widowhood, Giovanna suddenly revealed a more serious side and began endowing churches and charitable institutions. At her court the arts flourished, and learned and scientific men thronged Castel Nuovo as in her grandfather's day.

Much of the actual government she left to Acciajuoli. The feudal kingdom harbored many arrogant barons, who often took up arms, keeping the queen's troops fully occupied. Still, Acciajuoli made Naples a favorite port of trade by exempting it from taxation and securing its roads from fierce brigands.

For a few years suitors or their intermediaries flocked around the beautiful widow. King John II of France went to Avignon to ask Pope Urban V for Giovanna's hand for his fourth son, but fearing French influence, the queen refused. Instead she chose a good-looking frequenter of her court. James II of Majorca was a king without a kingdom, but his status did not concern Giovanna. With great splendor she married him in 1367. After three months, James, to whom status *did* matter, set out to recover the kingdom his uncle had usurped. Although his expedition failed, he continued to go on military adventures which often ended with his imprisonment. In the year of Giovanna's third marriage, her good friend Urban V decided to return to Rome. He sailed in a fleet of 23 galleys, his own having been supplied by the Neapolitan queen. When she came to Rome for a visit, Urban honored her with her second Golden Rose.

Back in Naples, Giovanna celebrated Charles of Durazzo's marriage to her niece Margaret. On this occasion she announced her intention of bequeathing her crown to the young couple. Shortly afterward, she learned to her dismay that Charles had entered the service of Louis of Hungary in his war against the Venetians.

That summer a Swedish noblewoman and prophetess, later canonized as St. Birgitta, arrived in Naples with her granddaughter, Catherine. While making friends with the queen, she lectured her severely about the court's frivolity

Giovanna I. Presumed portrait, based on church fresco, Naples.

and licentiousness. Sweetly Giovanna promised reform, but she became upset
when Birgitta prophesied Acciajuoli's imminent death. Following Acciajuoli's
burial not long afterwards, King John of France tried to wrest Provence from
the kingdom of Naples, but the queen was so ably supported by the pope and
her Provençal subjects that she forced a French retreat. No sooner had this
crisis passed than the Holy See's war with the Viscontis of Milan spilled over
into Naples. But when Ambrose Visconti entered the city, the veterans who
had served with Louis of Taranto decimated the Milanese army.

Urban V, Giovanna's most powerful backer, died in 1370 and was succeeded by Gregory XI, who refused to be friendly. Undaunted, she arranged
a treaty by which Frederick of Sicily acknowledged her as Queen of the Two
Sicilies on condition that she leave him in peaceful possession of his island. He

took the title of King of Trancoria and promised to furnish galleys and men-of-arms at the queen's request.

In 1371 Birgitta came again to Naples on her way to the Holy Land, this time accompanied by her sons, Birger and Charles. At 43 Giovanna was still astonishingly beautiful, and when Birgitta and her party received an audience, Charles fell in love. Although he had a wife and children in Sweden, as Birgitta constantly reminded him, he hardly left the side of the bewitching queen. But the romance was short-lived. One night when he did not appear at a grand ball, Giovanna, an elegant dancer, sent a messenger to command his presence. The man found Charles extremely ill; death came in two weeks. An anguished Birgitta scolded Giovanna and her whole court, and again the queen sweetly accepted every reproof but did not change her ways.

She needed distraction, for intriguing nobles constantly harassed her. When the Duke of Andria lay siege to the town of Tirani, the Neapolitans suffered from want of provisions, and the tall queen, majestic in armor, went from piazza to piazza heartening her people to hold out. After the siege ended, the Duke of Andria fled to Avignon, where Pope Gregory gave him money to raise a new army.

James died in 1375. As rebellions continued to burst out, Giovanna's advisers suggested she marry for a fourth time. Her choice fell on Otho, Prince of Brunswick, another frequenter of the Neapolitan court and well-known captain of a band of mercenaries. Of all her husbands she considered him the best.

She now had a new and very powerful enemy. Pope Urban VI, who succeeded Gregory in 1378, was Neapolitan born and had received many royal gifts. Nevertheless he immediately began plotting her downfall with the Duke of Andria, who again rose in rebellion against her. Urban's eagerness to invest Charles of Durazzo with Giovanna's crown stemmed from his belief that his own nephew would be allowed to share the kingdom.

Urban's election had been so disputed that certain cardinals elected an antipope, who took the title of Clement VII. Thus began the Great Schism, which with its two popes and two papal capitals, disturbed Europe for 39 years. After she and Otho had suffered various insults from Urban, Giovanna joined Clement's party.

The rival papal armies fought a bloody battle at Marino. Urban, using the services of the famous Sir John Hawkwood, was victorious. Clement then decided to retreat to Naples, where Giovanna sheltered him for some months in the Castel dell'Ovo.

Urban had threatened to put her in a nunnery for failing to pay him his feudal dues. Further angered by her hospitality to Clement, he now excommunicated her and declared her deposed. At this juncture Giovanna appointed a distant cousin, Louis of Anjou, brother of Charles V of France, as her heir, displacing Charles of Durazzo. On hearing of the queen's change of heart, Charles of Durazzo headed for Italy with Hungarian troops and a light body of German and Italian infantry. Along the way he gained Hawkwood's services.

Soon Charles lay siege to Naples. Giovanna had expected the Provençal fleet to arrive and escort her to Avignon and the antipope's protection while she waited for Louis of Anjou. But the fleet failed to appear in the Bay of Naples, and the queen and her ladies suffered the horrors of siege. Otho, while fighting against Charles, was taken prisoner, and his troops panicked. The next day Giovanna sent her surrender to Charles.

Too late the Provençal fleet showed up. When the queen begged her subjects to be loyal to Louis of Anjou, Charles was so furious that he moved her to the Castel dell'Ovo as a prisoner. In November 1381 he and his wife Margaret were crowned in the cathedral at Naples. Fearing that Giovanna's presence might inspire a rebellion, Charles put her in the Castel del Muro, a grim and gloomy fortress. Disillusioned and fearful, Giovanna sat for two months in prison but was allowed to pray in the chapel.

Finally Louis of Anjou arrived and threatened to restore Giovanna to her throne. Debating whether to end her life, Charles reached a firm decision when a message arrived from Louis of Hungary: "Let Giovanna die the same death which Andrew suffered through her."

He assigned the task to four Hungarians. On May 22, 1382, as two of them stood guard at the door of the chapel where she knelt in prayer, the other two threw a silken cord around her neck and strangled her.

On Charles's orders her corpse went on display for six days. The curious came, but few mourned the end of Giovanna's long and storm-tossed reign.

Maria
Queen of Hungary, 1382–1395

Because Giovanna I's implacable enemy, King Louis of Hungary, had no sons, he adopted Charles of Durazzo, who later became the Neapolitan queen's other great foe. Louis, however, reserved the right of succession for his daughters. Nonetheless, the adoption eventually jeopardized the throne of his daughter Maria and led to double murders.

The king and his second wife, Elizabeth of Bosnia, welcomed their second child, Maria, in 1371, the year after he inherited the Polish throne from his Uncle Casimir and his eldest daughter Catherine, was born. A third girl, Jadwiga (baptized Hedvig), arrived in 1373.

Louis, however, rarely appeared in Poland and left the government in the hands of regents, one of whom was his mother, Elizabeth. In 1374 he met with Polish representatives in the Hungarian city of Kassa and came to terms on a general charter of rights. By way of concession, the Poles promised that if Louis died, they would accept one of his daughters as sovereign. The same year he presented tiny Catherine to her future subjects. Next he turned his attention to planning suitable marriages for his well-loved daughters. For Maria he chose Sigismund of Luxembourg, son of the Holy Roman Emperor, Charles IV; for Catherine, Louis of France, later Duke of Orleans, son of King Charles V; and for Jadwiga, Wilhelm of Hapsburg, son of Leopold III of Austria. High festivity followed Sigismund and Maria's "infant marriage," and afterwards Sigismund stayed on at the Hungarian court, joined by Wilhelm of Hapsburg after his betrothal to Jadwiga. The children learned and played at Visegrad and Buda, in castles Louis had made centers of chivalry and culture. Although earning the sobriquet "the Great" for his martial exploits, Louis, owner of Europe's most valuable gold mines, resembled his great-uncle, Robert the Wise of Naples, in scholarship and patronage.

When Catherine died in 1378, Louis named Maria to the Polish throne; Hungary was to fall to Jadwiga. But the Poles, whose experiences with the Teutonic Knights had left bitter memories, were deeply suspicious of Sigismund's German background. At another conference with a delegation from

Cracow, they expressed strong opposition to Maria and Sigismund. Ignoring the protest, Louis ordered the city gate shut and would not allow any Poles to leave before they formally submitted to his will. Then he demanded that they render homage to eight-year-old Maria. Three years later he commanded certain officials to come to Buda to kneel before Sigismund.

Amid great national mourning, Louis died in 1382. But his careful plans for Maria to rule in Poland and Jadwiga in Hungary went awry. One day after his burial the Hungarian magnates elected Maria "king" with Elizabeth, her mother, as regent. Suffering through a civil war, the Poles refused to accept her unless she renounced the Hungarian throne and discarded Sigismund. To Elizabeth these terms were impossible. The Poles, however, were willing to accept Jadwiga. After some delays, Elizabeth sent her to Cracow in 1384.

For the new queen in Buda, wrangling began at once and continued for almost three years. "For one, to become the leader is the chief desire," wrote a Venetian diplomat. "This one wants a countship; that one strives for a principality. All struggle to get higher by displacing others. Ferocious jealousy possesses them. They hate each other, break into factions and divide the very population itself."

Some factions continued to champion Sigismund as consort; others wanted a son of the French king. Many were angry because the jealous and capricious Elizabeth seemed to be completely under the thumb of her reputed lover, Miklos Gara, the palatine or feudal lord of one of the great Hungarian families.

Meetings of the high nobility and principal churchmen expressed the initial discontent. The struggle intensified when lords from the south, led by the Croatian Horvatis, invited Charles of Durazzo, Louis's adopted son, to Hungary so that they could place him on the throne. Charles accepted their bid and with a mercenary army marched north.

Meanwhile Maria's marriage to Sigismund had taken place. To collect an army to oppose the advancing enemy and defend Maria's rights, Sigismund hypothecated a part of Hungarian territory to raise necessary funds, a transaction that dismayed the nation.

Charles entered Buda without resistance, at first declaring his friendly intention of helping the young queen "against all her molesters." But soon he showed his hand and on New Year's Eve 1385, he had himself crowned in the cathedral of Stuhlweissenburg in the presence of two humiliated and weeping queens. At her husband's grave Elizabeth vowed vengeance.

Charles had occupied the throne for only 39 days when Elizabeth asked him to a council chamber to discuss some matters of state. While she stood with Balazs Forgach and other lords, a royal cupbearer struck Charles on the head with a poleax. For good measure Elizabeth's cohorts then strangled the usurper.

The Horvatis and other magnates who had helped Charles with his coup

Maria. Woodcut from *Hungary in Greatness and Decline* by Domokos Varga. Hungarian Cultural Foundation.

d'etat were furious and joined forces with the Bosnian Prince Tvartko, Elizabeth's cousin, who had been fomenting unrest in Croatia. Accompanied by Miklos Gara, Maria and Elizabeth headed there to quell a fast-growing rebellion. One day on the road, the Horvati forces swooped down on the "queen women." Gara, pierced by arrows, set his back against their carriage but was brutally struck down, his bleeding head flung at Elizabeth's feet. Frantically the queen mother fell on her knees before her captors, shrieking that they should take her life and spare her daughter's because only she was guilty. Impervious to her pleas, the rebels imprisoned both queens in a castle on the Adriatic seashore near Novigrad. There, before Maria's horrified eyes, her captors strangled her mother and hung her body out on the prison walls.

The Venetians, angered by the alliance of Naples and Hungary, paraded their fleet in front of the castle and thereby saved Maria from being taken to almost certain execution in Naples. She was then locked into a new prison in Diakovar. While she languished there, the situation in Buda became even more chaotic. Some rebels tried unsuccessfully to bring Charles of Durazzo's son to court. Others spoke of summoning the Grand Duke Jagiello, whom Jadwiga had just married. To complicate the picture, enemies from the south and northeast threatened invasion.

To resolve its difficulties, Hungary decided to accept Sigismund and acknowledge him as king in the spring of 1387. Now tardily he set about liberating his wife. But the Venetians acted more quickly. Awed by their might, Maria's jailer handed her over to John Barbadico, captain of the Venetian Republic. Maria and Sigismund met near Agram in the summer of 1388, and Sigismund rewarded the Venetians lavishly. Then he and his wife returned to Buda.

Although Maria had promised not to take revenge, she did sit on a tribunal to determine the guilt of her erstwhile captors. An angry Sigismund ordered many heads chopped off, including those of several Horvatis.

Even as he brought the rebels to heel, Sigismund faced threats of a Turkish invasion. Resolute ruler though he proved to be, he was already leading a scandalous private life filled with too much drink and too many women. Maria, who remained childless, accepted her husband's affairs stoically.

She had long been separated from her sister Jadwiga. Some of her courtiers still resented the fact that the Polish queen had wrested from Hungary the province of Red Ruthenia at the very time Elizabeth was being strangled in prison.

In 1395 a meeting between the Polish and Hungarian sovereigns finally took place at Soncz, chiefly to establish friendly relations between Sigismund and Jagiello. After so many years, Maria and Jadwiga faced each other with sisterly affection. As a special gift for the Hungarian queen, Jadwiga had ordered a luxuriously padded saddle, covered in yellow velvet and ornamented in gold, with silk tassels on the reins.

Later that same year a pregnant Maria accidentally pitched from her horse and was killed. Her reign had been dramatic although short in accomplishment. But as the first woman sovereign of a major European country, she has a special niche in history.

Jadwiga
Queen of Poland, 1384–1399

At the age of 10, Jadwiga obeyed an order to sacrifice personal happiness for the good of her country and church. But in the end the marriage into which she entered so unwillingly helped make her a great queen.

Born at Buda toward the close of 1373, Jadwiga (Hedvig), youngest of the three daughters of Louis and Elizabeth of Bosnia, King and Queen of Hungary and Poland, was something of a disappointment to her father, who had ardently hoped for a male heir. Nonetheless, this baby, whose veins carried both Anjou and Piast blood, eventually became her father's favorite.

Like her sisters, Catherine and Mary, pretty Jadwiga enjoyed a nurtured childhood and went through a "marriage of the future" ceremony. In 1378 she was taken to the town of Hainburg on the Danube, where her hands were joined to those of young Wilhelm of Hapsburg, son of Leopold III of Austria. As custom decreed, Wilhelm, like Maria's betrothed Sigismund, then came to Louis's brilliant courts at Buda and Visegrad, where people were "as ready to dance as to say the rosary." Several times Jadwiga went to stay for extended periods with Wilhelm's family at the gloomy Hapsburg court in Vienna.

Her elder sister Catherine died at the age of eight in 1378, and Jadwiga and Maria became even closer companions. Their most important teachers turned out to be their father, called "the Great" for his skill in conquest, and their devout grandmother Elizabeth, who served as Polish regent on three occasions. She brought a Polish entourage to the court in Buda, where Jadwiga learned Polish.

Louis died in 1382, believing that Maria was to be queen of Poland and Jadwiga queen of Hungary. Disregarding his wishes, however, Hungarian magnates elected Maria "king" the day after his entombment. Louis had been an absentee ruler of Poland, and the Poles, who also distrusted Sigismund, would not consider another sovereign who lived in Hungary. One group put forward the name of the Mazovian duke, Ziemowit. But a majority insisted on honoring the promise made to Louis in 1374 to accept one of his daughters. They asked for Jadwiga, but said that she must remain forever in Poland.

During an interregnum that followed Louis's death, the Poles fought what amounted to a civil war, and to end it the nobles called a large assembly at Sieradz. Louis's widow Elizabeth sent her representatives there to demand that after Jadwiga's coronation she be allowed to remain for three years in Hungary. After Ziemowit's partisans almost took control of the stormy session, the delegates declared Jadwiga queen. When they demanded her immediate presence, Elizabeth delayed until she received an ultimatum: Jadwiga must come at once!

Civil unrest kept the queen mother in Buda, and after many delays the girl set out by herself for Poland in October 1384, riding in a retinue of Hungarian soldiers, and hoping for a speedy reunion with Wilhelm. Two days after her ceremonial entry into Cracow, she was solemnly crowned in the cathedral on the royal Wawel hill and again before the city hall, the first queen to sit on the Polish throne in her own right. Like Maria, she was elected "king."

After the coronation, the crown council and priests directed her studies and discussed the burning issue of her marriage. Ignoring Wilhelm, the Polish nobles who had recommended her for the throne wanted her to wed Jagiello, the Grand Duke of Lithuania. Such a marriage, they argued, would unite two neighboring states which frequently warred with each other. Brought together, Poland and Lithuania could present a common barrier to their great enemy, the Order of Teutonic Knights.

Jagiello, too, had compelling reasons. As the last pagans in Europe, the Lithuanians were continuously harassed by the Knights, who aimed to Christianize them by violent means. Jagiello had just murdered his uncle, whose son Witold had temporarily gone over to the Knights. As negotiations began, the Poles asked Jagiello to make certain concessions, primarily to associate his grand duchy with the Polish kingdom in a federal union and to accept the Catholic faith for himself and his countrymen.

Jadwiga felt betrayed. From all accounts, Jagiello was a rough pagan, 24 years her senior, who could not even speak her language. He was ugly, besides, and came from a violent family. Jadwiga continued to look on Wilhelm of Hapsburg, her beloved playfellow and dancing partner, as her intended husband and wrote her mother, pleading for support. But envoys she sent to Buda returned with Elizabeth's cold answer: "The young queen and the Polish lords must act according to what the welfare of Poland and the Christian commonwealth demand."

The devious Elizabeth soon did a complete turnaround. Uneasy at reports of Jagiello's negotiations with the Poles, Wilhelm's father, Leopold III of Austria, rushed to Buda to protest. On his demand Elizabeth drew up a fresh declaration, signed by Queen Maria, promising that the marriage between Jadwiga and Wilhelm would be fulfilled after all.

In the meantime, resplendent in mail and plumed helmet, Wilhelm arrived in Cracow with a large retinue and gift-laden wagons. Chronicles disagree whether he actually gained admittance to Wawel Castle and then escaped or from the beginning was forced back by guards. But Jadwiga seems to have met him several times at a Franciscan convent near the foot of the royal hill. Whatever his true story, for the next few months Wilhelm crept in disguise from one hiding place to the other.

In the autumn of 1385, word arrived that Jagiello and the Polish barons had come to final terms. He had in fact started out with a document that accepted him as King of Poland and gave him the "most illustrious queen in honorable marriage."

A desperate Jadwiga looked for a means of escape. Legend has it that one night, descending a narrow stairway to a usually unguarded room, she found it locked and protected by sentries. Her servants supplied her with an ax, and she struck at the door hinges. Just then an old noble, summoned by the sentries, pulled her back and led her to her apartments in the castle. For days her advisers and her confessor reminded her that if she married Jagiello, his nation would enter the Catholic church, new lands would be added to the Polish crown, and the Teutonic Knights would no longer be a threat. At last after unceasing prayer she bowed to her royal obligation. She did not know that in Buda her father's adopted son, Charles of Durazzo, had usurped Maria's throne on the last day of the preceding year and that Elizabeth had just summoned Charles to his murder.

In February 1386, Jagiello entered Cracow with a large entourage, and Jadwiga received him graciously. Three days later he was baptized and given the Christian name of Ladislaus. Within another three days the marriage was solemnized in the cathedral. First though, Jadwiga had to renounce her "infant marriage" to Wilhelm of Austria. At the beginning of March, Jagiello was crowned King of Poland, about the time Charles of Durazzo's partisans imprisoned Elizabeth and Maria.

Despite her reluctance to wed, Jadwiga resolved to be a good wife. To her pleasure, Jagiello began to "Polonize" himself almost immediately. For the next 13 years the pair would work side by side for political and religious goals. Shortly after their wedding, Jadwiga and Jagiello went to the troublesome province of Greater Poland to appease it. A legend attaches to their visit to Gniezno. The king became furious when the villagers refused to supply provisions for the royal household and ordered his officers to seize the cattle and drive them away. In retaliation, a parish priest closed all the churches. So that they might reopen, a troubled Jadwiga begged her husband to restore the stolen property. When he did, she still looked sad, saying, "You can give them back their cattle, but who will give them back their tears?"

In February 1387, Jagiello fulfilled his promise to bring Christianity to Lithuania. At Vilna he headed a stately concourse of Polish nobles and prelates who advanced to an oak grove where they cut down trees, destroyed idols, extinguished a sacred fire, and set a cross at the desecrated heathen altars. Afterwards, thousands of Lithuanians received splashes of baptismal water. Then, having laid the cornerstone of a Catholic cathedral, Jagiello signed an edict to give the Lithuanian people property rights and equality before the law.

Meanwhile Jadwiga faced a thorny issue. An old contested borderland, Red Ruthenia (East Galicia), which had become Polish under her great-uncle, Casimir the Great, had been ruled by Hungarian governors since Louis's day. The Poles wanted it back, and while Jagiello was absent in Lithuania, Jadwiga decided to solve the problem head on.

Accompanied by nobles and soldiers, the young queen rode into Red Ruthenia, more interested in peace than war. As she began to restore privileges abolished since Casimir's reign, people swarmed to her banner, and the Hungarian garrisons threw down their arms. Only one fortress held out; Jagiello then sent in Lithuanian troops, who speedily captured it. While on her Ruthenian expedition, Jadwiga received news of her mother's murder and in her grief made a truce with the Hungarians.

If Jagiello thought that his marriage might intimidate the Teutonic Knights, he was mistaken. They continued their acts of aggression against Lithuania and spread propaganda that the Lithuanians were insincere about their conversion. In Rome members of the Hapsburg family seized on the propaganda and persuaded Pope Urban VI to contest the validity of Jadwiga's marriage. The Hapsburgs insisted that she was Wilhelm's wife although no marriage had been consummated.

Suddenly Wilhelm's former confidant, Gniewosz of Dalewice, who had easily gone over to Jagiello, began passing out rumors that Jadwiga still carried on in secret with Wilhelm. An irate queen insisted on having her character cleared at a public trial, where Gniewosz was ordered to recant. By this time, thoroughly convinced that Jagiello's conversion efforts had succeeded, the pope gave his blessing to the marriage.

Wilhelm quickly faded from Polish view. When one of Jagiello's envoys offered him money, he threw the man in prison. He even refused a papal summons. Although co-workers, king and queen began a practice of traveling separately to their various castles. The musical Jadwiga invariably had an entourage of flautists and lute players. The court praised her charm, but she could show a streak of capriciousness. A palace account book noted that one day servants "were greasing the carriage because her royal Majesty wished to drive out, and she did not drive."

As the years passed, the stately Jadwiga grew in religious faith. For her charitable work and love of the poor, the Poles saw her as almost a saint. Once, it was said, she used her cloak to cover the corpse of a coppersmith drowned in the Vistula River. Another time she rested her shoe on a stone to tear off a golden spur for a poor mason. The cloak became a banner of the Coppersmiths' Guild; the imprint of her shoe was preserved in a church wall.

HEDVVIGE.

35

LVDOVICI Hungari natu minor (cum Sigismundum Cæsaris filium
ab Hungaro successorem destinatum, respuissent Poloni) An. 1384. Regina renunciatur, solemnique ritu coronatur Cracouiæ, Regni ampliss.t
gubernatione delata tenerrimæ etiamnum puellæ. Intestinis discordijs,
mutuisque dilacerationibus defatigatos Polonos cura incessit de adjungen-
do nouæ Reginæ marito, quo Regni mala quiescerent. Destinatus iam fuerat
HEDVVIGI sponsus ab Hungaro Rege Wilhelmus Austriacus. sed hoc
reiecto, quod parum præsidij regnum proprijs discerptum studijs
sibi polliceretur a Principe extero, ac tenuioris fortunæ, palmam præ-
ripuit omnibus Iagello Magnus Lithuaniæ Dux, qui amplis pol-
licitationibus se, suosque ad Christiana Sacra, Lithuaniamque
ad Polonici Imperij unionem perpetuo transitura, spopondit.

Jadwiga. Museum Narodowe, Wroclaw, Poland.

Her father had founded a university in Pecs, and she determined to emulate him. She began preparing to reorganize the university, begun by her great-uncle, Casimir, in Cracow. To it she attached a theological faculty and bequeathed money and her magnificent jewels. But she did not live to see the restored university, known as the Jagiellonian University, which opened a year after her death.

To instruct her subjects in another direction, she commissioned various Polish translations of devotional books. As her reputation for piety steadily increased, Pope Boniface IX gave her the power to nominate her own prelates under the Holy See.

In keeping with her intense religious spirit, Jadwiga also acted as peacemaker in her husband's family. His cousin Witold had always been a troublemaker. When Jagiello appointed his brother Skirgillo as governor of Lithuania, an enraged Witold allied himself with the Teutonic Knights and marched into Lithuania. Then suddenly he changed his mind and asked for peace. Jadwiga did not attend his meeting with Jagiello, but at her suggestion Witold was appointed viceroy of Lithuania. Thus she converted an enemy into a friend. Some years later, however, she opposed Witold's expedition against Tamerlane, the Tartar leader. As she foresaw, it turned into disaster.

Jadwiga finally faced a representative of the Teutonic Knights, the old enemy, in 1397. When a nobleman pawned to the order certain provinces he held as fiefs from the Polish crown, Jadwiga was determined to secure Polish rights and therefore demanded that she confer in person. At the parley she did not get those rights and prophesied the Knights' imminent destruction. Eleven years after she spoke, Jagiello crushingly defeated them.

Since her marriage, Jadwiga had been childless, but in 1399 she finally expected an heir. In June she gave birth prematurely to a daughter, Elizabeth, who died within three weeks. Jadwiga, whose health had been critical since her labor, immediately worsened. On her deathbed she told Jagiello to wed Anna, daughter of the Count of Cilly and granddaughter of Casimir the Great. Such a queen, she said, could transmit hereditary rights to him and their children.

In late July, the city of Cracow went into deep mourning for the 26-year-old ruler. Her will stipulated that half the proceeds from the sale of her possessions go to the poor; the other half she reserved for the university. As word of her passing spread, all Poland grieved. In the Latin calendar at Wawel Castle, a scribe noted the death of

> Jadwiga, Queen of Poland—unwearied creator of divine culture, protectress of the church, administrator of justice, servant of all virtue, humble and beneficent mother of orphans, who in her time had had no equal of royal blood in the eyes of men in the whole world.

Her cult had begun.

Margrethe
Regent of Denmark, Norway, and Sweden, 1387–1412

Margrethe of Denmark, one of the most indomitable women of the 14th century, learned her first politics from her remarkable father, Valdemar (IV) Atterdag, whom she resembled in drive, energy, and endurance. Denmark was an elective monarchy; when Valdemar was installed as king in 1340, most of the land had been mortgaged to Mecklenburg nobles. Eight years later, through armed might and shrewd dealings he won most of it back.

Margrethe, the youngest child of King Valdemar and Queen Helvig, was born in 1453 at the castle of Søborg in northern Zealand. The royal family already numbered a son, Christoffer, and a daughter, Ingeborg. Two other girls and a boy had died as small children.

In 1355, Queen Helvig suddenly left her family and entered Esrum Cloister as a lay sister. As Margrethe developed without a mother's care, her father described her as "Nature's error," one who should have been created a man.

She was, however, a useful political pawn. A treaty between Valdemar and Magnus Eriksson, King of Sweden, pledged the six-year-old girl to Magnus's 18-year-old son, Haakon, who had inherited the Norwegian throne through his mother, the granddaughter of Haakon V. Valdemar planned the betrothal to counter claims to the Scandinavian thrones made by the Dukes of Mecklenburg and certain noble factions within Scandinavia itself. He also hoped to regain Skåne in southern Sweden. Harried by his rebellious elder son, Erik, who ruled in the south, Magnus also welcomed the alliance. But six months later when Erik died and Haakon became co-ruler with his father, Magnus decided he no longer needed the King of Denmark's help. He preferred an associate like his brother-in-law, Duke Albrecht II of Mecklenburg. Hence he was taken by surprise when Valdemar conquered Skåne and surrounding areas in 1360–1361, using Albrecht as an ally. Indeed, the Danish king's about-face so angered him that he broke off the betrothal.

Just at this time Valdemar and his son, Junker Christoffer, sailed with the

Danish fleet to the island of Gotland, taking Oland along the way. Visby in Gotland was an important trading center for the Hanseatic League. Outside its walls, Swedish peasants tried to defend the city; the German merchants remained neutral. The peasants were massacred, and the Danish army marched into Visby. There, to keep their trading privileges, the merchants paid "gold, silver, furs of various kinds, and a great many other treasures." In 1362 the Hansa intervened, started a blockade of Denmark, and with Holstein and Sweden agreed on joint military action. Now negotiations were begun to obtain Elizabeth of Holstein as a bride for Haakon. Swedish nobles hoped to hurry them up by sending Elizabeth to Norway. During a winter storm her ship was grounded off Skåne, and the girl was taken to the Archbishop of Lund, who played politics and detained her.

Meanwhile the assault of Valdemar's enemies on Helsingborg never materialized because the Danes captured much of the Hanseatic fleet. King Magnus gave up his war plans, and the Hanseatic league soon signed an armistice with Valdemar. The two kings now felt free to arrange the wedding of Margrethe and Haakon in Copenhagen in April 1363. That same year Junker Christoffer died of a long-festering wound. In 1362 Ingeborg had been married to Heinrich of Mecklenburg, son of Duke Albrecht II.

While Margrethe was sent to Norway, Haakon and his father kept busy defending their throne against Swedish nobles, who dickered with Duke Albrecht's son, another Albrecht. Stockholm's German merchants hailed him as king in 1363, and the Swedish parliament elected him the next year. Then the two Albrechts inflicted an incisive defeat on Magnus in 1364 and threw him into prison. Haakon, however, held on to the Norwegian throne.

At Akershus, Haakon's castle in Oslo, Margrethe was put under the tutelage of Merete Ulvsdatter, daughter of the famous Birgitta of Sweden and the wife of a Norwegian magnate, Knud Algotsson. Together with Merete's daughter Ingegerd, the Danish girl came under strict discipline and developed a deep, lifelong piety. When Margrethe reached the age of 16, she and Haakon began to live together as man and wife. Their life, however, was anything but opulent. Dated 1369, a letter from the queen-consort's hand warns her husband that her servants will leave her because food is in such short supply in her household. She begs him to urge a local German merchant to give her some food on credit.

All this time she stayed keenly aware of her father's difficulties. In 1367 the Hanseatic League had joined again with Mecklenburg, Holstein, and Sweden against Denmark. As Valdemar's forces fought unsuccessfully, the castle in Copenhagen was torn down stone by stone, and in 1370 his chancellor, Henning Podebusk, signed the Treaty of Stralsund, ceding many castles in Skåne to the Hansa for 15 years. Three days later, Denmark signed a separate peace with Mecklenburg, by which Albrecht II promised to return the castles he had conquered. Valdemar and Duke Albrecht II shared a grandson, 10-year-old

Albrecht, Ingeborg's son; the Danes promised he would succeed to Valdemar's throne. The treaty, however, was never formally ratified. That same year around Christmas, Margrethe gave birth to her only child, a son named Oluf. Meanwhile she received word of her sister's death.

The Norwegian king was seldom at home. In Stockholm King Albrecht had surrounded himself with Germans, and Haakon marched on the city in 1371. Albrecht saved his crown only by granting more power to the Swedish nobles and freeing Magnus. Life at Akershus was lonely and deprived, but it made Margrethe self-reliant and strong. She had become a woman of powerful intellect and immense determination, prepared to take matters into her own hands whenever possible.

Magnus drowned in 1374; Valdemar Atterdag died in 1375. Margrethe was his only surviving child, but Danish law did not allow a woman to wear the crown. When certain leaders declared it should go to young Albrecht, as the late king had promised, Margrethe rushed to Denmark and set forth Oluf's claims. Making considerable use of her charm and magnetism, she arrived at some clever deals with the nobles and the Hansa and succeeded in having Oluf proclaimed the King of Denmark. Margrethe also received help from Podebusk.

After she and Haakon signed a charter confirming Oluf's privileges, they fought a not-too-serious war with the Mecklenburgs of Germany and Sweden. Meanwhile Margrethe stayed in Denmark and governed as her son's guardian. Five years later Haakon died, and Oluf was recognized as King of both Norway and Denmark with his mother the actual ruler.

By this time she had made a bitter enemy in Albrecht, the Swedish king, who spoke only German. Using his threats against herself and the Hansa, she maneuvered the league into yielding the castles it held in Skåne. Additional agreement with the counts of Holstein, giving them Schleswig as their fief, made Denmark's southern borders safe. Ever the opportunist, she now took advantage of Swedish discontent with Albrecht and set forth Oluf as a claimant to the Swedish throne.

The sudden death of her 17-year-old son in 1387 turned into more than a personal tragedy for Margrethe. It threw Norway and Denmark into political chaos. With no king, no heir in either country, talk surfaced again of electing her nephew, young Albrecht.

Since the Mecklenburgs were as unpopular in Norway as in Sweden, Margrethe realized she must act quickly. One week after Oluf's death, his mother, in black gown and veil, had herself declared "all powerful lady and mistress and the whole Danish kingdom's regent" with the right to name her successor. She chose six-year-old Bugeslav, son of Ingeborg's daughter, Maria, and Vartislav VII of Pomerania. Advantageously, the boy had no special ties to the Mecklenburgs. She adopted him and gave him the name Erik. Following the Danish declaration, Margrethe was named regent of Norway. Meanwhile her most trusted adviser, Podebusk, had died, to be succeeded by Bishop Peter Jensen Lodehat.

Next she formed common cause with the Swedish nobles who up until this time had supported Albrecht. New disputes had risen over the disposal of the lands of the late Bo Jonsson Grip, the powerful chancellor who had consistently opposed Albrecht. Quickly Margrethe gathered allies, among them Birger, Merete Ulvsdatter's brother.

She met the nobles at Dalaborg in 1388 and set down her terms. In keeping with the formula used in Denmark and Norway, she was hailed as "sovereign lady and rightful ruler of the Swedish kingdom." She also gained the major portion of Bo Jonsson Grip's vast land holdings.

After Dalaborg, civil war broke out. The ever taunting Albrecht called her "King Trouserless" and egged her on by saying she belonged in front of an embroidery hoop. Thereupon he sent her a grindstone to sharpen her needles. Piling on insults, he also called her "monk dough," alluding to her special friendship with her confessor, the Abbot of Sora. Albrecht went so far as to spread rumors that she had had children by the abbot.

But the Swedish king's forces had underestimated her toughness and resilience and could not defeat her. Except for Stockholm, which remained under German control, the cities and castles accepted her authority.

In 1389 Margrethe formally took over rule of Sweden. Now she commanded all the north. Various Mecklenburg princes and Wendish officials sent soldiers to help Stockholm. A new enemy appeared: both the Baltic and the North Sea suddenly swarmed with pirate ships of the Victual Brothers, who sought to supply food to Stockholm and thus save Albrecht. Nonetheless Margrethe routed Albrecht at the Battle of Fallköping and imprisoned him.

In spite of her victory, she faced a hard truth. The nobles would not allow a woman to be crowned in any of the three Scandinavian countries. So Margrethe had Erik proclaimed hereditary King of Norway in 1389 and recognized as rightful heir to the Swedish throne in 1390. During his minority she reserved for herself the office of regent.

Meanwhile she had to deal with her old enemy, Albrecht. In 1395, after Hansa intervention, he and Margrethe signed the Lindholm Treaty: Albrecht obtained his release after promising to pay a large ransom over the next three years. When he failed to do so, the Hansa gave Stockholm to Margrethe in exchange for commercial privileges. In these negotiations she again proved her superb diplomatic skills.

The German threat remained, however, and she envisioned a united defense, which would in addition keep peace among the Scandinavian countries. She proposed a coronation ceremony for Erik and a special meeting to formalize the union symbolized by the young king. In Kalmar, on the southern coast of Sweden, in June 1397, the Archbishops of Lund and Uppsala crowned Erik the King of Denmark, Norway, and Sweden.

Margrethe. Tomb effigy in Roskilde Cathedral. National Museum, Copenhagen. Photo: Lennart Larsen.

Powerful clerics and magnates had gathered for the ceremony, and afterwards Margrethe sat down with them to produce a coronation letter and the "union document." Almost a month after Erik was crowned, the letter, written on official parchment, was hung with 67 seals, those of two archbishops, 10 bishops, five lower clergy, 46 knights, and four squires. It declared that Erik, having been elected King of Denmark, Norway, and Sweden, had now been elected king of one union state. It did not send Margrethe into retirement; it warmly commended her and indicated that she would continue to rule.

The "union document," prepared by a smaller group of councillors, was not such a finished product. Written on paper, it was stamped with 10 seals, not the expected 17. Following a long introduction, the first of nine paragraphs describes what will happen after the king's death. Only one king will be elected so that the kingdoms will never be separated again. If the deceased king has had sons, one will be elected king; if he has had only daughters, the councils of the three kingdoms will unite to choose among his grandchildren. If he has had no issue, the joint council will pick the man most suited to the throne. Further paragraphs emphasize that the king must respect the laws of each country and that they cannot be transferred from one to the other. Another paragraph gives the king power to conduct foreign affairs, but declares that whatever council he has with him must agree to any declaration of war. Finally the document states that Margrethe will rule in full authority over all the territories she has acquired.

This "union document" has provoked endless debate among historians, who have wondered why it was left in a draft state and who stamped their seals. Much disintegrated, these seals are difficult to identify. They were long believed to have belonged to seven Swedes and three Danes, with the Norwegians left out. One modern scholar has offered convincing proof that one seal may be Norwegian. Vigorous debate seems to have been the reason seven councilmen did not signify their approval.

Margrethe, a champion of hereditary monarchy as in Norway, must have been unhappy over the provision that strengthened the nobles at the expense of royal power. But she was too wise to risk a rupture and did not force issues. Norway had been sparsely represented, and the document was sent there, presumably for more assent. It was returned to Copenhagen without approval in 1425, more than 10 years after Margrethe's death. But the incompleteness of the document mattered little to the regent. She ruled a union-in-fact. The coronation letter itself spelled her victory at Kalmar.

Even victors can be hurt. A cruel trick brought bitter memories to the regent in 1402, when some merchants in a Prussian country town claimed that a sickly beggar was her son. Oluf's sudden death in 1387 had given rise to rumors that he had been poisoned. Although the poor man made no pretenses, his benefactors spread the word that some other young man had been killed in Oluf's place and that the prince had slipped away. As more and more supporters flocked to the vagrant, he himself began to believe the story. After a time Margrethe called for him to be brought to Skåne. With a crown on his head and his clothing covered by letters he had sent to the regent, he was burned at the stake.

Margrethe was not loved, but she was respected and admired. Through a network of royal sheriffs she consolidated her administration. Since her resources had been stretched, she levied heavy taxes and despite her vaunted piety confiscated church property. At the same time, in St. Birgitta's memory, she sponsored convents and made charitable gifts. She paid particular attention to recovering for the crown all the landed property acquired by the nobles during Albrecht's reign. Her subjects, however, complained that she carried out her land reduction policy too vigorously. The greater part of Schleswig came to her through purchase.

But she was not always successful. In 1403 the Teutonic Knights, claiming that they had to protect Hanseatic merchants from pirates who fanned out from Visby, had occupied Gotland. Margrethe could not drive them out and finally paid them to leave in 1408.

The indefatigable regent also busied herself as a matchmaker, shrewdly planning many marriages among the children of the Scandinavian nobles. In 1405 her negotiations won for Erik an English bride, Henry IV's daughter, Philippa. When Erik went to Norway to receive the girl, Margrethe sent along a letter of directions because she feared that the Norwegian nobles might induce the impetuous young king to promise too much.

One paragraph reads:

> [I]f any clerk or layman comes to you and asks you for some privileges . . .
> you must hesitate as long as you can. If they insist on knowing your meaning,
> you must push them on me and say that you are expecting me every day, and
> as soon as I come you will readily do so, if I advise you to, but you cannot do
> anything before I come because I know more about the matters than you.

In spite of her policy of strict neutrality, a short war with Holstein broke out over the question of a successor to its count. Before the conflict was over, Margrethe died of the plague aboard a ship in Flensborg Fjord in 1412. She left large sums to those who had suffered from war. Far more, she left a union which with some interruptions lasted until 1523.

Giovanna II
Queen of Naples, 1414–1435

Unlike Margrethe, the Scandinavian regent, the second Giovanna allowed feudal anarchy to take hold. But even before she began her troubled reign, her life had been marked by bloodshed, crisis, and confusion. She was born in 1371 at the Castel Nuovo in Naples, the older child of Charles of Durazzo and his wife, Margaret, adopted daughter and niece of Giovanna I.

Charles, also adopted by Giovanna, was fighting for her old enemy, Louis of Hungary, in 1379 when she generously acceded to Pope Urban VI's request to send Margaret, young Giovanna, and two-year-old Ladislaus to Charles's camp. After her daughter became ill, Margaret took her children to Rome, returning to Naples in 1381 after Charles usurped Giovanna I's throne. The following year he arranged for her murder. He was also the adopted son of Louis of Hungary, and in 1385 he left for Hungary to seize the crown of Louis's daughter, Maria. But within a short while the partisans of the queen and her mother assassinated him.

He left his family in a critical situation. Famine, plague, and falling agricultural prices had decimated the Regno or Kingdom of Naples, whose barons controlled the peasants and brawled among themselves. In contrast to the visual splendor at court, the atmosphere was warlike; every man wore a suit of armor.

Young Ladislaus succeeded his father under the regency of his mother, but his accession was disputed by the advisers of Louis of Anjou, son of the Louis whom Giovanna I had adopted as her heir. When Urban supported Louis of Anjou, the differences widened into a war between two children, directed by their mothers. After Pope Boniface IX recognized Ladislaus's claim and crowned him at Gaeta in 1390, the French responded by sending troops to occupy Naples and the surrounding territory. Only in 1399 did Ladislaus succeed in driving out the princes of Anjou and taking over the kingdom. Like his courtiers, he delighted in intrigue, war, and conquest. Monogamy never suited him, and he kept a harem in the old Castel dell'Ovo. His own two marriages proved barren, and Giovanna, as promiscuous as her brother, became heiress-

Giovanna II. Drawing by John A. Houston after sculpture on tomb of King Ladislaus, Naples.

presumptive. Her first husband was Wilhelm of Austria, the prince who had been betrothed to Jadwiga before she became Queen of Poland. That marriage also was childless.

In 1408, Ladislaus set his sights on Rome, which seemed an easy target. For over 30 years, the Great Schism had weakened the papacy, pitting two popes, one in Rome, the other in Avignon, against each other. In the most renowned of Ladislaus's military adventures, he captured Rome, then stalked the city, demanding loot and beheading those who refused to give him money.

A conclave at Pisa in 1409 deposed the two rivals and chose another pope, Alexander V. Neither Gregory XII nor Clement VII would give up authority, and for a time the papacy had three incumbents. Then John XXIII, who had succeeded Alexander, hired a famous *condottiere*, Braccio da Montone, who drove the Neapolitans from Rome.

Later Ladislaus came to terms with John, who obtained some church property, only to quarrel once more with the Neapolitans. Again Ladislaus occupied Rome and sacked and burned it as John fled. Then the king overran the Papal States, invaded Tuscany, and threatened Florence. But on the heels of his successes, he fell gravely ill and was carried on a cumbrous litter from his Tuscan camp back to Naples, where he died in August 1414. By now a widow of 43, Giovanna became queen, knowing that she would have to rely on the strength of the *condottieri*. Two of them, Braccio da Montone and Muzio Attendolo Sforza, trained together, would play crisscrossing roles in Giovanna's troubled reign.

She celebrated her accession by taking a new lover, the 26-year-old Pandolfo Alopo, whom she named Grand Chamberlain in complete charge of finance and patronage. At the same time her eye fell on the tough and illiterate, but charming Muzio, who had fought valliantly for her brother. He had earned the cognomen Sforza (Force), which he passed on to his family. Alopo, however, saw him as a dangerous rival and put him behind bars, where Sforza learned to form the letters of his name.

Giovanna and Alopo knew little about running a government, and they devoted themselves to expensive, bawdy, and profligate entertainments. When rebellious barons took up arms against the misgovernment, Sforza was freed, on condition of his taking Alopo's sister as his bride. To bind their interests more closely, Alopo arranged for Sforza to be appointed Grand Constable.

The Great Schism had ended when the Council of Constance deposed John and elected Martin V in 1415. Giovanna's advisers now persuaded her to strike a bargain with Martin. Until he could enter Rome, Neapolitan troops would guard the city; he in turn recognized Giovanna's dynastic claim to the throne of Naples.

To aggrandize their feudal privileges, fractious and scheming barons at court laid new plans. Having agreed that the amorous and irresponsible queen must marry again so that a strong consort could take over rule of the kingdom, they settled on James, Count of La Marche, a Bourbon of French blood. Giovanna agreed to marry him, but on Alopo's advice refused to make him king, granting him only the titles of Vicar General, Duke of Calabria, and Prince of Taranto.

Met on the Adriatic coast by a noble escort in the summer of 1415, James quickly fell in with the schemes being hatched. Since Sforza was now considered Alopo's man, he was arrested. While James and his princely cavalcade moved toward the Castel Nuovo and his waiting bride, he had himself proclaimed King of Naples. Almost immediately after the wedding, Alopo was captured and put to death and Giovanna kept in semiconfinement.

The French usurper, however, lost his popularity when he began distributing honors and key posts to his countrymen. In 1416 a coup headed by Ottone Caracciolo set Sforza free and booted James and his proteges out of Naples.

Although restored to his office of Grand Constable, Sforza did not recover his old standing with the queen, who had a new favorite, with whom he could not get along—Giovanni Caracciolo, a cousin but no friend of Ottone Caracciolo, the coup leader.

Nonetheless Giovanna had faith in Sforza's military skill and sent him to Rome to hold it until Martin's arrival. On reaching the city, he defeated Braccio da Montone, his old friend, who was defending it in the pope's name.

Martin made his entry in 1420, but the harmony lasted only a short while. Both he and Sforza began to feel that the always excitable Giovanna had yielded too much power to Caracciolo. The pope withdrew his support and recognized Louis of Anjou as King of Naples. Then he commissioned Sforza to fight for Louis.

On Caracciolo's advice, Giovanna turned to Louis's cousin and rival, Alfonso, King of Aragon and Sicily, promising that if he would help her, she would name him as her heir. When he asked for guarantees, Giovanna assured him that he would receive both the Castel Nuovo and the Castel dell'Ovo the moment the Aragonese sails were sighted in the Bay of Naples.

To further strengthen her military position, Giovanna engaged Braccio's services, giving him Sforza's former post of Grand Constable. When Sforza invaded from the north, Braccio started fighting vigorously. Both Louis and Alfonso were encamped in Naples.

It proved to be a war not of movement but of stalemate. Braccio and Sforza soon became bored and besides, Braccio needed to look after his private interests. Easily he persuaded Sforza to make peace with the queen, but although Louis and Alfonso then promised to leave Italy, Louis proceeded no farther than Rome.

The queen now received Sforza with her old warmth because she needed his support against Alfonso, who did not keep his vow to stay away from Naples. His Catalan entourage caused friction among the Neapolitans, and to Caracciolo he seemed much too presumptuous. Giovanna began to regret that she had promised him her throne.

On hearing of her change of heart, an enraged Alfonso moved fast. When he arrested Caracciolo, whom he considered head of the opposition, Giovanna fled to the Castel Capuano, where Alfonso's troops besieged her. Again she called on Sforza. He attacked from behind and routed Alfonso's Catalan forces, but judged his own army insufficient to hold his position. Therefore he demanded that Giovanna withdraw to Aversa. First though, the queen insisted that Caracciolo be set free. To carry out her wish Sforza had to exchange his Catalan prisoners for her lover. Then to the surprise of even her closest advisers, the fugitive queen named her enemy, Louis of Anjou, her heir. Since the mercenary captains were always switching sides, Alfonso summoned Braccio. On his way to attack Braccio at the beginning of 1421, Sforza accidentally drowned while crossing a stream.

In mourning for the general who usually had stood beside her, Giovanna confirmed his 22-year-old son Francisco Sforza in possession of his father's lands and castles and treated him as though he were the commander-in-chief of her forces. The bloated queen, now 50, was highly attracted by the strapping young man and at her depraved court found every excuse to celebrate his military prowess. With the support of other forces, Francisco moved against Braccio, and in a fierce battle Braccio received fatal head wounds.

Alfonso decamped, the Neapolitans recovered Naples, and Giovanna returned to the Castel Nuovo, where she heaped still greater favors on young Sforza. But he soon left for Milan, where he was to gain fame as the greatest *condottiere* of all.

A few years passed in comparative quiet although life in the palace was still geared to royal indulgences. Then in 1432 Giovanna quarreled with Caracciolo, whom his enemies seized and murdered. As internal disorders broke out once more, Gian Antonio, Prince of Taranto, led a revolt against the queen in Apulia. Louis of Anjou, her heir designate, came to the queen's rescue with a campaign against the rebels, but died in the midst of it in 1434.

Giovanna named his son, René of Anjou, as her successor. After an inglorious reign of 20 years, she herself died on February 11, 1435. She had not reckoned with Alfonso, who seven years later finally captured Naples and occupied her throne as "il Magnanimo."

Blanca
Queen of Navarre, 1425–1441

Daughter of the most peaceable of kings, Blanca of Navarre detested military violence. It was her bad fortune, however, to marry an insatiable warmonger.

Granddaughter of Juana II, she was born in 1385 to Carlos, heir to the throne of Navarre ("par excellence un prince francais"), and his wife, Leonor of Trastamara, daughter of Enrique II, King of Castile. When Blanca was two, her grandfather, Carlos II (the Bad), died; her father became king. In contrast to his predecessor, who had almost continuously led his armored troops in battle, Carlos III (the Noble) had no interest in warfare. One observer likened his reign to a "peaceful, smiling morning that succeeded a tempestuous night." In trying to rebuild ties with France, he traded certain domains for an annual subsidy and his title of Count of Evreux for that of Duke of Nemours.

Chroniclers have left no record of Blanca's childhood. Presumably it was cosseted. Leonor of Trastamara, passionate lover of the arts, was described as "una buena madre y buena esposa." In 1402, when 16-year-old Blanca sailed to Sicily to marry King Martin, her father started building at Olite a splendid, multitowered palace, summoning—in a deliberate act of eclecticism—Mudejar craftsmen to decorate its fine apartments and terraces. Plans called for over 400 rooms and galleries, vast gardens set in classical symmetry, and a zoo to shelter exotic birds and animals. Building continued for the next 17 years. Carlos, acutely aware of appearances, loved ceremony and patronized French jewelers, artists, poets, and musicians. Amid great pomp he brought his princely ways to France as often as possible, leaving Leonor, a capable administrator, as regent.

Martin of Sicily was also heir to the throne of Aragon, and Blanca seemed destined to be queen there. But Martin's death in battle at the age of 35 in 1409 changed many destinies because it left his father, Martin the Humane, without a legitimate successor. When the Aragonese king died a year later, a committee of nine chose Don Ferdinand of Trastamara as king. He ruled for only six years, leaving behind two sons, Alfonso and Juan. Alfonso, who followed his father to the throne, later gained Naples as well and earned the title of Alfonso the Magnanimous.

Within months of her husband's death, Blanca became engaged to Louis of Bavaria, brother-in-law of the French king. But the marriage never took place, and she returned to her father's court at Olite. Two sisters, Maria and Beatriz, had died in her absence. The death in 1413 of her elder sister, Juana, heiress to the throne, pushed Blanca into the position of heiress presumptive. Meanwhile Juan of Aragon had become engaged to her younger sister, Isabel. Ever the political opportunist, he abandoned Isabel and began to court Blanca although she was 12 years his senior.

He did not come unchallenged. Juana's widower, the Count of Foix, also began wooing his sister-in-law, but Carlos turned him down because of Navarrese repugnance for French rulers.

Juan knew well what he wanted, an Iberian peninsula free of French domination. Marriage to the heiress of Navarre would give him the opportunity to rid the kingdom of French influence. But he carefully kept his ambition from the Francophile Carlos. The wooing went on for several years with Juan going back and forth to Aragon. It was interrupted by the death in 1415 of Leonor of Trastamara, followed by an extended period of mourning by her family. In finally accepting Juan, Carlos recognized the possibility that the Aragonese infante might someday become king and that Navarre might thus be made subject to the Aragonese crown. Therefore he ordered many safeguards for the independence of his kingdom written into the marriage settlement. All officers of the kingdom and court, as well as commanders of forts, had to be Navarrese. Juan was forbidden to allow Blanca to give up any part of the kingdom. Children of the marriage were to be reared in Navarre. If there were no children and Blanca died first, Juan would have no claim to the crown. But Carlos made no provision for what might happen if Blanca died first with heirs.

The marriage was celebrated at the castle in Olite in 1420. Almost immediately Blanca realized that her young husband had a burning desire to govern Castile as well. He and his brothers, King Alfonso, Enrique, and Pedro, believed that in accepting the Aragonese crown, their father, Ferdinand of Trastamara, had been cheated of the Castilian kingdom, where the family held huge possessions. Throughout her married life Blanca watched Juan make war.

After the couple's first child, Carlos, was born in 1421, the proud grandfather, whose two sons had died in early childhood, created the principate of Viana for his namesake. The next year a daughter, Juana, arrived. Then at the age of two the Prince of Viana received the oath of loyalty from the Cortes and was declared heir to his mother.

Two years later Carlos the Noble died, and Blanca was proclaimed Queen of Navarre; she and Juan were not acclaimed together until 1429. Juan had gone off with his brothers on more raids which culminated in a full-fledged war with Castile, 1428–1429. Although only titular king, Juan saw to it that he did most of the governing.

Blanca had borne another daughter, her namesake, in 1424, and as queen she gave birth to Leonor in 1426. Little Juana had died the same year as her grandfather. But Juan regarded his wife with scant enthusiasm. For his children he had even more negative feelings, disliking, and fearing all three. As legal heirs to their mother, the Queen Proprietress of Navarre, they threatened the total rule he wanted. Nevertheless he knew he could arrange dynastically advantageous marriages for them. With haughty self-confidence he first negotiated with the Count of Foix in southern France, and in 1434 eight-year-old Leonor and 11-year-old Gaston de Foix joined hands in a "marriage of the future."

He remained insatiably aggressive. While the Treaty of Mejare with Castile (1430) lasted, he once again joined his brothers on the Italian peninsula, where Alfonso had set his sights on the Neapolitan throne after the death of Giovanna II. Following a fierce sea battle off Ponza in 1435, the Aragonese infantes were taken prisoner for a time. Back in Navarre, Blanca lit candles for Juan's health and well-being. Returning home in 1436, Juan decided to strengthen the truce with Castile by offering his daughter Blanca to his nephew Enrique, the knobby young Castilian heir with a too-large head and broken nose. Riding hard into Castile on a more peaceful mission than usual, he expected a warmer welcome than he got since his sister Juana was the Castilian queen.

The chief opposition came from Alvaro de Luna, the King of Castile's stubborn majordomo, whom Juan of Aragon had long regarded as his chief enemy. Finally agreeing to the marriage, Luna wrenched some concessions from the Navarrese king consort and paid a token pittance for some appropriated lands.

In March 1437, a simple engagement ceremony took place in the chilly fields of Alfaro, near the Navarrese border. With servants and baggage, Blanca, by now excessively stout, accompanied her daughter, as did Prince Carlos and Pierres de Peralta, constable of Navarre, well known as Juan's hatchet man. Presents were exchanged, and the Bishop of Osma prayed over the hands of the young pair, both just 14 years old. Juan did not show up for the occasion.

The queen brought her daughter back to Olite to stay for the next three years. Despite the betrothal, Juan again thrust into Castile in 1439, and Blanca governed by herself, wanting above all security for her family and peace for her country.

Meanwhile Prince Carlos married Inez, Princess of Cleves. Blanca, whose piety had increased with her weight, had encouraged her daughter-in-law's religious studies. But Inez was more interested in enlivening her husband's studious, serious court circles at Olite and Estella.

Back from Castile, Juan did not hide his contempt for his son, weak of constitution and frequently of will. He would not allow Carlos to accompany his mother and sister to the wedding ceremony at Valladolid. With the banishment of Alvaro de Luna (an exile that proved to be only temporary), Juan had seen an opportunity to push ahead with Blanca and Enrique's marriage.

The wedding was fixed for September 1440, in Valladolid, On the way Pedro Fernandez de Velasco, Count of Haro, welcomed the mother and daughter to a series of brilliant fiestas at his ancestral palace in Brievesa. One chronicler has left a small vignette. As the two Blancas, one quiet and slim, the other loud and fat, sat at high table on a dais, the Navarrese queen invited Haro's wife to join them. The countess watched Blanca happily eat her way through an endless succession of "roasts, fowl, fish, pastries, and fruit." Four more days of celebration followed as silver fountains gushed red wine and masques, bullfights, and mock jousts were staged, each day ending in a lavish feast with tumblers and minstrels amusing the guests.

At Valladolid, Juan of Aragon coldly awaited his wife and daughter. In the midst of preparatory festivities several important figures at the Castilian court suddenly and mysteriously died, and a large church wedding was judged highly unsuitable. So the shy Blanca and the even shier Enrique were wed at an altar in the palace during a private mass.

That evening, according to royal custom, three notaries sat outside the drawn curtains of the great wedding bed, ready to attest to a moan from the royal virgin, and heralds stood beside the castle doors prepared to sound a fanfare once servants displayed the spotted sheets. But the wedding night proved a fiasco. Whatever psychological or physical inhibitions there might have been, Enrique was unable to perform. The court chronicler solemnly but neatly summed up the situation: "The princess remained exactly as she had been born."

As reports reached Juan that his daughter continued to be a virgin, he resumed his threats and his seizures of Castilian lands. An increasingly ailing Blanca, who had long surrounded herself with Jewish and Moorish doctors she had tried to convert, went directly from Valladolid to the shrine of Guadalupe. Still grieving over Juan's bellicosity, she continued on to Santa Maria de Nieva to offer prayers for him and for peace. She died there.

Her will made Carlos her successor to the Kingdom of Navarre and the Duchy of Nemours. After him his sisters were next in line, but she asked her son not to take the throne without his father's consent. That request presaged trouble.

Isabella I (Isabel)
Queen of Castile, 1474–1504

A secret wedding in Valladolid on October 19, 1469, proved to be the most momentous union in Spanish history. The bride was Isabella, half sister of the King of Castile, the bridegroom Ferdinand, son of the King of Aragon, Castile's great enemy. Juan II of Aragon had designated his son heir to his throne, but civil war in Catalonia made Ferdinand's position insecure. Isabella's chances of a crown were even smaller since her half brother, Enrique IV, wanted a daughter of doubtful paternity to succeed him. But within 10 years she and Ferdinand would be sovereigns of a united Spain.

Juan II of Castile and his second wife, the high-strung Isabella of Portugal, rejoiced at the birth of a daughter, Isabella, in Madrigal on April 17, 1451. Three years later the sybaritic king died, and Enrique, his son from his first marriage, became King of Castile. Isabella and her baby brother Alfonso then went with their mother to live in a gloomy castle in the little town of Arevalo.

There, despite a sporadic education under monk tutors from nearby villages, Isabella learned to enjoy poetry, music, and philosophy, to sew and embroider, and to become a fine horsewoman. On the whole, however, she led a lonely life, made more difficult by her mother's moodiness, partly attributable to a guilty conscience. As queen consort, Isabella of Portugal had helped bring about the downfall and execution of Alvaro de Luna, her husband's favorite. Brooding at Arevalo, one moment she loved, another moment hated her children. Fortunately young Isabella gained a lifelong friend in Beatrice de Bobadilla, a girl her own age and daughter of the keeper of the castle.

The careless and incompetent Enrique IV, dubbed "the Impotent" after his failed marriage to Blanca of Navarre, called for a great celebration when his second wife, Juana of Portugal, gave birth in 1462 to a daughter, Juana. But the baby was soon known as "la Beltraneja" for Beltran de la Cueva, the queen's lover, believed to be the father. Fearful that rebellious nobles might refuse to recognize Juana's legitimacy and then use his young half sister and half brother in their schemes, Enrique brought Isabella and Alfonso back to his dissolute court at his favorite *alcazar* in Segovia, where he usually appeared in Oriental costumes. But, having learned deep piety from their mother, the boy and girl could not be corrupted.

Refusing to recognize Juana la Beltraneja as the king's heiress, Castilian nobles settled the succession on Alfonso. At a mock ceremony outside the walls of Avila they dethroned an effigy of the king and paid homage to Isabella's young brother. Earlier, they had been moving around Castile, persuading various cities to rise against Enrique.

Shortly afterwards, the first skirmishes broke out. Although in a good defensive position, Enrique looked for any excuse to prevent war. He welcomed a move by one of his former supporters, the Marquis of Villena, who had gone over to the rebels. Villena offered to desert them and do everything to smother revolt if Isabella's hand were offered to his brother, Pedro Giron, Master of Calatrava. The prospective bridegroom was middle-aged and debauched, and Isabella did not want to marry him. But Enrique, who several times before had made Isabella a pawn in marriage maneuvers, went ahead with the negotiations. Her prayers for deliverance were suddenly answered when Giron, on his way to fetch her, was struck by a quinsy and died suddenly.

Now nobody talked about a truce. Young Alfonso donned boy-size armor, and the rival armies met at Olmedo. After a drawn battle, Segovia opened its gates to Alfonso. Isabella, who had remained at the castle with the queen and Juana la Beltraneja, joined her brother in time for his victorious entry. Then for a while they went to Arevalo to see their mother.

By summer news came that Toledo had declared for Enrique, and Alfonso's advisers decided he must march south and restore obedience. On the way, in the village of Cardenosa, he died suddenly and mysteriously. He was just 14. After the funeral Isabella shut herself in a convent in Avila. There Alfonso's supporters came to ask her to take the title of queen, but she rejected their offer. In her first recorded utterance she said,

> Return the kingdom to don Enrique my brother, and thus you will restore peace in Castile. But ... declare me successor to the realm.

A grateful Enrique agreed to recognize her as his heir, gave her several cities for her estate, and promised she would never be forced to marry against her will. In turn Isabella vowed never to marry without his consent.

All too quickly, however, he began to waver. He summoned the Cortes to approve Isabella's succession, but then tried to dismiss it before the matter could be considered. He also began to thrust prospective bridegrooms on his half sister, such candidates as Alfonso V of Portugal and the Duke of Berri, brother of the French king, Louis XI.

At this stage Isabella had decided that she wanted to marry her second cousin, Ferdinand of Aragon, a member of the same Trastamara house as she. Though she had never met him, she liked what she had heard about the young warrior, whose father the Aragonese king had often thrown his troops against those of Castile's. Politically astute, young Isabella also considered the possibility that Ferdinand might someday be King of Aragon. She herself was determined to be the Castilian ruler. Aragon (made up of Aragon itself, Catalonia, and Valencia) and Castile (comprising Galicia, Asturias, the Basque provinces, Leon, Old and New Castile, Estremadura, Andalusia, and Murcia) were the two largest kingdoms of the Iberian peninsula and, like her advisers, Isabella dreamed of uniting them. Juan of Aragon had long held a similar vision, and when Isabella sent word that she was prepared to face Ferdinand, the septuagenarian Juan happily agreed to her plan.

Nonetheless she feared that if she became openly disobedient to her half brother's wishes, he would take away her legal right to succession. The unhappy young woman joined her increasingly deranged mother in Madrigal and there wrote letters to Ferdinand and to prelates and nobles asking for advice. Ferdinand indicated that he was willing to marry her, but that it was impossible for him to come immediately because of problems in Aragon. Just as she agonized over this turn of events, Enrique persuaded himself that a marriage alliance with Portugal would be more favorable than with Aragon. Soon he threatened Isabella with imprisonment if she refused the Portuguese king. In desperation she sent a new letter to Ferdinand and also wrote the Archbishop of Toledo, who gathered a force, quickly joined by another, to provide an escort of 500, enabling her to leave Madrigal and to settle in Valladolid.

Ferdinand now realized that he must join her immediately. Disguised as a muleteer, accompanied by six companions dressed as merchants, and traveling by night, the Prince of Aragon and King of Sicily (as his father had designated him), bypassed King Enrique's men, who lurked everywhere, and safely reached Valladolid.

At the house of Juan de Vivero, where 18-year-old Isabella was staying, she and 17-year-old Ferdinand met for the first time. In a blaze of torchlight, he saw a plumpish girl of middle height, with copper-toned hair and the blue-green eyes of the Trastamara family; she saw a good-looking youth, stocky and swarthy, with his hair already beginning to recede. The same house provided the setting for the marriage ceremony, secretly presided over by Alonso Carillo, Archbishop of Toledo. But once the rites were over, the town openly celebrated.

While negotiations were going on, Ferdinand had signed a set of capitulations or agreements to allay Castilian fears of foreign intrusion. They made plain that he would never enjoy any rights to the Castilian succession. He would be considered only a consort.

Because the bride and bridegroom were relatives, the Archbishop of

Isabella I. Print Collection, Newark Public Library, Newark, N.J.

Toledo and Ferdinand's father had forged a papal bull that dispensed their kinship. Afterwards the young couple grew terrified at the thought the forgery might be discovered. Meanwhile Isabella concentrated on trying to gain her brother's approval. After she and Ferdinand approached Enrique and asked for his blessing, Louis XI of France persuaded him to officially declare Juana la Beltraneja his heiress and to promise her in marriage to the Duke of Berri, now Duke of Guyenne. Isabella received this news just after the birth of her first child, her namesake, in 1471.

To her relief, the country did not rally around Juana. Isabella's prospects brightened even more when Cardinal Roderigo Borgia (later Pope Alexander VI) appeared with a legitimate marriage dispensation. Juan II of Aragon, desperately fighting France for possession of Roussillon and Cerdagne in the northeastern Pyrenees, called on Ferdinand for help. After her husband left, Isabella rode about from town to town strengthening her position. Meanwhile she rejoiced that the ending of the civil war in his father's lands left Ferdinand as undisputed heir to the throne of Aragon.

Enrique's marriage plans for 10-year-old Juana collapsed with the death of the Duke of Guyenne. By the end of 1473 he accepted an invitation to a banquet with his half sister. Suddenly he was taken ill, and persuaded that he had been poisoned, he and his followers left in a huff. He recovered, but by the end of the year, he died from other causes.

Realizing she had no time to lose, Isabella had herself crowned queen in Segovia although Ferdinand was still absent. When he returned, he reacted bitterly to the report that she had usurped a male privilege by permitting the sword of justice to be carried before her. Indeed he became so enraged that he threatened to go back to Aragon unless he received certain perquisites.

With her usual tact, Isabella healed the breach immediately. She appointed two prelates to be arbiters in weighing her and Ferdinand's respective rights and working out terms to bolster his wounded pride. The capitulations were reconfirmed with new provisos that Ferdinand's name would precede Isabella's on all documents and moneys, that their arms would be painted on the escutcheon, and that justice would be administered by the king and queen acting as one person, unless they were apart. In that case, each would act with equal authority.

Reunited, the young people laid great plans for the kingdom. To their dismay they now learned that a new rebellion had formed around Juana la Beltraneja. Before dying, Enrique had placed her in the custody of the Marquis of Villena, who fomented an uprising with the help of other nobles. The rebels at once dispatched letters to Juana's uncle, Alfonso, King of Portugal, who obligingly declared war. When Isabella and Ferdinand sent ambassadors to Alfonso, he answered them that he considered his niece the Queen of Castile and that he meant to marry her.

Portuguese troops poured into Spain in the spring of 1575. With energy and determination, Isabella and Ferdinand faced a war of succession. As their first business, they divided the work of recruiting, and Isabella, donning armor, set out on horseback. One night she had a miscarriage, but climbed back in the saddle within two days.

After Ferdinand ordered a humiliating retreat, he and the queen turned with new determination to winning. Isabella now made a bold move. Promising to repay in three years, she requisitioned half the silver and gold plate of the church. Further decisive steps followed. The army was reorganized into a smaller, more efficient force; cannons were bought from Germany and Italy. Finally, at the battle of Toro in March 1576, Ferdinand won one of the most important battles in Spanish history. Nonetheless, the civil war went on for three more years until Portugal finally renounced rights to the Castilian throne and Juana la Beltraneja vanished into a convent.

That same year of 1479, Juan II of Aragon died and was succeeded in Aragon by Ferdinand and in Navarre by his daughter, Leonor. With Ferdinand's accession, Isabella finally realized her dream of joining the two most powerful Spanish kingdoms. Castile and Aragon, however, continued to operate as separate legal entities, and Ferdinand kept full authority in Aragon. Although he was co-sovereign in Castile, Isabella became dominant in its domestic affairs, leaving diplomatic dealings to him. Gradually Castile came to play the more important part in the union chiefly because the monarchical power was not limited as in Aragon.

In 1480 the Cortes of Toledo assembled, and working closely with its representatives, over the next few years Ferdinand and Isabella produced a torrent of laws, edicts, and ordinances that totally reformed the judicial, military, and monetary systems. Everywhere they centralized administration with a civil service of middle-class professionals in place.

A "law and order" queen, Isabella decided she must quickly stamp out feudal anarchy and restore royal authority. Under Enrique and during the civil war, the nobles had gained great individual power and considered themselves kings within their own estates. At her bidding, the Cortes rescinded many of the grandees' privileges and prohibited the building of new castles. Meanwhile the king and queen ordered that almost 50 of the most dangerous older ones be burned to the ground. As a further measure they sent small expeditions, chiefly financed by the church, to various regions to bring the nobles to heel. Help also came from the Santa Hermandad (Holy Brotherhood), which they reinstituted to perform police functions. Gradually Ferdinand made himself head of the three great military orders of Santiago, Calatrava, and Alcantara.

Unity and pacification became royal watchwords. Religion too played its part. Everywhere in Castile, Isabella sensed heterodoxy. The best antidote, she determined, would be to impose religious orthodoxy. From childhood she had been under the influence of friars and monks, especially an early confessor,

Tómas de Torquemada, an ambitious Dominican friar. He exhorted her to ask Pope Sixtus IV for permission to introduce into Castile an independent inquisition to persecute heresy. It applied most specifically to the Jews and the *conversos*, the converted Jews, who wielded great economic and cultural influence.

Torquemada's appointment as Inquisitor General in 1483 signaled the true beginning of the Spanish Inquisition, which with its refinements of torture and seizure of Jewish funds proved to be the perfect instrument for the queen's religious arrogance and financial needs. As the *auto-da-fés* (burnings at the stake) grew common, thousands died. Isabella wrote primly to the papal ambassador: "I have caused great calamities and depopulated towns, lands, provinces, and kingdoms, but I have acted thus from love of Christ and the Holy Mother."

The cult of the Virgin Mary had reached its high point in Spain. Dignified and decorous, unfailingly gracious, Isabella herself seemed an admirable combination of femininity and piety in a matriarchal country, where children carried the names of both father and mother. After the birth of her first daughter in 1471, she had borne her husband four more children, Juan in 1478, Juana in 1479, Maria in 1482, and Catalina in 1485.

As testimony to her incessant travels to observe her reforms permeating society, each confinement took place in a different region of Spain. There were even further reasons for movement. Castile had no fixed capital, and the royal couple settled variously in Seville, Madrid, Segovia, and – after its conquest – Granada. As she rode the long dusty roads on horseback, appearing in the simplest hunting attire, the queen became an ever greater symbol of unity and purpose. Still, when the occasion demanded, she could deck herself out in dazzling robes of state.

Beyond the Jews, she and Ferdinand had long sensed an even greater insult to Christianity in the Moorish kingdom of Granada to the south. After suffering numerous provocations, they made ready to attack in 1482, just as the Spanish Inquisition took shape. While Ferdinand rode at the head of his troops, Isabella acted as financier and quartermaster, importing German and Italian specialists, whose guns hurled larger projectiles than had yet been used. Even when pregnant, Isabella crisscrossed the country, recruiting and helping supervise battles.

In a war of atrocities and chivalry, Ferdinand, so skilled (if devious) at diplomatic dealings, proved to be but mildly successful as a military leader. Still by 1491 the Christian forces stood below the well-fortified city of Granada. At the start of the new year, 1492, the Moorish king Mohammed XI (Boabdil), handed over the keys of the citadel, and Isabella caused a great silver cross to be raised over the battlements. In the magnificent throne room of the Alhambra she and Ferdinand received the homage of their new subjects.

That same year of military triumph, at Torquemada's bidding, all the Jews who would not abjure their faith were expelled from Castile. But they were not driven out of Aragon until the reign of Ferdinand and Isabella's grandson, Charles.

On the heels of the conquest of Granada came an historic sponsorship. Encouraged by one of her ubiquitous confessors, Isabella agreed to finance the expedition of a Genoese captain, Christopher Columbus, who believed that he would reach the Indies and its spice trade by sailing westward from Europe. Columbus had begun his appeals in 1485, but the king and queen were too preoccupied with Granada to be interested.

He left with three well-equipped ships in August. In October he made landfall and claimed possession in the name of the Spanish crown. Then he sailed on among the islands which he believed lay near the Asiatic mainland. He would make three more trips to the "Indies."

By the spring of 1493, Columbus, accompanied by shivering Indians and carrying gold, presented himself at the Aragonese court in Barcelona. Believing that he had reached the Indies, the Spanish monarchs appealed to Pope Alexander VI to confirm their title to the lands discovered by their admiral so that no conflict would develop with Portugal. Portuguese explorers had already discovered the Madeira Islands and the Azores. The pope declared a line of demarcation, which granted to Spain all lands not already in the possession of a Christian prince, which lay more than a hundred leagues west and south of the Azores; all lands east of the line were to be claimed by Portugal. A year later that line was readjusted by common agreement.

In 1494 the pope rewarded the king and queen's zeal for their faith with the title of Los Reyes Catolicos—the Catholic Monarchs. Ferdinand and Isabella took it seriously. Her confessor, Francisco Ximenez de Cisneros, who had been elevated to Archbishop of Toledo, was an ardent church reformer. Although religious freedom had been promised in Granada, he began a program of fierce proselytization, ordering mass baptisms, bonfires of Arabic books and manuscripts, and forcing the people of Granada to choose baptism or exile. In 1502 Isabella expelled the Moors from all Castile. But Ferdinand, aware that the Moors provided cheap labor, told the inquisitors to leave them in peace in Aragon.

The Spanish sovereigns also busied themselves forming political alliances by marrying off their children. Father of at least three illegitimate daughters he had relegated to convents, Ferdinand schemed to encircle his great enemy, France, with Spanish allies—Hapsburg, Burgundian, and English—through marriage alliances for his legitimate children. So Juan the heir became the husband of the Hapsburg Archduchess Margaret; Juana was wed to Margaret's brother, Philip of Burgundy; Catalina was sent to England, first to marry Prince Arthur and secondly his brother, King Henry VIII. Isabel was wed to Alfonso, son and heir of King João II of Portugal, then after Alfonso's death to his uncle, the next king, Manuel I.

Aside from her political acumen, Isabella took a lively interest in music and humanistic learning and in middle age began to learn Latin. With her enthusiastic support, the Spanish Renaissance came to full flower. She herself collected paintings and fine tapestries. Spurred by her ardor, seats of learning flourished, literature took on a new vitality. But for the Catholic monarchs, culture and learning were inseparably tied to religious reform, promoted by the zealous Cisneros.

In her last years the triumphant queen was struck down by family tragedies. In 1497 the Infante Juan died at 19; some months later his wife gave birth to a stillborn son. The next year Isabel of Portugal died, followed two years later by her small son, Miguel. His death meant that the heiress to the throne of Castile was the unstable Juana, wife of a man far too ambitious for the queen's liking. The only one of Ferdinand and Isabella's children to enjoy much happiness was Maria, who married her widowed brother-in-law, Manuel I of Portugal, in 1500.

The multiple sorrows, one almost on top of the other, broke down Isabella's health. Swollen with edema, she died on November 26, 1504. As she had ordered, her body was taken to Granada. Pedro Martyr hailed her as the "world's noblest ornament," understandable hyperbole from a court observer. The actual picture was both black and white, for she had helped to write some of the most splendid and some of the most terrifying chapters in Spanish history.

Leonor
Queen of Navarre, 1479–1479

"Of all the kings and queens of Navarre," wrote historian José Moret, "she was the one who had the briefest reign after working for it the longest." In contentious times for the Pyrenean kingdom, her ambition eventually led her to murder.

Leonor, born in 1426, was the youngest child of Queen Blanca of Navarre and Juan of Aragon and with an elder brother and sister grew up in the magnificent castle of Olite, erected by her grandfather, Carlos the Noble.

Through her early years, Juan was absent for long periods, joining his brothers, King Alfonso V of Aragon, Enrique, and Pedro in raids against Castile, where they wanted to increase the land holdings acquired by their father. They also coveted its throne. In 1428 they waged full-fledged war with Juan II of Castile, but the fighting lasted only a year. Again in 1435 Juan and the princes of Aragon left for a campaign on the Italian peninsula; after a naval battle they were temporarily imprisoned.

Before sailing to Italy, Juan arranged for a "marriage of the future" between his youngest daughter and 11-year-old Gaston de Foix. His father, the Count of Foix, who lived across the Pyrenees, had once wooed Queen Blanca. On Juan's return to Navarre from Italy, he began negotiations for the marriages of his other two children. In 1437 Blanca was betrothed to Enrique, heir to the Castilian throne, and in 1439 Carlos, Prince of Viana, took Inez, Princess of Cleves, as his bride. Blanca and Enrique's wedding was celebrated in 1440, but the bridegroom's impotence spelled failure for the marriage.

The peace-loving Queen Blanca died in 1441, having named the Prince of Viana as her successor, but only with his father's consent, which Juan refused to give. Inordinately ambitious to rule Navarre on his own, he was jealous of all his children. But he reserved most of his contempt for his son, whom he considered ineffectual and weak-willed. The young man had had military training, but preferred literature and the arts to battle.

In the year of Queen Blanca's death, Leonor and Gaston consummated their marriage and went to live in the Foix-Béarn domains in southern France.

From 1443 to 1464, Leonor bore 10 children—Maria, Gaston, Jeanne, Jean, Pierre, Margareta, Catherine, Eleanor, Jaime and Ana.

Before becoming King of Naples in 1442, her uncle Alfonso had named her father lieutenant general to govern Aragon in his stead. Somewhat grudgingly, Juan then appointed Carlos governor in Navarre. In 1447 the widower married the ambitious Juana Enriquez, daughter of the Admiral of Castile. The advent of this stepmother triggered a chain of events that ultimately brought Leonor to the throne of Navarre.

Juan reappeared in Navarre in 1450, demanding that his wife share duties with Carlos. But the prince rebelled, and two powerful factions, whose enmity had originated in a family feud, chose sides, the Beaumonts pledging loyalty to Carlos and the Agramonts supporting Juan and his queen.

When Carlos' forces besieged Juana Enriquez at Estella, Juan rushed to her aid. At a battle near Aybar in 1452, he defeated his son, whom he captured and kept behind bars until public outrage forced the prisoner's release. Loyally, Carlos supported his still-virgin sister Blanca when she returned to Navarre in 1453, divorced, disgraced, and scorned by her father and sister.

Fighting between Beaumonts and Agramonts proved inconclusive, and in 1456 Juan dangled an enticing offer before Leonor and Gaston de Foix. If Gaston would lead an army against Carlos, Juan would name the Count and Countess of Foix heirs to the throne of Navarre. They were quick to accept. Gaston swept down across the Pyrenees and soundly defeated his brother-in-law, who slipped away from the battlefield outside Estella.

Carlos had already connived with Enrique, his former brother-in-law, who had become King of Castile in 1454; they stripped Juan of much of his Castilian patrimony. To carry out his promise to Gaston and Leonor and vent his anger against Carlos and Blanca, Juan convened an Agramont Cortes at Estella in 1457. It disinherited Carlos and Blanca and designated Gaston and Leonor as heirs to the Navarrese crown. Defiantly a Beaumont Cortes assembled at Pamplona to swear loyalty to Carlos.

After escaping from Gaston's victorious troops, Carlos had vainly sought help from Charles VIII of France and Pope Calixtus III; finally he found refuge in Naples with his uncle Alfonso, who drove him around the streets in a flower-banked chariot and murmured comforting promises of both the Navarrese and Aragonese thrones. Alfonso died in 1458, leaving Naples to an illegitimate son, Ferrante, and the Aragonese throne to Carlos' 60-year-old father. The prince moved on to Sicily where his mother had been queen during her first marriage. Alarmed by his son's popularity there, Juan lured him back to the Spanish mainland by hinting at a possible reconciliation.

Catalonia was politically linked to Aragon, and when Carlos came ashore in Barcelona, the Catalans hailed him with fervor, seeing him as a useful instrument in a planned revolt against Juan who they believed was taking away their privileges. Enthusiastically they supported the Prince of Viana's request that he also be named heir apparent to the crown of Aragon, a title Juan and Juana Enriquez wished to reserve for their son, Ferdinand, born in 1452.

While in Barcelona, Carlos began negotiating again with Enrique of Castile, this time asking for the hand of the king's young half sister, Isabella. Juan, who had already picked her as the future wife of young Ferdinand, became enraged and asked his son to meet him at Lerida. On arrival, the unsuspecting prince found himself clapped in irons and confined to the castle tower. With the news of Juan's treachery, revolution broke out on Barcelona streets. When the revolt spread alarmingly throughout Catalonia, the king released his son.

Back in Barcelona, Carlos sent off some haughty demands to his father. But before he could take any further steps, he fell gravely ill of pleurisy and died in September 1461. Rumor persisted among the Catalans that his stepmother had arranged to have him poisoned. Now more than ever the Catalans hated Juan; they were to keep their revolution going for 10 years.

On his deathbed Carlos dictated a will making his sister Blanca his heiress; that stipulation sealed her fate. Many of the Beaumonts stood ready to press her claims, and a jealous Leonor, who had returned to Navarre, agreed with her father that her sister must be kept a prisoner at Olite. When Leonor's 17-year-old son Gaston was married to Madeleine, sister of the French king, Louis XI, in 1462, Louis and Juan signed a treaty delivering Blanca into her sister's custody to prevent her from contracting a marriage that might endanger Gaston and Leonor's succession.

Pretending that he had negotiated a marriage between her and Louis' brother, the Duke of Berri, Juan spirited Blanca away from Olite and arranged for her transportation across the Pyrenees to St. Jean Pied de Porte in Basse Navarre. There Blanca wrote a letter transferring her rights to her former husband.

Leonor and Gaston's emissaries then brought her to the castle of Orthez near their Chateau of Pau in Béarn. Stories surfaced over the next two years that Blanca had been tortured and subjected to sexual assault. She died there in 1464; everybody believed that Leonor had bribed a servant to poison her. Just at this time Leonor bore her last child, who was stillborn.

Now the Count and Countess of Foix assumed the title of Prince and Princess of Viana, and as titular king Juan allowed Leonor to take over the governorship of Navarre under his direction. The Catalan revolution continued, and he was busy intriguing with the French monarchy for aid. Gaston de Foix may have been egged on by his father-in-law or the King of France when, in the midwinter of 1466, braving blizzards and snowdrifts, he brought an army across the mountains to seize certain Navarrese forts occupied by the Castilians. He conquered Calahorra and moved on to Alfaro, where at the last moment more than 6,000 Castilians marched up to challenge him. Even women joined the battle, hurling rocks at Gaston's troops. He raised his siege, decamped from Calahorra, and sulkily retreated into Béarn. But the passage of his army through Navarre had left deep scars and embittered the people. Juan's henchman, Pierres de Peralta, stabbed to death the Bishop of Pamplona, who collaborated with Gaston.

While Leonor governed, always thinking of the day the crown would be hers, Gaston recovered the city of Viana in 1468, thus provoking renewed conflict between the Agramonts and the Beaumonts, who chose him as their leader. At various stages he even thought of usurping the Navarrese throne from his father-in-law, whom the Agramonts continued to support. After the breakdown of accords reached at Tafala in 1469 and Olite in 1471, the Beaumonts declared themselves ready to submit to Leonor as queen, not as somebody governing in her father's stead. Juan found the offer unacceptable.

In 1467, Leonor lost her firstborn, Maria, Marques of Montalfeltre. In 1470 her son Gaston died during a tournament; she mourned her husband two years later. As the Beaumonts had allied themselves with her half brother Ferdinand, Leonor turned more to her father and to the Agramonts. In 1476 she met with Ferdinand and Juan at Viana to settle the succession to the throne. She wished to name her grandson, Francisco Febo, as her heir, and Ferdinand and Juan agreed.

Leonor remained under her father's thumb for the next three years, waiting more and more impatiently for her royal turn. Finally, when the nearly blind octogenarian Juan died at the beginning of 1479, Leonor was proclaimed queen by the Cortes at Tudela, where she resided. But she had little time to enjoy her throne. Fifteen days after her investiture she died, leaving Beaumonts and Agramonts unreconciled and Navarre in a state of anarchy.

Catalina (Catherine de Foix)
Queen of Navarre, 1484–1512

It was Catalina's unhappy destiny not only to be driven from her Kingdom of Navarre but to see it annexed to the Castilian crown. During the few years of life that remained to her, the queen-in-exile never gave up trying to retrieve her crown.

Only daughter and second child of Gaston, Prince of Viana, and Madeleine, sister of King Louis XI of France, Catherine de Foix was born in 1469, when her grandmother, Leonor de Foix, governed Navarre for Juan, King of Aragon, and titular King of Navarre; Catherine's grandfather, Gaston de Foix, was seigneur in Foix-Béarn, which would eventually be her inheritance. Within a year of her birth her father died after being wounded while jousting, and Madeleine took her baby daughter and three-year-old son, Francisco Febo, to live at the Chateau of Pau, the family seat in Béarn.

At the beginning of 1479, Leonor became Queen of Navarre, but died 15 days after gaining the throne. She left it to 12-year-old Francisco Febo, but Madeleine did not bring him to Pamplona until 1482 because the Beaumonts and Agramonts were still fighting. Weary of the continuing turmoil, the young king and his mother stayed only three months and then returned to Pau. Two years later the golden-haired king died there, probably of tuberculosis although poison was rumored. He left his rights to his sister. Catherine, called Catalina by her new subjects, was acclaimed in 1484, with Madeleine (Magdalena) as regent. When the Navarrese expressed fear that Magdalena's brother, King Louis, would pressure her into granting him wide powers, Catalina's uncle Jean, Viscount of Narbonne, conveniently overlooked the fact that his mother, grandmother, and great-great-great grandmother had been regnant queens and cited the Salic law against female inheritance of the throne. He also laid claim to Catalina's French fiefs. Although the Castilians and Navarrese supported her, the Viscount of Narbonne kept pressing his demands for ten years. Her only recourse was to take up arms against him.

Other powerful uncles also intervened in the queen's life. Cardinal Pedro de Foix and his brother, Jaime, entered into elaborate negotiations with

Ferdinand and Isabella on the future marriage of their niece to the Spanish rulers' young heir, Juan. Influenced by her brother, Magdalena favored a French candidate, Jean d'Albret, son of Alain d'Albret, feudal lord of a considerable territory. Since the Navarrese Cortes approved the Spanish infante, Magdalena convened the three Estates of the fiefs of the House of Foix and gained their approval of Jean d'Albret. Catalina was married to him at Orthez in the summer of 1484, and Jean, whom the Spanish called Juan Labrit, became co-ruler.

Ferdinand, no longer a likely father-in-law, turned into an adversary, who occasionally changed his colors. At times he and Isabella supported Catalina with arms against her uncle; but Ferdinand had inherited Juan II's obsession with controlling Navarre, and whenever possible he intervened in its affairs. With the Inquisition in full swing in Castile, he charged Tudela with giving asylum to fleeing heretics. Defiantly the city fathers stood up for their rights, but found no backing in Pamplona. In 1488, under threat of excommunication, they finally submitted to Ferdinand and Isabella's demand to surrender the heretics. Navarre, however, never accepted the Inquisition.

Catalina and her young husband, both criticized as haughty, signed a treaty with France in 1491, infuriating Ferdinand. Much of the time they were absent from Pamplona, taking care of the fiefs threatened by her uncle. They were also rulers of Andorra, Assus, Béarn, Bigorre, Foix, and much of Gascony, Perigord, and Limousin. Despite so much traveling through their domains, they produced 11 children over a span of almost 20 years.

Because of the ongoing conflict between the Beaumonts and Agramonts, Catalina and Juan could not be crowned until 1484 during a brief lull in the fighting. Magdalena, their sage adviser, died the next year. Their acceptance of a Castilian protectorate, a transaction she no doubt would have opposed, enraged the French king, Charles VIII, who threatened to dismember Navarre. The accession of Louis XII in 1498 brought some relief, but a rupture with France recurred because Navarre participated with Ferdinand in his Italian wars out of gratitude for his help against the Viscount of Narbonne.

Seventeen-year-old Cesare Borgia, son of Pope Alexander VI, had been named Bishop of Pamplona in 1492, but had seldom appeared at his post. In 1506, however, by then a famous *condottiere*, he arrived in Pamplona once more to offer his services to Juan Labrit, who was fighting the Beaumonts, long opposed to the d'Albret-Foix alliance. Before winning any sweeping victory, however, he was killed at Viana. He left a widow, Juan Labrit's sister.

To escape from both France and Spain, Catalina and Juan allied themselves with Austria that year, again angering Ferdinand, who began plotting actively against them. In 1511 he badgered Pope Julius II into excommunicating the Labrits because they had once been allied with Louis XII, who had given sanctuary to an antipope. The bill of excommunication gave Ferdinand his main claim to Navarre.

Isabella of Castile had died in 1504, and three years later Ferdinand had married Germaine de Foix, daughter of the Viscount of Narbonne. Supported by Louis XII, Germaine's brother, another Gaston de Foix, took up his father's claims against the Labrits. But he was killed at the Battle of Ravenna during an Italian campaign in the spring of 1512.

Suddenly Navarre had nothing to fear from the French. Indeed, Louis XII, well aware that Ferdinand and Henry VIII were conniving to regain Guyenne (lost to England during the Hundred Years War), welcomed an alliance with Navarre. Shortly after the Battle of Ravenna, the Labrits sent emissaries to Blois to open negotiations.

In June an English fleet transported 10,000 men, under the command of the Marquis of Dorset, to Guipuzcoa with plans to link up with Ferdinand's forces under the Duke of Alba. Thereupon Ferdinand asked the Navarrese rulers for free passage through their country on his way to Guyenne. He also demanded the right to choose Navarrese officers to hold six fortresses as guarantees of the Labrits' neutrality. As bait he offered them membership in the influential Holy League.

Catalina and Juan declined; meanwhile they waited for word from Blois. In July they instructed their envoys to sign a treaty by which France and Navarre agreed to defend each other if either came under attack. The accord also prohibited either nation from allowing passage by an enemy of the other. As a final point, Navarre promised to declare war on England. Through secret channels, Ferdinand learned of its contents before the treaty was signed; furious, he ordered Alba to invade Navarre at once. The day after Alba entered Pamplona, the city surrendered. The Labrits, with their children, servants and small army, fled to the Chateau of Pau. Alba conquered more territory, expecting help from the English. But believing that he had been duped, the wrathful Marquis of Dorset sailed back to England with his troops.

Alba had promised the Navarrese that their *fueros* would be upheld. Initially the Pamplonese held back from accepting Ferdinand as King of Navarre because Juan Labrit was still living. Finally, however, Ferdinand's lawyers successfully presented his case, and within a few months the Estates of Navarre swore allegiance.

In September 1412, Louis XII, having finally decided to help the Labrits, assigned a French general to lead Juan's army through the Valley of Roncal for an attack on Pamplona. Juan tried to put the city under siege, but his army was an undisciplined group of Gascon and Béarnais volunteers, German and Albanian mercenaries, and French men-at-arms. The Duke of Alba arrived in Pamplona before the invading forces and secured the city. Nevertheless, Juan's army left devastation in its wake. Undaunted, he and his French general tried again in November; their attack failed badly. With their ragged army he retreated across the Pyrenees; on the way all were attacked by mountain-dwellers. Wounded and weary, the company struggled into Bayonne.

As Ferdinand solidified his power in Navarre, Catalina and Juan tried to interest the Holy Roman Emperor Maximilian, his grandson Charles in Brussels, and the new pope, Leo X, in their cause. Most of all they wanted the pope to revoke the bill of excommunication because many potential supporters stayed away from them for fear of being excommunicated too.

The Labrits met little success. Louis XII promised to assist them through a truce he negotiated with Ferdinand in 1513, but the signed paper said nothing about the deposed king and queen.

At the little court they set up in Pau, Catalina and Juan received more bad news. By 1514 Ferdinand had won the allegiance of the nobles in Basse Navarre. The next year he incorporated the entire Kingdom of Navarre into Castile.

For the Labrits, letter writing and negotiating went on constantly. In 1514 they had begun dealing with the next French king, Francis I, who in the end did nothing for them. Ferdinand died in 1516, but his grandson, the Archduke Charles, delayed in coming to Spain. During the interregnum, Juan Labrit made a third strike—encouraged, he thought, by Francis. He also believed he would have help from both the Agramonts and Beaumonts, who hated the occupying army. But troops never came from the French king. Juan's tiny volunteer army captured one fort and slowly advanced. Then many recruits began deserting, reinforcements never arrived, and a Castilian general quickly defeated the remnants of Juan's troops. He retreated to Pau, where a few months later he died bitter and discouraged, six months after Ferdinand.

Refusing to give up, Catalina sent an emissary to Brussels and obtained Charles's promise that he would not keep the throne of Navarre if there were proof that she had a just claim. Still trusting his word, she died in February 1517. Her 14-year-old heir, Henri, promised to carry forward her quest.

Juana
Queen of Castile, 1504–1555

Her countrymen called her Juana la loca, loca da amor—Juana the mad, mad for love. Fated always to be at the mercy of others, Ferdinand and Isabella's second daughter is the most tragic queen in Spanish history. She may have been less a madwoman, however, than the victim of her son's ambition and the political rivalry between her husband and father.

She was born November 6, 1479, in the palace of the Count of Cisfuentes in Toledo, and named for her maternal grandmother. That year Ferdinand succeeded his father, Juan II of Aragon, uniting the crowns of Aragon and Castile, and Portugal and Castile signed a peace treaty, ending a long war. Even as Isabella lay in childbed the great Cortes assembled at Toledo to help her and her husband set the foundation for security and national unity.

By 1585 Isabella had completed her family. Often she took her five children with her on journeys through her realm, making them equally accustomed to military encampments and royal residences. Like her sisters, Juana was well taught by the famous Italian humanists Antonio and Alessandro Gerardino. The Spanish court showed special pride in dark, high-strung Juana, who conversed fluently in Latin, danced gracefully, and played clavichord, small organ, and guitar. But it also noted that like her maternal grandmother at Arevalo, the long-nosed girl often preferred solitude and was prone to moodiness and melancholy.

She was 16 when her parents betrothed her to Philip of Hapsburg, only son of Maximilian I, the Holy Roman Emperor. By inheritance from his mother, Mary of Burgundy, young Philip was sovereign of the Low Countries. In August 1496, a vast fleet carried Juana and her imposing retinue from Laredo to Flanders. Her parents may have planned her marriage as a prosaic, political alliance, but when she saw the blond, dangerously handsome Philip for the first time, she fell deeply in love. He was less fervid in his feeling although her adoring looks caught his fancy. Both impatiently awaited their wedding, which was celebrated in October at Lierre. Five months later Philip's sister, the Archduchess Margaret, arrived in Spain to marry Juana's brother, the Infante Juan.

After her honeymoon, a progress with Philip through his domain, Juana settled down in the huge ducal palace in Brussels, trying hard to cope with a new and bewildering environment in which she was surrounded by Flemings. Even her chief duenna was Flemish. All too soon, in October 1497, word came of Juan's death. Three months later his widow gave birth to a dead son. Thereupon the Cortes of Castile recognized Juana's elder sister, Isabel, the Queen of Portugal, as heiress to the throne. In August 1498, however, Isabel died in childbirth, leaving a sickly son, Miguel. Three months later, with easy labor, Juana delivered her first child, Elinor.

Marriage did not change Philip's philandering ways. His flirtations aroused Juana's jealousy, and the Flemish court gossiped freely about her rages. Well aware of her daughter's reputation, an anxious Isabella dispatched an emissary, Tómas de Matiezo, subprior at Segovia's Convent of Santa Cruz, to watch and report. He later told the queen that contrary to her expectations, her daughter was too unstable to extend Spanish influence in the Low Countries.

In February 1500, in Ghent, the unhappy young wife gave birth to a son, Charles, and felt a momentary triumph at having so easily produced an heir. Revelry exploded in the streets and within a couple of days a glowing Philip and Juana showed themselves on the palace balcony to their exuberant subjects. Five months later, messengers arrived in Brussels to announce that Juana's nephew Miguel was dead. After three years of unremitting family tragedy, the again-pregnant Juana emerged as heiress of Ferdinand and Isabella.

She bore her second daughter, Isabel, in 1501. That year, in November, she and Philip were summoned to Spain, but they were forced to leave their children behind. During the summer, Isabella had sent another envoy, her first chaplain, Juan de Fonseca, Bishop of Cordova, to advise her daughter and to enjoin her at departure time to enhance Spanish prestige wherever she could on the journey through France. It included a stay at the Chateau of Blois, where Philip and the French Queen Anne, acting in place of an ailing Louis XII, signed a contract for the eventual marriage of young Charles to the baby princess, Claude.

After some delays, Juana and Philip made a ceremonious entry into Toledo in May 1502. It was Philip's first glimpse of his wife's homeland which she had not seen in six years. Their reception, however, was shadowed by word that Arthur, Prince of Wales and husband of Juana's youngest sister Catalina (Catherine), had died.

After suffering through the blistering Spanish summer, Philip declared he must return to his own country which he claimed needed him badly. But Queen Isabella demanded that Juana, who was pregnant once more, remain behind until her baby arrived. Smoldering over Philip's decision, Juana quarreled violently with him. After he stormed off, she fell into deep melancholy.

In the spring of 1503 she gave birth to a second son, Fernando. Her anger abated, she wanted to return to Philip. But Isabella acutely feared her son-in-law, who stood in line to inherit Austria and the title of Holy Roman Emperor. If he were to rule Castile jointly with his wife, it might become an appendage to Flanders and Austria. Nor did the astute Spanish queen approve of Philip's partiality toward the French. Sternly she insisted that her daughter remain separated from her husband for a time in order to prepare for queenship.

Sure that Philip surrounded himself with buxom beauties back in Brussels, the love-starved Juana let herself be tormented by jealousy. It was a miserable period also because she continued to be at odds with her ailing mother and bitterly resented being sent under Juan de Fonseca's care to the lonely castle of La Mota, outside Medina del Campo.

At last Philip sent an emissary to bring her back to Flanders. While Isabella delayed giving her daughter permission to leave, Juana in her usual, headstrong way began to prepare for her journey. When on Isabella's instructions Fonseca tried to stop her, she rushed up to the battlements and collapsed there. Isabella arrived by litter and tried to reason with her, but Juana hurled such abuses at her mother that reluctantly the queen gave in.

Almost as soon as Juana was reunited with her husband, she learned that he had taken a mistress. She reacted by falling on her rival and cutting off the young woman's long flaxen hair. Then, to win back Philip's favor, she began to use love potions and other sorceries devised by some Moorish prisoners she had brought along as serving maids. A disgusted Philip ordered the girls dismissed, and when Juana refused to let them go, he confined her to her room, where she promptly went on a hunger strike. Within a few days, the pair reconciled, but more quarrels followed, usually occasioned by Juana's intense jealousy.

Queen Isabella died in November 1504. Toward the end she had added a codicil to her will that if Juana could not or would not rule, her father should. Dutifully Ferdinand proclaimed his daughter Queen of Castile but started drawing in his own reins of power. On the day of Isabella's burial he asked one of his officials to read to the Cortes a diary kept by Juana's Spanish treasurer, Martin de Moxica, in Flanders. It so graphically portrayed the heiress's instability that the worried Cortes decided to name her father curator.

Ferdinand left no stone unturned. Next he sent councillors to Flanders, where they encouraged Juana to write a letter giving him full authority to govern while she was absent from Spain. In spite of his distaste for the Spanish climate, Philip was just as greedy for control. He intercepted the letter, then forced his wife to write a new one to his plenipotentiary in Spain. After expressing hope that time would heal her, Juana declared that nothing would induce her to deprive her husband of his governing role in Spain. Even with this message dispatched, Philip held his wife practically incommunicado for fear that Ferdinand would again try to influence his daughter. In this depressing atmosphere, Juana gave birth to a third daughter, Mary, in 1505.

Now Philip fell victim to his father-in-law's intrigues. Always the wily and masterful diplomat, Ferdinand had functioned well with Isabella, but with her steadying hand gone, some of his headier impulses took over. Considering marriage to young Germaine de Foix, niece of Louis XII, he signed a treaty with the French monarch, who had stood behind Philip's claims to Castile. Within a few months, confident of Louis's continued support, Ferdinand asked Philip to put his name to the Treaty of Salamanca, instituting joint rule of Castile by Philip, Juana and himself. Philip obligingly signed.

At the beginning of January 1506, the royal couple boarded ship off the Flemish coast, sailing again without their children, whose upbringing their twice-widowed Aunt Margaret began to supervise. Little Fernando lived in Spain, where he had been left at his grandfather's request. During a blinding storm, through which Juana alone remained calm, the Flemish fleet found safety in English waters. Philip went on to Windsor, where he agreed to free one of his prisoners, an English nobleman, in exchange for Henry VII's promise to help him hold power in Castile. Throughout most of the attendant festivities, Philip left Juana on the English coast, but finally brought her to Windsor to sign the treaties and enjoy a brief reunion with her sister Catalina, the young widow whom the English called Catherine of Aragon.

On reaching Spain in April, Juana declared that she had come only to consult with her father, not to supersede him. She had always preferred him to her mother and was not unhappy that he was planning to marry Germaine de Foix. An angry and anxious Philip now isolated her more than ever. But she did gain a point in refusing to ride into Corunna with her Flemish court ladies, jealously insisting they remain aboard ship.

As Castilian nobles flocked to the Flemish standard, Ferdinand decided he must meet with Philip as soon as possible. Without hesitation Philip accepted his gracious and conciliatory invitation to confer in a rural spot. Accompanied by many Castilian nobles, he approached his father-in-law in full panoply of war, which made him look slightly ridiculous since Ferdinand came riding a mule in the company of a small group of unarmed men. After the meeting, both principals withdrew to nearby villages, and for a few days letters flew back and forth. The final agreement declared that Ferdinand would leave Castile and that Juana did not want to participate in administrative affairs. No sooner had Ferdinand signed this treaty than he lodged a formal protest. Nonetheless he left for Naples, where his troops had been victorious. When the treaty was brought to Juana in Puebla da Sanadora, she reacted furiously. She fled on horseback, but did not ride far. She was soon discovered hiding in a bakehouse.

Somehow Philip managed to calm her, and heavily veiled and five months pregnant, she made her state entry with him into Valladolid. They stayed in separate houses as Philip hurried about his business. Once the members of the Cortes had given their oath of fealty, he asked them to declare the queen incompetent and to assign the entire rule to him. In the next few hours, Juana's supporters argued violently with Philip's advisers, and finally Philip's request was denied. But he remained king consort, and conscious of his power acted swiftly to replace Spanish officials with Flemings and award castles and land to his favorites.

From Valladolid the pair moved on to Burgos, where Philip determined to have his wife placed under restraint. There, in September, after a lavish banquet and a strenuous game of pelota, he began suffering from chills and a fever. Juana forgot all she had endured at his hands and stayed constantly at his bedside. Six days later he died at the age of 28, and his widow gave way to a storm of grief.

From now on she wore only black, and her enemies spread stories that she viewed the corpse daily. Actually, she did not order the coffin opened until five weeks after the tragedy, in this way responding to rumors that Philip's courtiers had spirited away his body. To her servants' surprise she kept her control as she darted a glance at her husband's remains.

With Philip's death, Castile once again headed for anarchy. The worst disorders broke out in Burgos between Flemings and Ferdinand's followers. At this juncture Isabella's old henchman, Ximenes de Cisneros, the powerful Archbishop of Toledo, set up a council of regency with himself as head and then declared martial law. He wanted the Cortes convoked, but Juana refused to act, claiming she must wait for her father's return from Naples. Cisneros went ahead nonetheless and summoned some of the deputies, who received only her accustomed answer, "Wait."

To escape this climate of dissension and menace, Juana fled to a country house nearby, but found little relief from claims and counterclaims. She now decided to honor Philip's will, which had requested his burial in Granada if he died in Spain.

In great haste Juana returned to Burgos, dissolved the Cortes, and with a stroke of her pen annulled all Philip's governmental acts and grants and appointments to foreigners, whom she forbade to hold any office. Resolutely she announced that when her father returned he must find the country as it had been under Isabella.

This business behind her, she felt ready to start on her journey to Granada. But the Bishop of Burgos told her it was against canon law to move a corpse for six months. Although Juana disregarded his warning, she grew terrified by new reports that Philip's corpse had been stolen. She ordered the coffin opened for a second time.

Her journey began in dense December fog, and before long she and her party had to stop. With improved weather, they pushed on, but at Torquemada, about 35 miles from Burgos, Juana's strength gave out, and she realized she would have to stay there to wait out her confinement. Catalina, her last child, was born in January 1507. During the Torquemada halt, which

Juana. Print Collection, Newark Public Library, Newark, N.J.

lasted four months, Juana held many midnight vigils in the parochial church, where she had placed Philip's elaborately draped coffin in front of the altar and had forbidden any woman to come near it.

One late April afternoon she started out again with the coffin. Suddenly a storm broke, and she decided to take shelter in a religious house. But when she realized it was a nunnery and not a monastery, she ordered all her entourage out into the fields. Once more, without giving any reason, she had the coffin opened. The party stayed out all night in the wind and rain, pressing forward when they could.

By morning they reached a desolate village, Hornillos, where a weary Juana decided to stop, keeping the coffin with her at the farmhouse where she stayed. Early in the summer she received word that her father was coming home and wanted to meet her in Tortoles. After opening the coffin a fourth time, she set out for the reunion, which resulted in her turning the government over to Ferdinand as regent.

Father and daughter set up court in Santa Maria del Campo, but that autumn Ferdinand left Juana in Arcos, a village a few miles outside Burgos; Philip's coffin had followed her. More than once her father had suggested that she marry Henry VII of England, but she had pointed out that a widow could not remarry while her husband's corpse remained unburied. Each time Ferdinand brought up the subject of marriage, Juana used the same argument.

In the next year he took bolder measures. He was planning a punitive expedition against Andalusia, and worried that certain nobles would rally to his daughter in his absence, he decided to put her in the remote castle of Tordesillas. Armored troops took her there in February 1509, and Juana felt completely betrayed. At the castle her guardian was Louis Ferrer, one of Ferdinand's favorites. Immediately he invoked rigorous discipline, and Juana reacted by going on a hunger strike and refusing to bathe, change her clothing, or sleep in a bed. In spite of her protestations, Philip's coffin was placed in a nunnery.

Within seven months her father visited her at Tordesillas. But instead of being given better treatment, she was moved to an inner apartment, where she could no longer look out on the panorama between castle and river. Ferrer may also have subjected her to physical violence. Later Ferdinand paid her a surprise visit, bringing with him a group of the most prominent nobles, who saw their queen looking distraught and disheveled. Suddenly realizing his trick, Juana hurried to put on proper clothes in an attempt to seem regal. But it was too late to correct the impression she had made.

Ferdinand moved on to new victories. In 1512, he conquered Navarre, becoming the ruler of Spain from the Pyrenees to Gibraltar, but still thirsting for control of the Mediterranean and all of Italy. The son Germaine de Foix had given him in 1509 died at birth, and the certainty that his Hapsburg grandson Charles would succeed to the Spanish thrones gnawed at him constantly.

Ferdinand himself died in January 1516, having left orders that Juana not be told of his passing. Cisneros became regent again. Fortunately for Juana, a new jailer, Hernan Duque, replaced the brutal Ferrer.

Almost two years after his grandfather's death, young Charles arrived in Spain with his sister Elinor, and the pair paid a dutiful visit to their mother whom they had not seen in 12 years. If they found her sunken eyes and withdrawn expression shocking, they showed little sympathy. Almost at once they made clear their purpose: Juana must delegate to her son the authority to rule. She obeyed, and the Castilian Cortes as well gave him the right. A few days later Cisneros died.

Charles was appalled at the lonely life of his little sister Catalina at Tordesillas and ordered the girl taken away. But Juana reacted so violently that Catalina came back. Like their two sisters, Isabel and Mary, Charles and Elinor had been brought up in Flanders to believe that their mother was mad, and he was convinced he must continue her imprisonment, no matter what.

After the death of his grandfather Maximilian, Charles was crowned Holy Roman Emperor in 1520. (The Aragonese Cortes took longer to submit to his rule.) His advisers, notably the Burgundian Grand Chancellor Chevres, suggested that Juana's freedom would hinder his plans for Charles to use Spain as a springboard to world domination. Juana commanded, begged, complained, threatened, implored, and raged in vain.

For all her misery, the prisoner of Tordesillas had become a symbol of right and justice. When rebellion broke out in 1520 against Charles's absence in Flanders and against Adrian of Utrecht, his deputy in Spain, the comuneros vowed to set Juana free and restore her to sovereignty. Conveniently forgetting they had declared her insane, Charles's men asked her to issue an edict against the rebels dissolving their junta, but she refused. Now for the first time she learned that both Ferdinand and Maximilian were dead.

The Marquis of Denia, a new guardian appointed by Charles, fled as the comuneros arrived. When they summoned the Cortes in Tordesillas, Juana presided over the governing body for the first time. As an official spokesman knelt before her and delivered a pledge of loyalty and obedience, she said, "I am most pleased that you have undertaken to right all the wrongs. . . . I shall aid you the best I can."

Back in Flanders, Charles was now galvanized into action. To remove the comuneros's chief complaint that foreigners ruled the kingdom, he directed Adrian of Utrecht to ask two great nobles, the Admiral and the Constable of Castile, to join a triple regency.

Meanwhile spies inside the castle daily reminded Juana of her royal blood and loyalties. Torn between the two factions, she had new qualms. Then she grew angry because the comuneros sent physicians and priests to try to restore her mental and emotional health. In protest she refused to sign any document that ordered the royalists to disband.

The rebellion had begun in August 1520, but by November the royalists had a strong new army in shape. That December a battle broke out in Tordesillas. With confusion in the castle, Juana escaped and ran through the streets to get Philip's coffin at the nunnery. But the Mother Superior told her that the cart to transport it had fallen apart. The first royalist soldiers to reach the castle found her in the courtyard, passive and remote.

Bent on revenge, the Marquis of Denia immured her in a room lit only by candles. Visitors were forbidden. Juana never knew that in 1525 Philip's coffin had finally been removed to Granada. In a special blow, Catalina was taken away to marry another King of Portugal, João III. Each year Juana's slovenly habits worsened; she regularly ate crouched on the floor, throwing her dishes against the walls.

In spite of her powerful relations, she was never set free or given any medical treatment. Her sister Catalina had married Henry VIII and become queen-consort in England. Her daughter Elinor first wed Manuel I of Portugal, her aunt Isabel's widower, then Francis I of France. Isabel, another daughter, was queen-consort in Denmark; the third, Mary, sat with her husband on the thrones of Hungary and Bohemia. Charles's reign as Holy Roman Emperor, however, brought a succession of political and military crises, exacerbated by the Reformation. He paid little attention to Spain.

His mother survived in her living tomb for 35 years. She died of gangrene on April 12, 1555, at the age of 75. A few months later a world-weary and withdrawn Charles abdicated and sought peace in a house on monastery grounds in Yuste. His brother Fernando took over as Holy Roman Emperor; his son became King Philip II of Spain.

Despite his years of neglect, Charles made sure that his mother's coffin was properly entombed in the Royal Chapel in Granada beside Philip, whom she had loved too wildly, and in the close company of her parents, who had helped build her tragedy.

Mary
Queen of Scotland, 1542–1567

> I did not think that the Queen, my sister, would have consented to my death,
> who am not subject to your law and jurisdiction; but, seeing her pleasure is so,
> death shall be to me most welcome; neither is that soul worthy of the high and
> everlasting joys above, whose body cannot endure one stroke of the
> executioner.

So Mary Stuart said with dignity just before she died. "Sister" was a
figurative term, for Elizabeth I, who ordered her death, was the cousin of
Mary's father, King James V of Scotland, son of Henry VIII's sister, Margaret
Tudor. Mary's claims to the English throne through this grandmother led in-
exorably to the execution block.

Completely broken by the defeat the English had inflicted on his army at
Solway Moss, James V lay dying at Falkland when his wife, Mary of Guise,
gave birth to a daughter, Mary, in the palace of Linlithgow in West Lothian,
on December 8, 1542. "It came with a lass, and it will gang with a lass," he said,
remembering the Stuarts's descent from a daughter of Robert the Bruce.
Within six days the baby succeeded her father. Nine months later she was
crowned at Stirling Castle, where she lived the next five years.

Meanwhile James Hamilton, Earl of Arran, leader of a pro–English,
pro–Reformation faction, became regent and offered the young princess as the
future bride of Henry VIII's son, Edward. But the day before Mary was
crowned, Arran suddenly gave up his Protestant faith, abased himself for
apostasy, and asked Cardinal David Beaton and Mary of Guise to join the
regency. Although the English wooing continued, it now assumed the rough
form of raids on Scottish border towns and farmlands. In anger the Scottish
parliament declared the English marriage plans moot. When Beaton instituted
excessively harsh religious policies, his enemies soon murdered him. Fearful of
losing the influence they had gained through Mary of Guise, the French
rushed to Scotland and captured the assailants. As the English continued to
make raids, the Scots called for further French help, promising their little

queen in marriage to the Dauphin Francis, son of Henri II and Catherine de Médicis.

In 1548, along with her maids-in-waiting, Mary Fleming, Mary Seton, Mary Beaton, and Mary Livingston—"the four Maries"—Queen Mary was whisked off by galley to France. Brought up at the luxurious court beside her future husband, she learned to speak three or four languages well, to write stylish poetry and prose, and to carry on sparkling conversations. By her teens she was facile enough to accompany her sweet singing voice on lute, harp, and viol.

Her powerful relatives, the Guises, also had a hand in her education. In addition to admiring the pretty child, the French found her a useful political instrument. On her 12th birthday in 1553, their lawyers had declared she was the right age to choose the sole governor of Scotland, and in accordance with their wishes she had appointed her mother.

Mary and the dauphin were married in Notre Dame Cathedral in Paris in 1558. Within a year the bridegroom succeeded his father, and Mary was hailed as queen-consort. In Scotland, meanwhile, civil war had broken out between supporters of the Protestant reformer, John Knox, and the regent's forces. The English came to the aid of the reformers, and Mary of Guise, mortally ill, agreed to talks. But she died before any could be arranged. Elizabeth, the new English queen, and her chief mentor, William Cecil, pressed on the Scots the Treaty of Edinburgh, which provided that foreign armies would leave Scotland and that Mary would abandon her claims to the English throne. Although the late regent had never ratified the treaty, it went into effect and broke France's hold on Scotland.

During Francis's brief reign, power had been in the hands of the Guises. But when the sickly young king died in 1560, it passed to his mother, Catherine de Médicis, who assumed the regency on behalf of her next son, Charles IX.

Now came another surprising turn in Mary's life. As John Knox remarked, the French king's premature death "made great alteration in France, England, and Scotland." Her mother's death had left Scotland without a government, and the young widow returned to Edinburgh, which received her with "fires of joy." At 18 the auburn-haired Mary stood almost six feet tall—a longish nose and heavy-lidded eyes kept her from being truly beautiful, but her lively charm captivated everybody. Even the formidable Catherine de Médicis had acknowledged it.

Settling in at Holyrood Palace, Mary created a highly graceful court life of masques, dancing, and plays, interspersed with hunting and hawking. At council meetings, where she often sat demurely with her embroidery, her comments showed that the Guises had trained her well in state affairs.

Since the Scottish Parliament appeared to sanction Reformation doctrine, Mary did not try to force the Catholic religion on her country. She asked only

Mary (Scotland). National Portrait Gallery, London.

to have mass celebrated in a private chapel at Holyrood for herself and her French followers. Still John Knox went to the palace to lecture the queen and from his pulpit thundered that a mass was more fearful than 10,000 armed enemies. After one of his interviews with the queen, he claimed there was so much "womanly weeping . . . that her chamberboy could scarce get napkins enough to dry her eyes."

Mary chose as her chief minister her illegitimate brother, James Stuart, a Protestant, whom she created Earl of Murray. Although for a time he had professed religious tolerance, he invited the queen to make a progress to watch him repress the power of the greatest Catholic family in the North, the Gordons, particularly that of their chief, the arrogant Earl of Huntley. Mary accepted with pleasure since the Gordons represented a threat.

She left Holyrood several more times for progresses around her country. Meanwhile marriage proposals arrived almost daily in Edinburgh. Candidates included the Kings of Sweden, Denmark and France; the Archduke Charles of Austria; the Dukes of Ferrara, Nemours, and Anjou; and the son of the Earl of Arran. Some were simultaneously wooing England's Elizabeth, who even offered Mary her own favorite, the Earl of Leicester. For a time the Scottish queen seemed to prefer feeble Don Carlos, the tragic heir of Philip II of Spain.

Then in 1565 her cousin, 19-year-old Henry Stewart, Lord Darnley, second after Mary in succession to the throne of the childless Elizabeth, returned from exile in England. Son of the Earl of Lennox and Margaret Douglas, he was extremely good-looking, even "lady faced," but uncommonly weak, indolent, and arrogant. Disregarding the advice of the Scottish nobles, Mary wrote to the pope for permission to marry him. By the time the dispensation arrived, however, she had become Darnley's bride. The wedding so incensed Murray and certain Protestant nobles that they raised a rebellion, known as the Chaseabout Raid. With the queen riding in their midst, her troops drove Murray across the border into England.

All too quickly, disgusted by her bridegroom's debauchery and insistent demands that the crown be secured to him for life, Mary fell out of love. Still she gave him the title of king and allowed him to sign state documents. Since he seldom turned up to do so, she ordered a stamp of his signature. Nonetheless Darnley loudly complained of being left out of state affairs.

Meanwhile, Mary had begun to place most of her trust in her secretary, the Italian-born David Rizzio, who had first entered her service as a musician. When she showed signs of pregnancy, Darnley willingly believed rumors that she was carrying Rizzio's child. Jealousy led him to participate in a political plot led by the Earl of Morton, Lord Ruthven, and Maitland of Lethington. On a March evening in 1566, they broke into the queen's cabinet in the tower of Holyrood Palace, dragged Rizzio into an antechamber, and stabbed him to death.

Showing great composure, Mary somehow lured Darnley into escaping with her to Dunbar on a wild, cold, five-hour ride. Barely a week later she returned to Edinburgh at the head of an army against the rebels, who fled. The reconciliation with Darnley, however, was short-lived. When their child, James, was born that June, Mary had begun to hate her husband.

After recovering from a severe, stress-related illness, Mary looked to the power-hungry and virile James Hepburn, Earl of Bothwell. Toward the end of November he and his allies proposed to the queen that if she would pardon Rizzio's murderers, they would help her end her marriage. At first Mary hesitated, fearful that an annulment might render her son illegitimate. Finally, she pardoned the men.

And Bothwell acted. In the new year of 1567, syphilis struck Darnley in Glasgow. Visiting him there, Mary arranged to have him carried to Kirk o' Field, a house in Edinburgh, where she saw him daily. One February night Kirk o' Field was blown up in a terrific explosion, and the bodies of Darnley and his valet, both strangled, were found in the garden. Everybody believed that with Mary's knowledge the vicious and boastful Bothwell had murdered the king.

Now events moved with dizzying speed. Mary fell ill again and in March left for the countryside to recuperate. After a mock trial in April, Bothwell was acquitted; four weeks later he carried off the queen to Dunbar. Quickly he divorced his newly acquired wife, and pardoning his seizure of her person, Mary created him Duke of Orkney. In a Protestant ceremony in the great hall of Holyrood she married him, just three months after Darnley's death. Furious at this hasty marriage, the Scottish Protestants mustered an army, and Mary and her new husband countered by raising one in Hepburn territory. A battle was expected at Carberry Hill, but it was delayed while talks continued over a proposed single combat between Bothwell and one of the Protestant nobles. During the negotiations, Mary's army began to disappear. The queen surrendered only after watching Bothwell escape from the field. She never saw him again.

First taken to Edinburgh in filthy clothes, Mary was subsequently imprisoned in the island fortress of Lochleven. There she signed an abdication decree in favor of her infant son. On the same day she suffered a miscarriage, losing twins. Meanwhile Bothwell, landing in Norway, had been taken to Denmark and imprisoned in Dragsholm Castle. He was to die there, completely insane, five years later.

Always able to fascinate men, Mary persuaded her jailer, George Douglas, a brother of Sir William Douglas, Lord of Lochleven, to help her escape by the following May. Murray, returned from exile, had declared himself regent of Scotland, and within a few days Mary mustered an army of 6,000 men and marched against him. But her poorly organized forces were speedily routed at the Battle of Langside, which she anxiously watched from a nearby hill.

Desperately she rode across the Scottish border to ask Elizabeth to hear a "just case." The English queen responded by sending "two torn shifts, two pieces of black velvet, two pairs of shoes, and nothing else." Mary's arrival highly embarrassed her, and months dragged on while she wondered what to do. Finally Mary agreed to an inquiry at York. She was never allowed to speak although the "judge," the Duke of Norfolk, was so charmed that he eventually became her suitor. On the other hand, Murray appeared and produced poems and the so-called "Casket Letters," purportedly written by Mary to Bothwell and showing an adulterous relationship. In spite of such evidence, Murray's case went badly.

An impatient Elizabeth transferred the hearing to Westminster, but Mary still did not appear. Nor was she allowed to speak to the queen. Again the dubious "Casket Letters" were presented, to no avail, and the arguments proved inconclusive.

Nonetheless Elizabeth kept her under house arrest with various titled families. Mary was moved to several different castles, but stayed mostly at Sheffield with the Earl of Shrewsbury as her jailer. During the long and wearisome years of captivity, she found some much-needed consolation in her needlework, her lap dogs, and her singing birds. But deprived of the exercise she craved, she grew stout, and her good looks gradually faded. She had last held her son, James, in her arms when he was one year old, and she would never see him again.

Even Mary's imprisonment did nothing to quell Elizabeth's uneasiness about her, seeing her as the focus of Catholic hopes to regain the English throne. When her pleas for release went unanswered, Mary willingly entered into plots. The first, the Ridolfi conspiracy, had led to Norfolk's arrest and execution in 1570. Other plots followed, confirming Elizabeth's conviction that Mary must be kept a prisoner for life. Following her wishes, the English Parliament passed an act to allow for Mary's trial and execution if any plot to kill Elizabeth were discovered.

Mary's last warder, Sir Amyas Paulet, remained quite immune to her charms and placed increasingly strong restrictions on her. In 1586 Anthony Babington and certain friends conceived a new scheme to assassinate Elizabeth and deliver Mary from prison. Letters of approval from Mary fell into the hands of Elizabeth's spy master, Sir Francis Walsingham.

Never before had Mary been so directly implicated, and she was brought to trial in September 1585. The court pronounced a sentence of death against her, but Elizabeth delayed in signing the warrant of execution. Finally her secretary carried it into effect.

One week later, on February 8, 1587, the drama played out in the great hall of Fotheringay Castle. Wracked with rheumatism (and possibly porphyria) and gray haired under her auburn wig, Mary laid her head on the execution block. She was clad in her customary widow's weeds which were burned afterwards lest they become relics. Two hundred knights and gentlemen showed mixed emotions as they watched her die.

Once she had presciently embroidered the words, "In the end is my beginning." The world has never forgotten Scotland's romantic and tragic queen.

Mary I
Queen of England
and Ireland, 1553–1558

Daughter of Henry VIII and Catherine of Aragon, Mary was the first queen to rule England in her own right. She began her reign on a tidal wave of popularity, but died five years later, detested and reviled.

This granddaughter of Henry VII and Elizabeth of York and of Ferdinand and Isabella was born at Greenwich Palace on February 18, 1516. At her christening Henry, who had longed for a son, declared hopefully, "If it was a daughter this time, by the grace of God the sons will follow." But Mary proved to be her parents' only surviving child. Watched over by a studious mother and coddled by an often boisterous father, she passed her early childhood in a luxurious household.

In 1525 Henry named her Princess of Wales and considered betrothing her to her first cousin, the Holy Roman Emperor, Charles V. But Charles demanded too large a dowry, and Henry quickly abandoned the suit. That same year, having dallied with Mary Boleyn, he became infatuated with her sister, the nubile Anne, one of his wife's ladies-in-waiting. But he waited until 1527, when Catherine was beyond the age of childbearing, to ask her for a divorce on grounds that their union was invalid because she had been his deceased brother's wife. With papal backing, Catherine held her ground, and Henry exploded in anger. Meanwhile she encouraged her precocious daughter in the Catholic faith and a study regimen, supported by a high-born governess, that eventually included astronomy, natural sciences, mathematics, Latin, Spanish, Italian, and Greek. Musically gifted like all the Tudors, Mary had a fine contralto voice and learned to accompany herself well on the lute and virginal.

Events soon crowded fast on the royal family. Henry, still smarting but undaunted, insisted that Thomas Cardinal Wolsey, Archbishop of York and Papal Legate, get him an annulment; when Clement VII refused him, Wolsey was dismissed. Wise to the royal temper, the new Archbishop of Canterbury,

Thomas Cranmer, obligingly declared the king's marriage to Catherine void. In January 1533, Henry secretly married Anne, who gave birth to their daughter Elizabeth the following September. Four months earlier Mary had suffered the humiliation of seeing her hated stepmother crowned Queen of England.

Continuing to move against Rome, Henry persuaded Parliament to pass the Act in Restraint of Appeals, denying all jurisdiction of foreign powers in English affairs. By the Act of Supremacy, Parliament named him Supreme Head of the Church in England. Still another parliamentary act gave him the right to make all ecclesiastical appointments. Finally he dissolved most of the monasteries and confiscated their land and wealth.

Henry also struck at his daughter. On Anne Boleyn's demand he stripped Mary of her title as princess and through the Act of Succession declared her illegitimate. In yet another attempt to demean her, he forced her to leave her household and move in with the infant Elizabeth. Separated from her beloved mother, Mary could not get his permission to see Catherine during her mother's long and ultimately fatal illness.

As her father stepped up his demands that she recognize him as Supreme Head of the Church, Mary gave him soft answers but stubbornly went on resisting him, although such obduracy often resulted in her being locked in her room and deprived of food and warm clothing. Then in 1536 three events ended her persecution. Catherine died; Anne Boleyn, accused of adultery, lost her head on the chopping block; and Henry married the delicate Jane Seymour. One week after the wedding Mary yielded and acknowledged her father as "Supreme Head in Earth under Christ of the Church of England." At the same time she signed a document admitting that her parents' marriage had been illegal. Her surrender may have had multiple causes—pressure from her cousin, Charles V, grief over her mother, relief that the mischievous Anne had disappeared for good, exhaustion, illness. Ever afterwards, however, Mary was consumed with a sense of guilt for her action.

Although she reentered the court as Queen Jane's companion, she was left with a concentrated bitterness time would not erase. Still, she and the gentle queen got along well, and proudly she stood as godmother to Edward, the long-awaited heir. Within a week of the baby's birth however, she wept as one of the chief mourners at his mother's funeral.

Like Jane, the homely and sensible Anne of Cleves, Henry's fourth wife, was kind to her stepdaughter, and Mary regretted the subsequent divorce. She did not get along with the king's fifth wife, the flighty and beautiful Catherine Howard, who followed Anne Boleyn to the block. During Catherine's brief tenure at court, Mary became even more religious and secretly vowed to avenge the insults to the Roman Catholic Church. After Henry's sixth marriage to the even-tempered Catherine Parr in 1543, 27-year-old Mary was restored to the royal succession.

Mary I. National Portrait Gallery, London.

In breaking with Rome, Henry had intended only to exclude the pope and to keep the English church Catholic, but long before he died in 1547, Protestant influences had seeped into ritual. Reluctantly he had allowed his son Edward to be educated as a Protestant, and when the boy became king at the age of nine, the Catholic religion in England went underground. Mary refused to subscribe to the new Protestant service and battled with the Privy Council to retain her license to hear mass. For taking this stand she placed herself in considerable danger, but she thought her cousin Charles V would invade England if any harm came to her. Such defiance boosted her popularity, and she was seen as a bastion against the young king's second protector, the power-hungry Duke of Northumberland. Whenever Mary appeared in public, Londoners hailed her enthusiastically. After Edward died in 1553 at the age of 15, North-umberland tried to put his young daughter-in-law, Lady Jane Grey, on the throne. But Lady Jane, a great-niece of Henry VIII spent her nine-day "reign" in the Tower of London, where the Lord Protector kept her during his coup d'etat.

Meanwhile Mary had made her bid for the crown and at Framlingham Castle in East Anglia had been gathering an army. When Northumberland left London to lead his soldiers against her, the lords of the Council dispatched the Earl of Arundel to Framlingham with a letter declaring that all along they had been "true and humble believers" in their hearts. The same day the Garter Knight of Arms proclaimed a new sovereign—Mary.

She began a triumphal progress in late July. Outside London she met her half sister Elizabeth, and together they rode on horseback into the city on August 3, to be greeted by ringing church bells and wildly cheering crowds.

After Northumberland's capture and speedy execution, Mary, short, grave, and myopic, was crowned with due ceremonial. Ireland belonged in her title because Henry VIII had proclaimed himself king there in 1541. She knew whom she wanted as consort, and soon negotiations began for her marriage to Charles V's son, Prince Philip of Spain, a 26-year-old widower.

As part of the marriage settlement, the Spaniards demanded the death of Lady Jane Grey in order to rid England of a rival claimant to the throne. At first Mary showed reluctance to act against her, declaring that "she could not find it in her conscience to put her unfortunate kinswoman to death, who had not been an accomplice of Northumberland, but merely an unresisting instru-ment in his hands." But after some weeks, tremendously eager for her own wed-ding, Mary agreed to bring the girl to trial. As a consequence, Lady Jane, her husband, Lord Guildford Dudley, and her father, the Duke of Suffolk, went before the executioner.

Too quickly Mary presumed that her public support implied acceptance of all her beliefs. Within months she asked a new Parliament, led by Lord Chancellor Gardiner, to repeal the religious decrees of the old Parliament and to annul her parents' divorce.

When Mary's resolve to restore the English Church to the jurisdiction of Rome became known, riots flared, and scurrilous pamphlets were circulated. Sir Thomas Wyatt, a champion of Protestantism, who wanted to break off the Spanish match and set Elizabeth on the throne, headed the most savage upris-ing. His rebels even bombarded the windows of Whitehall Palace with arrows as Mary watched in consternation. Once her soldiers had stopped the violence, Mary suspected Elizabeth of complicity and placed her first in the Tower and then confined her under house arrest at Hatfield Palace for two years.

Announcement of the queen's betrothal gave her subjects, terrified of Spanish influence, new cause for widespread outrage. But Mary went stubbornly ahead. On July 25, 1554, she married the darkly handsome Philip in a splendid ceremony at Winchester Cathedral. Like her aunt, Juana la loca, she was completely lovestruck. But the prince showed little interest in his scrawny, neurotic bride and felt he had made a huge personal sacrifice in order to keep England as an ally against Spain's great enemy, France. Still, by November Mary believed herself pregnant.

That same month a formal ceremony of reconciliation with Rome took place, and with the help of Gardiner and the newly-arrived Cardinal Pole, Mary revived medieval heresy laws. They came into effect with the new year, and Protestant heretics once more faced burning at the stake. Over the next three years 300 men and women would perish in the flames including such famous clerics as Cranmer, Nicholas Ridley, and Hugh Latimer. Rich Protestants having usually escaped abroad, many of the victims were humble and poor. Soon the heretics were considered political martyrs as well, for to the majority of Englishmen submission to Catholic authority meant betrayal and turning the nation over to foreign and papal influence.

As the English Inquisition began, Mary's private life turned bitter. Her vaunted pregnancy turned out to be a "phantom," actually the first signs of ovarian dropsy. To add to her depression, Philip left England to assume new duties as King of Spain and the Netherlands after his father's abdication. Mary saw him again for three and a half months in the early part of 1557 when he returned to pester her for money to finance a war against France. After his visit she thought herself pregnant again, only to find her hopes dashed.

She had reconciled with Elizabeth, and at midsummer entertained her at Richmond. Elizabeth reciprocated at Hatfield Palace with a bear-baiting exhibition and a play performed by the choirboys of St. Paul's Cathedral. But all around her Mary could sense the deep disenchantment of her subjects. They openly practiced the Protestant religion again. They howled and raged even more after learning that France had taken advantage of Philip's preoccupation with the war to seize Calais, the last English possession in France, in 1558. Mary felt so humiliated she declared that when she died, the word Calais would be found written on her heart.

By autumn 1558, her spirit was completely broken. On her deathbed she heard that a Protestant, anti–Spanish court had begun forming around Elizabeth. When "Bloody Mary" died on November 17, joyous bells pealed and Londoners danced in the streets. Five years earlier, the same sounds and sights had punctuated her accession.

Jeanne d'Albret
Queen of Navarre, 1555–1572

When Jeanne d'Albret was born on November 16, 1528, her father, Henri, was still trying to regain the kingdom his parents had lost. Sixteen years earlier, the army of Ferdinand of Aragon had conquered Haute Navarre, the larger Spanish portion, and the smaller part, Basse Navarre, in France, sending Queen Catalina (Catherine de Foix) and her nine-year-old heir pell-mell across the Pyrenees to the Chateau of Pau in Béarn, which remained a family fief. In 1521–1522, Henri had attacked Haute Navarre but after early success had suffered miserable defeat. It was as king-in-exile that he married the French king's sister, the widowed Marguerite d'Angoulême, ten years his senior. Jeanne, their first and only surviving child, was quickly separated from her parents. Henri d'Albret kept busy fighting his battles, taking new hope in 1530 when Charles V turned Basse Navarre loose. Henri was now king *de jure* of the northern segment and still in possession of the fiefs belonging to Foix-Béarn and Albret.

Jeanne's mother was equally occupied. A correspondent of scholars like Erasmus and Theodore Beza, Marguerite showed her extravagant devotion to her brother, Francis I, by an intense preoccupation with public affairs. The little princess was placed under the care of a friend, Aymée de Lafayette, at the castle of Lonray in the Norman countryside. After Marguerite and Henri's infant son died on Christmas Day, 1530, their relations became strained, with the result that the little girl saw even less of her father and remained distant from the emotionally cool Marguerite.

Early on, Jeanne showed signs of the tuberculosis hereditary in her family. A sensible and highly intelligent child, she remained isolated, never having playmates or experiencing any kind of family life. Only brief visits to the court broke her solitude. After 1538, however, when she and Aymée lived in the somewhat forbidding Chateau Plessis-les-Tours, she spent more time in the company of the French royal family. During this period Nicola Boulin, a noted humanist, supervised the girl's education.

She now began to figure in her father's political schemes. Henri d'Albret wished to offer her hand in marriage to Charles V's son (later Philip II) in the hope that the Holy Roman Emperor would restore Spanish Navarre to the young bride. But he was opposed by his brother-in-law, King Francis, who brought Marguerite over to his side.

In 1540 Francis carried out his own plans to marry his niece to William de la Marck, Duke of Cleves in the Rhine Valley and brother of Anne of Cleves, fourth and unwanted wife of England's Henry VIII. William asked for an immediate ceremony, but agreed that because of Jeanne's age and frail health, the marriage would not be consummated until later.

In vain Jeanne declared herself fiercely opposed to the match. In December 1541, the wedding came off at Chatellerault with great pageantry. Immediately afterward Duke William left for Cleves, which was threatened by Emperor Charles V's troops, and Jeanne returned to Plessis.

After a few years, however, he became impatient and asked for his bride, offering to send a delegation to escort her to Cleves. Meanwhile Jeanne had prepared an official document declaring she had never freely consented to the marriage. When William capitulated to Charles and surrendered his lands, an angry Francis announced that he had no further obligations to the frustrated bridegroom. The marriage was dissolved in 1545 on grounds that Jeanne had never ceased protesting it and that it had never been consummated.

Francis died in 1547 and was succeeded by his son, Henri II. With the new reign came a new suitor for Jeanne's hand. The Duke of Vendôme, Antoine de Bourbon, tall, handsome, and animated, had won recognition for his military exploits. This time the plain-faced Jeanne did not object and soon bloomed with the romance. After the wedding at Moulins, Henri II wrote to his Grand Constable, Anne de Montmorency: "I have never seen a happier bride than this one; she did nothing but laugh." The young poet Pierre de Ronsard had composed an epithalamium; its joyous lines were echoed through the festive journeys the bride and bridegroom made throughout the province of Béarn and to Antoine's family.

A year later Marguerite died, mourned by her devoted retainers and the humanists and scholars who made up her intimate circle, but not by her husband or daughter. Jeanne had hardly known her.

Soon Antoine became involved with his father-in-law, Henri d'Albret, in threats against Spanish Navarre. As war between Spain and France broke out in 1551, the two men saw an opportunity to strike. Before long the Navarre Question faded away in personal concerns. That year Jeanne gave birth to a son, Henri, with the father at her bedside. For the next 15 months Antoine, in the French king's service, kept constantly on the move. Jeanne willingly traveled from camp to camp in Picardy, but husband and wife could arrange only infrequent meetings.

She was pregnant again when her first born, the 23-month-old Duke of Beaumont, suddenly died in August 1553. She always believed that responsibility rested on her foster mother, Aymée, who had taken exaggerated measures to keep the child from catching cold; she had placed him in overheated rooms at the height of summer.

A second son, also given the name of Henri, was born in the Chateau of Pau on a cold December night in 1453. According to legend, Jeanne while in labor sang an old country song that called for help from the Virgin of Jurançon: "Beg God to deliver me quickly of the fruit of my womb, and may He give me the gift of a son."

Henri d'Albret took charge of his young grandson when Antoine resumed his command in Picardy, and Jeanne paid visits to friends throughout France and met her husband when possible in the rough and tumble camps. The old king gave the boy an almost peasant upbringing. Time would show that he also bequeathed his Gascon lightheartedness and toughness to the future King Henri IV of France.

In 1555 Jeanne gave birth to a third son, the short-lived Duke of Marle. Her father's death sent her hurrying back to Pau where she styled herself "reine et dame souveraine" of Béarn, Soule, and Basse Navarre. In addition to her father's fiefs, which also included the counties of Foix and Bigorre and the duchy of Albret, she had inherited from her mother the counties of Armagnac, Rodez, and Perigord and the viscounties of Limoges, Quercy, and Marsal. Antoine was feudal lord in the duchies of Vendôme and Beaumont and the county of Marle. At once Jeanne called on the Estates to accept her husband as joint ruler of Navarre. At first reluctant to assent to Antoine's role, parliamentarians finally did.

To Jeanne's dismay, he soon precipitated a crisis inspired by the French crown. Henri II tried to persuade him to give up the province of Béarn in exchange for certain areas in central France. Although Antoine refused, some of the leading Béarnais *seigneurs* attempted to stage a military coup. Bernard, Baron d'Arros, foiled it, but Jeanne had to handle the political implications. To prevent a general defection of the nobility, she awarded the faithful and kept the would-be traitors in office.

Again in 1556, she lay in childbed. But soon Antoine wrote to Montmorency; "God today took a little girl to whom my wife gave birth two weeks ago tomorrow." When they had recovered from their sorrow, the King and Queen of Navarre visited the towns in Basse Navarre and took part in enthusiastic Basque ceremonies. By autumn they left on a leisurely journey to present their son Henri to the French court, where Henri II and his wife, Catherine de Médicis, were much impressed with the attractive, lively heir.

Before long, Antoine began playing politics again. Never forgetting his eager collaboration with his father-in-law on the Navarre Question, he held several meetings with a Spanish envoy in the hope of obtaining the restitution of Spanish Navarre in return for territorial concessions in France. But Spanish stalling, Antoine's own overconfident demands, and a growing desire for peace

Jeanne d'Albret. Bibliothèque Nationale, Paris.

between France and Spain made the Navarre Question fade away once more.

Meanwhile in Pau, Jeanne faced administrative, judicial, and fiscal problems to which she gave immediate attention. As soon as she had consolidated her power, she began to gain the same kind of respect and loyalty her father had enjoyed.

Disheartened and angry over his failure to resolve the Navarre Question, Antoine found a new vehicle to satisfy his ambitions, the Protestant religion. Roman Catholics had given the name Huguenots to the Protestants who believed the teachings of John Calvin. During the reign of Henri II, they had become a large and influential political group in France.

Jeanne too showed interest in the sect, but not for any political reasons. Molded by sorrow, the laughing bride had become a serious woman, spare and angular, temperamentally and intellectually ripe for Calvin's logic and rigid strictures. In La Rochelle she and Antoine attended a public Huguenot service. Antoine did not say, however, that he had turned Protestant like many people in his domains. In fact he soon showed more interest in jockeying for royal power than in the future of the Huguenot movement. In 1557 Henri II received a mortal wound in the eye while jousting at a tournament. For a time Antoine, First Prince of the Blood and direct descendant of Louis IX, involved himself in the intrigues initiated by the Guises, the uncles of Mary Stuart, soon-to-be bride of the new king, Francis II. The Guises, however, went out of their way to humble the King of Navarre. Meanwhile Jeanne, who had borne a daughter, Catherine de Bourbon, that year, remained in Pau, devoting herself to administration and the education of her son, Henri.

Huguenots soon organized in opposition to the arrogant Catholic Guises. Antoine's brother, the Prince of Condé, was considered their "silent chief." But Condé was led off to prison after the Huguenots failed in their attack against the Chateau Amboise, the court's temporary residence, in the early spring of 1560.

By the end of the year, young Francis II was dead, and his brother, Charles IX, a mere child, was king. Their mother, Catherine de Médicis, took over the regency, deeply humiliating Antoine.

In reaction his wife became a Calvinist, and once converted, she decided to participate in the national religious scene. But six months passed before she could leave for the French court. Many Huguenots looked to her husband for leadership. Antoine, however, kept protesting his orthodoxy and attended mass regularly. In a move to conciliate the opposing factions, Catherine de Médicis named the King of Navarre the Lieutenant General of France. To her daughter Elizabeth she wrote scornfully: "[He] is entirely in my hands and deprived of all power and authority except through my good pleasure."

While Jeanne made her way up the Loire Valley, Antoine seemed increasingly drawn to the Catholic side and even boasted that he would bring his brother and wife along with him. Regularly, however, he broke his marriage vows. Soon he had a son by one of Catherine de Médicis's ladies-in-waiting.

As Huguenots gained more converts, even at court, the Catholic powers outside became alarmed and threatened invasion to keep France in the Catholic fold. Antoine served as principal pawn in the struggle. Led by Jeanne, the Huguenots mounted an intensive drive to secure his leadership. But intrigues on the Catholic side, replete with plots and offers of another kingdom in place of Navarre, tempted the Lieutenant General. He no longer felt any loyalty to his wife; his only interest lay in her title and her kingdom. When the Spaniards dangled the possibility that finally he might gain the French regency, Antoine became zealous on the Catholic side. Years later in her memoirs, Jeanne wrote: "The withdrawal of the former king, my husband, from his first zeal for the Religion, was for me a very sharp thorn, not a thorn which pierced my foot, but one which entered my heart."

When he could not persuade Jeanne to give up her new faith, he made her position at the French court untenable. Finally Catherine de Médicis gave in to his insistence to send Jeanne away. Antoine, who issued the direct command by letter, demanded that young Henri be left with him.

The complete disintegration of a once-happy marriage coincided with the outbreak of the First Civil War between the Huguenots and the Catholics in 1562. Carrying her tiny daughter, Jeanne returned to Pau by a roundabout, often dangerous route, threatened by Blaise de Montluc, Antoine's equerry.

Under Antoine's command, the royal Catholic army laid siege to Rouen. Before long he was shot in the shoulder and lingered for a month. As he was taken on a barge to Paris, he asked his physician to read a passage from St. Paul. "You see," said the dying man, "that God wishes women to obey their husbands." Quickly the doctor retorted, "But Scriptures also say, 'Husbands, love your wives.'"

With Antoine's death, Jeanne could freely negotiate with Catherine de Médicis, who allowed her to resume charge of Henri's education under a Huguenot tutor. Alternately brought together or driven apart, the two women had common goals, to bolster their kingdoms against powerful neighbors and to assure their sons' successions. When Pope Pius IV threatened Jeanne with excommunication and confiscation of her lands, Catherine successfully remonstrated, and Rome dropped the matter.

In 1564 the Queen of Navarre allowed her son Henri to leave in Catherine's entourage on a two-year progress throughout France. At one point she herself joined the retinue. When Catherine was received by the seer Nostradamus, the old man predicted that Henri of Navarre would someday be King of France.

Unlike her brother, Catherine de Bourbon spent much time at her mother's side, but did not get much attention. Small and frail, she had a too-short leg that caused her to limp. Nonetheless Jeanne saw to it that her daughter received a good humanist education.

For her own poor health, Jeanne frequently drank spa waters. But she never neglected her duties. From 1563 to 1567 she took several decisive steps to establish Calvinism in her kingdom and increase the autonomy of Béarn. New administrative, judicial, and legislative reforms also claimed her attention.

In 1566 she paid her longest visit to the French court, but constantly fell out with officers of the crown and her in-laws. Tart-tongued and easily offended, she regarded anybody who crossed her as a personal enemy. Back home, she had to deal with difficult problems in her various domains, mostly relating to Calvinism.

Resistance to Jeanne's religious programs was the alleged cause of the Oloron uprising of 1567 and that of Basse Navarre, which followed. As soon as she had pacified the Oloron rebels, the Second Civil War between the French Catholics and the Huguenots broke out in 1567. Occupied with the new rebellion in Basse Navarre, Jeanne maintained a position of strict neutrality in the war, which lasted only six months. Meanwhile her son Henri returned to Pau.

Once Basse Navarre was pacified, Jeanne joined her brother-in-law, Condé, at La Rochelle. It was considered the Huguenot capital of France, and Jeanne occupied the center of its so-called court. The Third Civil War had begun in 1569.

After her departure for La Rochelle, the French crown sent an army under Antoine de Lomagne, Seigneur de Terride, to reconquer Béarn for Catholicism. In the spring of 1569 Terride's troops occupied all of Béarn except for one fortress. Jeanne commanded Gabriel de Lorges, Count of Montgomery, to strike swiftly and hard with troops staffed by crack Gascon captains. After a week's campaign, Béarn lay completely in Jeanne's hands once more.

The night before the official restoration of Jeanne's authority, six prisoners taken at Orthez, including three well-known Béarnais rebels, were killed. When Jeanne's enemies charged that the men had been massacred, she countered that they had been shot trying to escape.

Soon after her arrival in La Rochelle, Jeanne had drafted her memoirs, actually a political manifesto to justify her joining Condé. She had delivered her son, she wrote, to the "tutelage and valor" of his uncle. She herself, she noted, was living in semiretirement "deprived of the pleasures of my own house, but only too happy to suffer for my God." Increasingly busy with her pen, she dispatched countless requests to foreign powers and allies for help.

Unfortunately for the Huguenots, the Prince of Condé was again taken prisoner at the Battle of Jarnac in March 1569 and was treacherously killed. Jeanne felt his death keenly, but pulled herself together to work on the Huguenots's peace strategy; she failed, however, to gain concessions she had demanded. Still the Treaty of St. Germain gave Huguenot nobles more privileges than they had expected—full liberty of conscience, the right to worship publicly on the outskirts of two towns in each province, a general amnesty, and the restitution of their confiscated estates.

On her return to Pau, Jeanne found herself in great financial hardship. Nonetheless she put at the disposal of the Calvinist clergy the former wealth of the Catholic Church. She seemed tireless, but her health had broken down. Summoning all her strength, she engaged in long negotiations with Catherine de Médicis for the marriage of her son Henri to Catherine's daughter Marguerite. The wedding supposedly would bring about a reconciliation between Huguenots and Catholics. Jeanne came first to Blois, then continued on to Paris, bewildered and disgusted by the licentiousness at court.

After a shopping expedition on an extremely hot day, Jeanne became ill and died on June 9, 1572. Poison was rumored, but doctors ascertained that her old pulmonary disorder had reasserted itself. She would have been horrified to know that Henri and Marguerite's marriage, which took place two months later, would be followed in four days by the massacre of the Huguenots on St. Bartholomew's Day.

Twenty-eight years later, Jeanne's son, then Henri IV of France, promulgated the Edict of Nantes, which at least for a century established the position of the Huguenots in France. Henri has gone down in history as a notable statesman, soldier, planner, builder, administrator. Toward the end of his life, which an assassin's knife cut short in 1610, he said that his mother was responsible for everything he had achieved.

Militant Calvinist and able administrator, Jeanne d'Albret left her own enduring mark. But perhaps her biggest accomplishment was grooming for great kingship her only surviving son.

Elizabeth I
Queen of England
and Ireland, 1558–1603

The November day Mary Tudor died, the lords of the council set out posthaste for Hertfordshire, and Hatfield Palace, where they found her half sister Elizabeth walking in the leafless park. As they knelt before the auburn-haired young woman, they were unaware that their cry of "Long live the queen!" was ushering in a glorious era of English history. They knew only that high drama had already stamped much of her life.

Born at Greenwich Palace on September 7, 1533, Elizabeth was not even three years old when her father, Henry VIII, accused her mother, Anne Boleyn, of adultery and imported a skilled French headsman to dispatch the queen. The day after the execution, the king wed his mistress, Jane Seymour, and almost immediately declared Elizabeth, as well as Catherine of Aragon's daughter Mary, illegitimate. After Jane died giving birth to Edward, the heir, Henry married and divorced Anne of Cleves, and then fell violently in love with young Catherine Howard, who became his fifth wife. She was executed for adultery when her stepdaughter was eight. With a happy sixth marriage to Catherine Parr, Henry restored his daughters to the succession.

Like their bluff father, the children traveled regularly from one royal residence to another. Elizabeth's favorite was rose-bowered Hatfield Palace, which her half brother Edward would later convey to her. Its red-brick walls blended gracefully into the fields and woods, where she was taught to ride well.

In whatever palace she lived, Elizabeth plunged eagerly into her studies. She had begun to learn mathematics, history, geography, architecture, astronomy, and four modern languages: French, Italian, Flemish, and Spanish. When a young Cambridge scholar, William Grindal, pupil of the celebrated Roger Ascham, began teaching the princess Greek and Latin, Ascham generously gave advice.

After her father's death in 1547, Elizabeth entered the household of

Catherine Parr. Not long afterwards, the dowager married Thomas Seymour, brother of Jane and Edward Seymour, Earl of Hertford and Duke of Somerset. At once Edward Seymour made himself Lord Protector for his nephew, the 11-year-old King Edward VI. Soon scandalous rumors arose that the high-strung Elizabeth romped regularly in her bedchamber with the handsome, lively Thomas Seymour, Lord High Admiral of England. After Lady Seymour's death in childbed, her widower was accused of planning to marry Elizabeth and overthrow the government of his brother, the Lord Protector.

As the case against Seymour proceeded, Elizabeth kept herself from being named an accomplice in his plot, but she watched helplessly as members of her household were taken to prison. Seymour was executed in the spring of 1549. Although under great strain, Elizabeth received the news bravely.

She found consolation in her lessons. Ascham, who had been appointed her tutor following the death of Grindal the previous year, warmly praised his royal charge's power of application, quick apprehension, and retentive memory. She could even extemporize in Latin.

In a sudden turn of fortune in 1552, Edward Seymour was displaced by the Earl of Northumberland and executed; young Edward reported the event matter-of-factly in his journal. Elizabeth sided with her half sister Mary against Lady Jane Grey, Northumberland's daughter-in-law, whom he unsuccessfully tried to place on the throne after Edward died in 1553. The next year Mary, the new queen, suspected Elizabeth of complicity in Thomas Wyatt's rebellion against the crown and confined her in the Tower of London for two months. For much of Mary's reign, her young half sister was kept at Hatfield, far removed from the English Inquisition the queen set in motion.

From such a difficult and unhappy youth, Elizabeth gained a worldly wisdom and wiliness beyond her years. She put these to good use when she succeeded to the throne on Mary's death in 1558. The problems facing the 25-year-old monarch were immense. A contemporary account summed them up: "The realm exhausted. The nobility poor and decayed. Want of good captains and soldiers. The people out of order, justice not executed. The French king bestriding the realm, having one foot in Calais and the other in Scotland."

Pale and frail Elizabeth may have looked weak, but she showed her political strength at once. When signing a public document, she dispensed with the "Supreme Head of the Church" title used by Henry VIII and Edward VI and contented herself with "&c.," thereby making both Catholics and Protestants happy. Then determined to gain the affection of her people and well aware that she was already a powerful national symbol, she set off on an extravagant precoronation parade from Hatfield to London. In an even greater display of magnificence, she was crowned on January 15, 1559, at Westminster Abbey. The Count of Feria, the Spanish envoy, wrote of the occasion: "She is much attached to the people and they to her, for they love a display of pageantry; and here they have seen such goings and comings and such musick and soundings of cannon, and nosegays and banners, that they are hoarse with their responses and doubt not that she will outwit her sister in rulership."

While still at Hatfield in November 1558, Elizabeth had appointed William Cecil (later Lord Burghley) as her chief minister of state. Devotedly he remained at her side for the next 40 years. Both political pragmatists, minister and queen realized they must balance Spain and France, England's two greatest enemies, against each other. They quickly brought the ongoing war with France and Scotland to an end, getting favorable terms for England. In still another area the young queen triumphed. Despite her own extravagant tastes, especially in gems and wardrobe, Elizabeth had a passion for solvency, and having inherited a bankrupt treasury, she next charged Sir Thomas Gresham, a financial wizard, with establishing a sound currency.

Her first parliament helped her continue steering a middle course between Catholics and Protestants. The religious settlement of 1559, enshrined in the Acts of Supremacy and Conformity, enforced the Protestant religion by law, declared the celebration of the mass illegal, and made Elizabeth Supreme Governor of the Church, not Supreme Head. Four years later, the Thirty-nine Articles enforced the teachings of Anglicism. But the government did not interfere with private masses, and Catholics who did not put in their monthly obligatory appearance at a parish church were subject only to minor fines. In the liturgy, Protestant doctrine combined with Catholic ritual.

To ensure proper succession to the throne, the new Parliament also concerned itself with finding a suitable consort for Elizabeth. Mary's widower, Philip II of Spain, presented himself as an early suitor, and ambassadors also came on behalf of Eric of Sweden, Duke Adolphus of Holstein, and Philip's nephew, the Archduke Charles of Austria. Elizabeth warmed to none of them, being far more interested in one of her own courtiers, Robert Dudley, her virile Master of the Horse, whom she had known since childhood. Cecil, however, cautioned her against considering him as a bridegroom after he fell under suspicion in the mysterious death of his wife, Amy Robsart, in 1560. Still Dudley continued to ride with Elizabeth and to partner her at the balls she doted on. She made him Earl of Leicester in 1564.

In 1567 she found herself with the recently deposed Queen of Scotland on her hands. Mary Stuart, a devout Catholic, was a claimant to the English throne and had French connections besides. She asked for asylum and support, but as a precautionary measure, Elizabeth placed her under house arrest at Carlisle. As various Catholic rebellions burst forth in her behalf over the years, Mary would find herself a prisoner for life in a series of castles. When she was first confined, the pope retaliated by excommunicating the English queen and issuing a bull that absolved English Catholics from allegiance to the crown, thereby making them potential if not actual traitors.

Elizabeth I. National Portrait Gallery, London.

As England continued to enjoy prosperity, these were the years of the queen's most splendid summer progresses to the estates of her nobles. No entertainment exceeded that of Leicester, who in 1575 hosted her at Kenilworth Castle for 19 days, running up expenses the equivalent of three million dollars.

Another generous admirer was Sir Christopher Hatton, later Lord Treasurer, who each year gave the queen a valuable piece of jewelry. Brilliant men at court like Francis Bacon, Walter Ralegh, Sir Nicholas Throckmorton, William Davison, and Francis Walsingham, the royal spymaster, showed her exceptional service.

Accustomed to Leicester's attentions, Elizabeth fell into a rage when he married Lettice Devereux, widow of the Earl of Essex, in 1578. By the next year, however, she had a new suitor, the 24-year-old Duke of Alençon, puny and pock-marked. She had already turned down his brother, Prince Henri, the Duke of Anjou (later King Henri III). Their resolute mother, Catherine de Médicis, had long negotiated with the English court for a union between one of her sons and Elizabeth. Surprisingly, the Tudor queen warmed to Alençon's wooing and seemed increasingly attracted to the political values the ardent little "Frog Prince" offered. But suddenly a friend's death called him back to France. As soon as he left, the Puritans, who feared any French alliance, raised a great uproar. After one of their spokesmen, John Stubbs, published a pamphlet warning of the danger of Alençon's suit, the queen's judges found him guilty of seditious libel and ordered his right hand cut off.

Meanwhile Elizabeth's attention had been fixed on daring maritime enterprises. Between 1576 and 1578, Martin Frobisher searched the North American coast for a Northwest Passage to Asia; from 1577 to 1580, Francis Drake circumnavigated the globe; other English sailors roamed the high seas, seeking new lands and trade routes.

When Alençon returned to London in 1583 and Elizabeth gave him a ring, Leicester and Hatton protested vehemently. The next day she sent a message to the "Frog Prince" that she was afraid she did not have long to live. To get rid of him, Lord Burghley paid him an ample sum. By the next year he was dead. So in middle age came Elizabeth's famous remark to her Parliament: "I am already bound unto a husband, which is the kingdom of England."

In 1587, declaring that "great things are done and more are afoot," a court annalist presented a telling picture: "Her majesty quits her bed early and retires to it late. She is at her virginals and her needle plies exquisitely, and she dances to the viola with the air of a young girl; her huntsmen are outwitted by her in their pursuits and her council lords fear her anger. But that she is troubled no one doubts; that she is forbidden by nature to fawn before Spain, neither that she seeketh a conclusion for the prisoner."

That prisoner was Mary Stuart. Plots to usurp the English throne still centered around her. After Mary involved herself in an assassination conspiracy, Elizabeth signed a death warrant, but left it lying on the floor. When her secretary picked it up and brought it to the Privy Council, she exploded with anger, pretending she had never meant the document to be acted on. Nonetheless, one week later, on a February morning in 1587, an executioner cut off Mary's head. Sterner measures against the Catholics followed.

For many years, with encouragement from the queen, English captains like Francis Drake, John Hawkins, and the "sea dogs" from Devon had preyed on Spanish shipping. Finally in 1588, Drake attacked the Spanish in the harbor of Cadiz, boasting of having "singed the King of Spain's beard." Philip's answer was to send the Invincible Armada against England.

As the Spanish fleet approached, Elizabeth came to Tilbury, where her army engaged in maneuvers. There, "attired like an angel bright" on her spirited white horse, she made a famous speech:

> I am come amongst you resolved, in the midst and heat of the battle, to live or die amongst you all; to lay down for my kingdom and for my people, my honor and my blood, even in the dust... I know I have the body but of a weak and foolish woman, but I have the heart and stomach of a king, and of a king of England too; and think foul scorn that Parma, or Spain, or any prince of Europe should dare to invade the borders of my realm; which, rather than any dishonor shall grow by me, I myself will take up arms, I myself will be your general.

Her army, however, saw no action. Thunderstorms in the North Sea and superior English seamanship sent the Great Armada limping back to Spain in a pitifully reduced state. The queen went to St. Paul's Cathedral for a thanksgiving service, and bonfires blazed everywhere in England. Grief, however, succeeded victory: Leicester suddenly died of an undisclosed illness.

Mary Stuart's removal as a threat to the throne and the defeat of the Armada brought a surge of nationalism and pride. England was now Mistress of the Seas, her colonial empire expanding. The euphoric mood resulted in a golden age of lyric poetry and drama, led by Edmund Spenser (who called the queen "Gloriana"), Sir Philip Sidney, Christopher Marlowe, and William Shakespeare, whose plays were often performed before the queen.

At the opulently dressed court, life was equally vigorous, with a continuous program of dancing, cards, chess, bull and bear baiting, all inspired by Elizabeth's pungent oaths, remarkable vitality, wit, and fire. But to all this power and unity there was a dark underside. The war with Spain had depleted the treasury, and through the last decade of the century England rocked with financial crisis. At court people became more corrupt and grasping. Elizabeth herself quarreled with Parliament over the granting of monopolies.

One handsome young man meant heartache for her, Leicester's spoiled stepson, the Earl of Essex, 33 years Elizabeth's junior. After his introduction at court, he quickly won her favor, and she chose him as commander of troops, fighting the rebels in Ireland, led by the Earl of Tyrone. On his return from an unsuccessful campaign, Essex took part in a feeble rebellion, and an unforgiving queen sent him to the block in 1601. Her subjects, however, overlooked her foolish if heartbreaking infatuation. In spite of her vain, capricious, devious, and often insincere personality, the "Virgin Queen" enjoyed an overwhelming popularity. In 1602 she celebrated 44 years on the throne.

Early in 1603, when she took ill with a cold and fever, she stubbornly refused medicine and food. Propped up on her cushions, she approved James VI of Scotland, Mary Stuart's son, as her successor. On March 24 she died, "mildly like a lamb, easily like a ripe apple from the tree." Two years earlier, to a deputation of her last Parliament, she had made her "Golden Speech," containing a nugget that might have been her epitaph: "This I count the glory of my crown, that I have reigned with your loves."

History has given her name to a resplendent age.

Catherine de Médicis
Regent of France, 1561–1563; 1574

Between 1572 and 1583, frequently interrupted marriage negotiations went on between the Duke of Alençon and England's Elizabeth, raising the possibility that she might become the daughter-in-law of the most powerful woman in France, Catherine de Médicis. The failure of that suit provided another setback for Catherine, who earlier had vainly proffered Alençon's older brother, Henri, the Duke of Anjou, as the Virgin Queen's wooer. "Such a kingdom for one of my children!" Catherine had once exclaimed.

Since she was a foreigner of lower rank, this granddaughter of Lorenzo the Magnificent had climbed long and arduously to royal power. She was born April 13, 1519, in the Medici Palace in Florence to Lorenzo de Medici, the Duke of Urbino, and his French wife, Madeleine de la Tour d'Auvergne. Twelve days later, the mother died, followed in less than a month by the tubercular Lorenzo.

The orphaned Catherine spent her first years in Rome under the careful eye of her great-uncle, Pope Leo X. Then she was brought back to Florence to live with her wealthy aunt and uncle, Clara and Filippo Strozzi, in their imposing palace. In 1527 when the Holy Roman Emperor, Charles V, stormed Rome, its citizens rose in bitter protest against the House of Medici. For a time the young heiress went into hiding, but was then placed with Dominican nuns in the Convent of Santa Lucia, only to be moved to the Sanctissima Annunziata del Murate. Because its nuns were faithful adherents of the House of Medici, reprisals were threatened against young Catherine, who had to be returned to the Santa Lucia convent.

Pope Leo X had died in 1521 and was succeeded by Adrian VI, who soon was followed by another Medici relative, Clement VII. He ordered the girl back to Rome to live with her aunt, Lucrezia Salvati. The auburn-haired Catherine, already inclined to be dumpy, did not have a pretty face, but with her fortune Clement saw her as a matrimonial prize and arranged for her marriage to Henri, Duke of Orleans, second son of the French king, Francis I, of the House of Valois. The pope himself presided at the wedding at Marseilles

Cathedral in October 1533, when both bride and bridegroom were 14. Three years later Henri became heir apparent after his brother Francis died.

Because of her Florentine background, Catherine was unpopular at the French court, where nobles jeered at her large, hooked nose. Nevertheless the sophisticated king was genuinely fond of her, praising her intelligence and charm as well as her skill in hunting, hawking, and dancing. Her young husband she adored, even when, scarcely three years after their marriage, he fell deeply in love with an ageless beauty, Diane de Poitiers, 19 years his senior. Learning to exercise will power and self-control, the young *dauphine* forced herself to stand by in dignified silence as her husband showered attention and the crown jewels on the blond favorite. Court painters soon depicted Diane sitting naked at her dressing table or in her bath.

Another compelling reason for Catherine's unfavorable reception within court circles was her apparent sterility. For 10 years she showed no signs of pregnancy. In vain she tried magical potions, prayers, and astrological charts. There was talk of sending her back to Florence, but Catherine threw herself on the king's mercy. Francis allowed her to stay, and Catherine returned to her potions. Finally, in 1544, a sickly heir, Francis was born. Over the next 12 years Catherine would prove her amazing fecundity, bearing nine more children: Elizabeth, 1545; Claude, 1547; Louis, 1548 (died in infancy); Charles (Charles IX) 1550; Edouard Alexandre (Duke of Anjou, Henri III), 1551; Marguerite, 1553; Hercule (Duke of Alençon), 1555; and Jeanne and Victoire, twins, 1556 (died in infancy).

The dynamic King Francis died in 1547, and his son was crowned as Henri II. Immediately on his accession he named Diane de Poitiers the Duchess of Valentinois and allowed her to take precedence after the queen on all public occasions. Catherine appeared to accept this new situation with her customary equanimity. But one day her disdain burst out: "I have read the histories of the kingdoms," she told Diane, "and I have found in them that from time to time at all periods whores have managed the business of kings." The Duchess of Valentinois also took her turn as governess to Catherine's children. A huge canvas by Clouet shows her, jeweled and again naked, as Pharoah's daughter receiving the infant Moses (the Duke of Alençon); in the background stands the baby's sad-eyed mother.

When not preoccupied with his mistress, Henri II involved himself in wars with Spain and Austria. Catherine mourned for the massive French defeat at the battle of St. Quentin in Picardy in 1557, and from then on she harbored a perpetual fear of Spain. But her spirits rose when the French recovered the port of Calais from the English while the Spanish were wasting time with local victories. Still the treaty of Cateau-Cambesis with Philip II in 1559 gave humiliating terms to Henri, who had to surrender all the conquests the French had made in Italy over the preceding 80 years.

During this period Catherine became a voracious reader and indefatigable

la reine mere du roi

Catherine de Médecis. Bibliothèque Nationale, London.

letter writer, frequently referring to her maternal anxieties. Every few months she moved her sons and daughters with furniture, trunks, tapestries, and wardrobe from chateau to chateau to allow for frequent housecleaning. On occasion Catherine swallowed her disdain and let them stay with Diane de Poitiers in her luxurious castle at Anet. Possessed of enormous family pride, Catherine showed extreme care for her children's health and training, providing them with the finest tutors. Since 1548 young Mary Stuart, intended bride of the heir apparent, had lived at court and been given the same advantages as well as extra care by her Guise relatives. But Catherine was never loving and often treated her brood too strictly.

In 1559, during festivities for the marriage of his daughter Elizabeth and Philip II of Spain, widower of Mary Tudor, Henri was wounded in the eye while jousting with the young Count of Montgomery. For ten agonizing days Catherine watched him die. From this bereavement she never fully recovered. But she quickly took revenge, appropriating Diane de Poitiers's jewels and her chateau of Chenonceux and retiring her to a small estate in Normandy.

Even though the new king, Francis II, gave his mother the title of governor, he was controlled by the powerful uncles of Mary of Scotland, whom he had married in 1558. The Duke of Guise, hero of Calais, took over the military command, and his brother, the Cardinal of Lorraine, the realm's finances and internal policies.

Within a year Catherine's fortunes began to change. The frail boy-king died of mastoiditis, and Mary returned to Scotland because her mother, the regent, also had died. Since Catherine's next son, Charles, was only 10, she now demanded the regency. Once before in 1552, while on campaign, Henri II had allowed her a short period of ruling.

Aside from the shame of the recent peace treaty, Catherine had to face the rivalry between two great houses, the Guises and Bourbons, who were involved in the fast-growing conflict between Roman Catholics and Huguenots, the leading Protestants. The Catholics were led by the Cardinal of Lorraine and his brother, Francis, Duke of Guise; the Huguenots by the Bourbon Prince of Condé, brother of Antoine, King of Navarre. Another brother, Admiral de Coligny, later became a pivotal figure in the wars of religion.

During these political-religious struggles, Catherine was obsessed with the idea of keeping royal authority intact. Through the dynasty, she believed, she served France. Shortly before Francis II died, the signs looked ominous. A Huguenot named La Renoudie plotted to remove the king's advisers, the Guises, but his uprising was easily crushed, and a forest of gallows quickly surrounded the chateau of Amboise, where Francis and his mother were staying.

Catherine heeded the advice of Chancellor Michel de L'Hopital to avoid taking sides and to pursue a policy of moderation and compromise. As one step they suggested that the terms Huguenots and Catholics be replaced by one word Christians. She wanted the Protestants neither to gain the upper hand nor to be crushed since she believed they kept the Guises from assuming too much power. The Colloquy of Poissy (1561) was designed to effect religious conciliation, but fell apart because of Guisard opposition.

In another attempt at reconciliation, Catherine offered the Edict of January 1562, which gave Huguenots licensed coexistence with certain safeguards, but which the Catholics rejected. Still it often formed the basis for future Huguenot demands.

Further chances of reconciling faded the next year when followers of the Duke of Guise massacred 200 Huguenots at Vassy. In the ensuing civil war, the duke and the King of Navarre were killed. The Peace of Amboise came a year later, granting freedom of worship to Protestant nobles in their houses.

Despite being allowed freedom of conscience, the Huguenots insisted they wanted the fuller terms of the Edict of January.

In the summer of 1563 Catherine declared Charles IX of age. Although her regency had officially ended, she continued as the power behind the throne. The next spring she led the sullen young King Charles, her daughter Marguerite, her two other sons, Henri and Hercule (now using the name of Francis in honor of his dead brother), and the late King of Navarre's son Henri on a grand tour of the kingdom. Traveling through Champagne, the two Burgundies, Lyons, Provence, Languedoc, and Guyenne, they were accompanied by a large, fabulously equipped retinue, including Catherine's "Flying Squadron," a bevy of about 80 painted young beauties who were rumored to ensnare noblemen and princes Catherine exploited to increase her own authority. The progress gave Catherine the opportunity of visiting two married daughters, Elizabeth, the wife of Philip II of Spain, and the lame Claude, Duchess of Lorraine, but Catherine did not meet with her Spanish son-in-law, whom she intensely disliked. She made a special stop at Salon to consult with Nostradamus, the physician and astrologer. He had once cast a horoscope revealing that three of Catherine's four sons would be kings and two of her three daughters would be queens. This time he predicted that young Henri of Navarre would rule France.

In 1567 war broke out again after the Huguenots, in a plot called "the enterprise of Meaux," tried to kidnap the king and capture Paris. The queen mother, who had reluctantly decided to use force, proffered the Peace of Longjumeau the next year, promising to restore the conditions of Amboise, but the pact proved ineffectual.

With scarcely a breathing spell, hostilities were renewed in 1569. The Prince of Condé, still the Huguenot leader, lost his life, and his brother, Coligny, was wounded. Although Henri, Duke of Anjou, demonstrated his military prowess, his jealous brother, King Charles, did not follow up on his victory. Coligny defeated the royal troops in Burgundy, and in 1570 a peace was signed at St. Germain granting the Huguenot nobles more privileges—full liberty of conscience and the right of worship on the outskirts of two towns in each province. Coligny also gained La Rochelle, an Atlantic port through which he could receive supplies from the English and Dutch.

Suddenly he found himself in favor with King Charles, but not with the queen mother. The unstable young ruler saw merit in Coligny's proposals to begin a scheme of colonization and join the Dutch rebels against religious persecution waged by the Spanish Duke of Alba. Catherine meanwhile had decided that in the name of peace she would marry her exquisitely lovely daughter Marguerite to young Henri of Navarre, who had become king after his father's death. With his staunchly Protestant mother, Jeanne d'Albret, she now opened negotiations. At the same time she planned to marry the Duke of Anjou to Queen Elizabeth. Anjou, however, insisted he could not reside in a country where he could not publicly practice his Catholicism. Alençon was less adamant, and slow bargaining began in 1572.

An unsuccessful attempt on Coligny's life stirred up the Huguenots, who allegedly threatened the extinction of the entire royal family as well as a new war. Catherine was among those authorizing the death of Coligny and the other Protestant chiefs. A royal marriage ceremony seemed to offer the perfect opportunity to strike. Huguenot leaders flocked to Paris for Marguerite's wedding to Henri of Navarre on August 18, 1572, and festivities continued for days. On St. Bartholomew's Day, August 24, Coligny, still recovering from his wounds, was murdered and his body flung out of a window.

Other Huguenot leaders also met death. Then, apparently unauthorized by the court, Catholics, overcome by long simmering hatreds, began slaughtering Huguenots in general, and over the next six weeks the massacres spread to the provinces. At swordpoint Navarre promised to convert to Catholicism, but Catherine kept him more or less a prisoner in the Louvre. Also placed there under strict surveillance was her always restive son, Alençon, who had protested Coligny's murder.

The massacre sparked a brief but savage fourth war. It ended in the Peace of La Rochelle, which promised the Huguenots liberty of conscience throughout France, but liberty of worship only in La Rochelle and Montaubon.

By 1574 a moderate Catholic element known as the *politiques* was engaged in a plot to free Navarre and Alençon, whom they wished to make their figurehead. At the same moment, however, Alençon confessed to his mother.

Within days of the uncovering of the *politique* plot, Charles, still haunted by memories of St. Bartholomew's Day, died of tuberculosis at the age of 23. He left only a daughter by his second wife, Elizabeth of Austria. Since 1573 his successor, his brother Henri, had been in Poland, where Catherine's tireless diplomatic maneuvering and outlay of money had procured his election as king. Forgetting his Polish crown, Henri set out for Paris by a rather circuitous route.

Until his return Catherine assumed the regency once more. One of her first acts was to order the execution of the Huguenot Count of Montgomery, who had been imprisoned since accidentally killing her husband 23 years earlier. The Protestants vowed revenge and announced a new war. Soon after the new king came back to Paris, Alençon escaped from court and turned up in a Huguenot camp. Some months later Navarre also got away, recanted his Catholic conversion, and joined the Huguenot chiefs. But during a truce Catherine appeared at the camp where Alençon was staying and induced him to return with her by promising him the title of Duke of Anjou and tripling his appanage. Alençon's submission to his mother induced the Huguenots to accept an accord, which some of his followers called the Peace of Monsieur. Better known as the Peace of Beaulieu, it assured universal freedom of conscience and worship except in certain restricted areas. But in the end both sides showed dissatisfaction.

Conservative Catholics had by now formed the Holy League against heresy and allied it with the pope and Philip II of Spain. Its real aim was to depose Henri III in favor of young Henri, the Duke of Guise. To control the Guises, the king in a show of good faith waged a sixth war, which concluded in the Peace of Bergerac and revoked many of the Beaulieu conditions, but granted the Huguenots the right to live unmolested in any part of France although still restricting public worship to certain places. Henri III took little interest in implementing the terms.

War or no war, Catherine had made the Valois court the most brilliant in Europe. She had inherited the Medici taste and refinement and delighted in the role of patroness to scholars, artists, and poets, notably La Pleiade, a glittering group of seven poets dominated by Pierre de Ronsard and Joachim de Bellay. Ceaselessly, as distraction from factional hatreds, she organized extravagant balls, banquets, and masques. These bled the treasury almost as much as Catherine's frenetic building schemes, which included a rotunda for Henri II's tomb, the palace of the Tuileries, and improvements to the various chateaux along the Loire River. Invariably, Italian architects received her commissions.

Under Henri III, the court became increasingly a center of sexual intrigue and vice. Of all Catherine's children, he had the most fantastic personality. A military hero, he was nonetheless preoccupied with costume and personal appearance. He had married Louise de Vaudemont of the House of Lorraine and taken a mistress, but after his accession his quiescent homosexuality burst forth; he became a transvestite, appearing in sweeping skirt and décolletage, painting his face, and surrounding himself with his *mignons* or favorites, cruel young fops whose only duty was to please him.

On questionable pretexts, war between the Holy League and the Huguenots kindled again in 1580, but was quickly halted by the Peace of La Fleix. Catherine now turned her attention to England. After years of exchanging negotiations, in 1579 Alençon began an active courtship of Elizabeth and came to London twice, apparently making a favorable impression on her. Hoping to profit from the advantages of such a union, the Flemings asked Alençon to intervene in their continuing struggle for liberty. After his troops massacred a great many inhabitants of Antwerp in 1583, his wedding plans evaporated.

By this time Catherine had outlived six of her children. Elizabeth, the Queen of Spain, had died in 1568; Claude, the Duchess of Lorraine, in 1575. The queen mother was stoical. But Alençon's death in 1584 precipitated a royal crisis. Henri III had no children, and his childless sister Marguerite was not acceptable as his successor because women could not reign in France. Although Henri of Navarre had become a Huguenot chief, he now was considered the heir apparent, and Catherine negotiated with him endlessly. The

Holy League objected, wanting to place the Duke of Guise on the throne. Henri finally admitted Guise's pretensions and forbade the exercise of all religions except the Catholic. Infuriated, the Huguenots took up arms in the War of the Three Henris (Henri III, Henri of Navarre, and Henri of Guise). Henri of Navarre defeated the royal favorite, the Duke of Joyeuse, but Henri of Guise bested the German auxiliaries of the Huguenots. Guise, wildly popular, then came to Paris.

An alarmed Henri fled to the Chateau of Blois and convened the Estates General. Catherine was also at Blois, enormously stout, old, and ailing. For years her apartments there boasted concealed cabinets, opened by secret pedals, where she kept gems and—rumor had it—vials of poison. On December 23, 1588, in the royal bedchamber, the king's bodyguard killed Guise and his brother, who had been summoned there. Catherine was reported to have said to Henri, "Well done, my son, now you have to sew up the pieces."

On January 5, 1589, she died of pneumonia. Eight months later a fanatic monk stabbed Henri III in the stomach. Before dying, the king named Catherine's son-in-law, long estranged from Marguerite, as his successor.

To this day Catherine remains a figure of controversy with perhaps more detractors than champions. For some her name evokes legends of perfidy. Yet even her critics allow that—whatever her motivation and methods—she tried to reconcile civic and religious conflicts that tore at France in her time.

Kristina
Queen of Sweden, 1644–1654

Like Mary Stuart, Kristina relinquished her throne. But unlike the Scottish queen, who fled under duress and ran into imprisonment, the Swedish ruler left by her own choice and moved around Europe for the rest of her life, cutting a flamboyant swath.

Born December 6, 1626, in Stockholm, Kristina was the only surviving child of famous warrior-king Gustavus Adolphus and his wife, Maria Eleanora of Brandenburg. A national hero who had welded his country into a great power, the "Lion of the North," became the leading champion of Protestantism during the Thirty Years War. In 1630, marching off with the strongest army he had ever mustered, he exacted a promise from his nobles to accept Kristina as their ruler in the event of his death.

Two years later, while leading a cavalry charge in the Battle of Lützen, he lost his life. Immediately the government of Sweden passed to a regency of five nobles, headed in absentia by the king's devoted friend, Axel Oxenstierna, who remained in Germany.

Maria Eleanora, who had made a grueling journey to accompany her husband's body home, became completely unnerved by her grief, and during 24 long months of official mourning, the court helplessly watched her hysterical and eccentric behavior. Over the bed, where she slept with her little daughter, she hung a golden casket holding the king's heart. Her apartments she draped entirely in black, and she permitted no light other than candles. There she wept incessantly, and there she immured Kristina, giving her only the company of repulsive dwarfs. Thus the little girl grew painfully aware of her deformity, one shoulder higher than the other. But even as she planted the seeds of her daughter's neurotic development, Maria Eleanora considered marrying her off to a Danish prince.

On his return to Stockholm in 1636, Oxenstierna rescued Kristina and placed her under the authority of the regents as her father had wished. He banished her mother to a country estate and sent the nervous little princess to her Aunt Catherine, the Countess Palatine, at Stegeborg, where Kristina

Kristina. The Swedish Institute, Stockholm.

enjoyed the companionship of her cousins, Maria Euphrosyne and Charles Gustavus. In 1638 Catherine died, and Kristina returned to Stockholm.

Now in accord with her father's wishes, Oxenstierna thrust her almost wholly into a masculine world. She had her blond hair cut short, wore a boy's clothes, and learned to handle any horse and any gun. With her tutor, Johannes Matthiae, the court chaplain, she assiduously studied mathematics, foreign languages, sciences, history, diplomacy, and listened as well to generals lecture on military strategy. Years later she wrote, "My personal inclinations seconded my father's designs in the most marvelous manner, for I had an unconquerable antipathy to all women's sayings and doings."

The masculine traits intensified as she grew older. Adoring the memory of her father, loathing her mother, she hardened herself by keeping her rooms cold in winter and exercising violently. She spent her free time in the royal stables and restricted her diet to army food—salt herring, dried beef, and bread and cheese. Her manners were said to be those of the cavalry troopers of Gustavus Adolphus' elite corps. Meanwhile Oxenstierna, a master diplomat, tutored her in politics.

Over the years Kristina had paid only brief visits to her mother's estate. When her daughter was 16, Oxenstierna finally permitted Maria Eleanora to come to the palace in Stockholm. Greatly shocked at the change in Kristina, she told Oxenstierna that nobody would want to marry a princess who looked and acted like a man.

The chancellor, eager for the girl to enter into a politically advantageous match, quickly arranged for two noblewomen to instruct her in the feminine arts and ordered her to wear women's clothes except when she exercised. Trying to follow the new instructions, Kristina felt herself torn between two personalities, for her voice, walk, and gestures remained masculine. Besides, she continued to be indifferent to hot and cold, stayed long hours in the saddle, and slept only five hours a night.

In 1643 she became infatuated with her cousin and childhood playmate, Charles Gustavus. But the soldier prince womanized freely, and when Kristina tallied up his affairs, she lost interest.

At 18 she became queen, but the luxurious pageantry of the coronation had to wait because the Thirty Years War dragged on. Meanwhile she quickly showed Oxenstierna that she had determined to rule in her own way. An early letter to him notes, "I can judge by your procedure that you have completely understood my will." As her first act she sent her mother back to the country; as her second she opened negotiations to end the war. But after the Peace of Westphalia in 1648, her critics charged that she gave away everything that her father's military genius and Oxenstierna's careful planning had won. Indeed an angry and aging chancellor believed that a capricious and overbearing young woman had ruined his life's work.

That summer her subjects felt deep sympathy for her after a madman slipped into the royal chapel and advanced on the queen. Kristina, kneeling on a dais, shoved the captain of her guards so that he threw himself on the intruder, who carried two knives. The next year she named Charles Gustavus heir apparent. Ambitious for the throne, he had persisted in paying court to her. But she had found a real love in Magnus Gabriel de la Gardie, another childhood playmate. She showered gifts and favors on him and made him ambassador to France, but lacking the privileges of rank, he could not be considered as a possible consort. Worse still, he did not love her, and in the end handsome Magnus married Charles Gustavus' sister, Maria Euphrosyne.

Kristina derived some comfort from the companionship of a new and beautiful lady-in-waiting, Ebba Sparre. Noble claimants for her hand swarmed around her, but cherishing her freedom, she determined to remain single. Still, it was agreeable enough to have admirers who could be dismissed if they grew tiresome. Rumored to the contrary, she remained sexually continent.

Despite her youth, Kristina was known as "the Minerva of the North," a formidable intellect. Since few of her countrymen could match her education, she began corresponding with foreign scholars, authors, and philosophers. Her greatest catch proved to be René Descartes, who accepted her invitation to visit Sweden in September 1649. The French savant balked at being shown off in court, yet busied himself with writing a ballet libretto, drawing up statutes for an academy, and making barometric notes for Blaise Pascal. In December he began holding conversations with the queen in her library, only to be disappointed at her lack of interest in philosophy. Literature engrossed her. But the stark weather ("Here a man's thoughts freeze in winter just as water freezes") took its toll, and after four months Descartes fell ill with congestion of the lungs. Ten days later he died.

Other foreign scholars Kristina lured to court over the years did not meet such a tragic end, but all missed creature comforts. Meanwhile she found one native-born genius, Georg Stiernhielm, who wrote poetry and studied archeology, languages, and the natural sciences.

Her coronation finally took place in 1650. The first years were peaceful. Fisheries and the timber industry boomed, new mines opened, trading ships sailed with lucrative cargoes, towns grew, and artisans' guilds received help from the royal treasury. Meanwhile the queen had reduced the Privy Council to a secondary position and restored the strength of the Vasa monarchy.

Now she wanted an even more secure title for Charles Gustavus, that of hereditary prince. To get it, she engaged in some clever manipulation. While showering generosity on her favorites, she had also encouraged agitation of the lower Estates, who were unhappy over the alienation of Crown property through her gifts and outright sales to the nobility. In a "Protestation" presented to the Riksdag (Parliament) in 1650, the three lower Estates demanded reforms as well as the return of the Crown lands to increase state revenues. Encouraged by her councillor, Adler Salvius, Kristina saw her chance and promised to abandon the cause of the burghers and farmers if the nobles approved Charles Gustavus as hereditary prince. Anxious to preserve their properties, the nobles sealed the bargain.

In 1651, paying the price of overwork, Kristina developed a severe nervous condition, but was brought back to health by a persuasive Frenchman who called himself Doctor Bourdelot. Although many accused him of being a charlatan, Kristina found herself infatuated. Soon he and the queen were inseparable, and she appointed him as her personal physician. Then Bourdelot began to exert an influence that enraged Oxenstierna and the other royal ministers, who saw Kristina's behavior become more frivolous by the day. It seemed most shocking when during church services she read the classics or played with her lap dogs or giggled with Bourdelot.

In desperation the ministry called on Magnus de la Gardie to get rid of the Frenchman. He tried to accuse Bourdelot of slander, but his suit went nowhere. Oxenstierna then orchestrated a rising tide of opposition to Bourdelot, and finally in 1653 a sorrowing Kristina bowed to the inevitable and sent her favorite on his way. But she saw to it that he left Sweden a wealthy man.

For distraction she sought other favorites and soon formed close ties to Don Antonio Pimentel de Prado, the newly arrived Spanish envoy, to a gallant young gentleman named Claes Tott, and to Count Raimondo Montecuicoli, ambassador of the Holy Roman Empire. Various swashbucklers also joined her intimate circle.

As early as 1651, Kristina had begun to hint that she wanted to abdicate and lead a more private life, but her advisers had prevailed on her to stay. Her reaction was to become increasingly extravagant and unstable. Oxenstierna warned her that her lavish entertainments and the gifts and Crown lands she showered on her friends would soon drive Sweden into bankruptcy. He took further alarm when she secretly signed a treaty promising to ally Sweden with Spain in a war against Portugal. Hastily he saw to it that both houses of the Riksdag repudiated the accord. But he acted too late to stem Kristina's declining popularity. Her subjects blamed her for all the economic ills now surfacing, and even students in the universities she had tried to improve angrily turned against her.

Meanwhile, rebelling against the Protestant beliefs long forced on her, she had shown a penchant for Catholicism, a faith Swedish law forbade her to embrace. The Jesuits had even sent two priests in disguise to Stockholm to instruct her. They succeeded so well that when Oliver Cromwell's envoy, Bulestrode Whitelaw, appeared at court in 1653 to negotiate an alliance, Kristina said she hoped that England would grant tolerance to Catholics.

Through Pimentel she tried to get the King of Spain, Philip IV, to support her conversion, but he refused. Pimentel's chaplain described her at this stage: "There is nothing feminine about her except her sex. Her voice and manner of speaking, her walk, her style, her ways, are all quite masculine. Though she rides sidesaddle, she holds herself so well and is so light in her movements that unless one were quite close to her, one would take her for a man."

In spite of all the foreshadowings, her abdication and conversion shocked the Swedish nation. In a simple ceremony at the royal palace at Uppsala in June 1654, the queen, dressed in white taffeta, left the coronation robe, crown, and scepter to Charles Gustavus. She tarried for a few days in Stockholm, then set out for Holmstadt, and at Båstad crossed the border. Calling herself Count Dohna, she disguised herself as a knight with sword and gun and mounted a horse for a six-day trip to Hamburg.

In Brussels the following September, Montecuicoli, Pimentel, and a few other witnesses solemnly stood at attention as Kristina abjured her faith and with little fanfare was received into the Catholic church. At Innsbruck, on her way to Italy with a polyglot entourage, she made her first public abjuration in the court church.

Ostentatious display marked her entry into Rome in December 1655. The sculptor Bernini had decorated the Porto del Popolo with the words, "Felice fastoque ornata ingressui" (to a happy and well-boding entry), and Pope Alexander VII escorted her to the high altar of St. Peter's. In contrast to the overdressed Italian nobility, Kristina wore a simple gray dress, her customary black scarf, and a plumed hat, restricting her jewelry to a gold ring.

Almost as soon as she had moved into the palazzo Farnese, she singled out the young, brilliant Cardinal Decio Azzolino for her special good will. With time he would control her finances, eventually all her affairs. She was more than a bit in love with him. Until Azzolino took his post, Kristina managed her money affairs badly and pawned her dresses at least once. Gossiping about her debts, Roman society also criticized her for lack of manners, vulgar speech, and disdain for religious practices.

Although she did not wish to return to the Swedish throne, she was eager enough to be queen elsewhere. On a visit to France in 1657, she won Cardinal Mazarin's promise to give her the crown of Naples if the French wrested the city from the Spaniards. When the Marchese Gian Rinaldo Monaldesco, her equerry, betrayed the plot, Kristina considered his act treason and arranged to have his throat cut, a murder that turned Catholic Europe against her. She had once written, "I love the storm and fear the calm," but at this point she welcomed Azzolino's help in picking up the pieces.

In 1660 Charles Gustavus died, and his sickly, four-year-old son, Charles XI, succeeded him. Fearing for her pension, Kristina left for Stockholm. Since she had named Charles Gustavus as her heir, she felt entitled to ask to be made heir to little Charles XI. In Stockholm when the people cheered her in the streets, she believed they wanted her restored to the throne, and quickly she changed her mind about ruling again. With her usual impetuosity she announced she would seek legal assistance in drafting a document to rescind her abdication. But with Monaldesco's murder still fresh in the regents' minds, she faced a stone wall of opposition from them as well as from the Lutheran Church.

When the Bishop of Abo declared that she had admitted being sorry she had changed her religion, Kristina fired back a letter threatening his person. At once public opinion solidified against her, and the regents enjoined her to leave the country at once. For a time she led a dissipated life in Hamburg, but when the pope indicated he did not want her to return to Rome, she modified her behavior so successfully that she received his permission to come back in 1662. Triumphantly she moved into a new home, the palazzo Riario, filling it with books and art. Her collection, begun in Stockholm with paintings looted by Swedish armies during the Thirty Years War, was especially impressive, boasting Titians, Corregios, Holbeins, and Michelangelos. The palazzo gardens also claimed her attention.

In 1664 Kristina paid a second visit to Sweden, badly bungled because she insisted on bringing a priest with her. Again, both humiliated and irked by her countrymen's coldness toward her, she left for Hamburg.

Pope Alexander VII died in 1667, and to celebrate the accession of her good friend, Clement IX, she gave an extravagant fete at her Hamburg palace. Guests drank too much wine, and when rioting erupted, the ex-queen calmly ordered her gentlemen to fire on the unruly crowd. Eight persons were killed.

About this time the throne of Poland fell vacant, and Kristina, once again enamored of royal trappings, offered herself as a candidate, believing that the pope would support her. When he refused, her plans came to nothing. Still she felt sure of his warm welcome if she returned to Rome.

Back again in the palazzo Riario, she became absorbed by astronomy, alchemy, and archeology. She alternated study with unstinted hospitality, for she kept a magnificent table and threw open her doors for splendid entertainments. Composers dedicated their operas to her; she patronized young Arcangelo Corelli and appointed Alessandro Scarlatti as her music master. Bernini created sculptures for her; a select group of churchmen, artists, writers, and musicians met regularly in her salon. In the 1670s, under the capable Charles XI, long restored to health, Sweden once again had a sound economy and Kristina a secure pension. Her financial situation brightened still more when the Danish-Swedish war ended in 1679.

Confidently she now turned her formidable energies to writing. Responding to Azzolino's encouragement, she had begun her memoirs in Hamburg but had quickly become discouraged. In 1680 she plunged in again, first making a synopsis of the chief events of her reign. Her autobiography did not get beyond her first six years. Writing an entire book was hardly suitable to her nervous temperament, and she happily found a new literary form, a collection of maxims. Set in the context of her life, some of those she produced sound ironic: "One never repents of pardoning offenses, but almost always of having punished them" or "A prince must consider himself the crowned slave of the public."

During her last years Kristina lost most of her masculine attributes, and the city knew her as a graying, stout little lady who always appeared in beautiful gowns. After a stroke she died on April 19, 1688, having referred to herself as "one of the monuments of Rome." She was buried with crown and scepter and in a white robe and purple-trimmed cloak. After 34 years of self-imposed exile, stubborn and fiercely independent, she remained a queen.

Sophia
Regent of Russia, 1682–1689

The year Kristina died, the regent Sophia Alekseevna, another woman of formidable intellect, was deposed in Moscow by her half brother Peter, known to history as "the Great." Her rule had lasted only seven years, but had been marked by surprising innovations. Indisputably, the cold-hearted Sophia had triumphed in a role previously out of bounds to Russian women.

The granddaughter of Mikhail I, founder of the House of Romanov, she was born September 27, 1657, the fourth child and third daughter of Czar Alexei and his wife, Marya Miloslavskaya. Since her mother was frequently ill or pregnant, Sophia came under the care of her aunts, Irina, Agnes, and Tatiana, in the *terem*, the women's quarters in the Kremlin.

There the *czarevnas* led a cloistered life. Rigid court etiquette demanded they follow a regimen of solitude, fastings, and devotions. They heard religious services only through a curtained balcony; they could ride out only in closed sleighs. Marriage could have provided an escape, but because of their superior lineage it was difficult to find suitable husbands, and many *czarevnas* ended up in nunneries. Their education, however, could not be faulted. Sophia was an apt pupil of the brilliant Semyon Polotsky, her brother's tutor. Like him and her father, she admired Western thought and became an excellent linguist.

The long-ailing Marya Miloslavskaya died in 1667, followed by the junior Alexei, heir to the throne. In 1670 Czar Alexei married a young beauty, Natalia Naryshkina, who bore him a vigorous son, Peter, in 1672. Since Natalia's family was as ambitious as the Miloslavskys, open hostilities quickly flared.

Czar Alexei died in 1676, leaving his crown to his frail second son, Fedor. A mysterious, scurvy-like illness frequently confined the 14-year-old boy to bed, and Sophia broke precedent by coming into his bedchamber to nurse him. Gradually she stepped in as intermediary between him and his ministers, clearly seeing her brother as the instrument by which she could grasp power and break away from the *terem*.

Even at 19 she possessed a gift for intrigue. Natalia's foster father, Artemon Matveev, who had served Czar Alexei well, was honorary head of the

Apothecaries' Hall, and Sophia dropped a hint or two about the doubtful benefits of the medicine sent to Fedor and reportedly prescribed by Matveev. Before long Matveev found himself banished to the north.

Next Sophia cleverly arranged for the departure of all the Naryshkins, including Natalia and Peter, from court. She then saw to it that many Miloslavskys assumed positions of power. In the *terem*, life had changed with the death of the martinet aunt, Irina. Although Aunt Tatiana became the nominal head, Sophia took charge and gave the other *czarevnas* more freedom.

Fedor III died in 1682 without naming an heir. Next in the dynastic line, however, stood his and Sophia's brother Ivan, a "sad head," a half-blind epileptic. At Fedor's funeral, Natalia joined the train in a covered litter, but Sophia and her court ladies, only half veiled, marched on foot. Stepdaughter stared down stepmother, and Natalia hurriedly withdrew.

Dismayed at the thought of Ivan on the throne, Patriarch Joachim and the Duma (legislative assembly) summoned several Naryshkins, including Natalia and young Peter, to Moscow. The influential council of the *boyars* (nobles) decided, however, that it could not choose between Ivan and Peter. When the patriarch asked a crowd assembled before the cathedral whom it wanted, it roared back, "Peter!" The patriarch then blessed the boy, and his mother immediately assumed the regency.

Matveev returned from exile, and fearful that they would lose their important posts, the Miloslavskys started to plot with Sophia, who suggested stirring up the *streltsi* (palace guard), which nursed several grievances against the Naryshkins. As enticement she promised the musketeers pay raises.

When the Miloslavskys spread rumors that Ivan had come to grief, the *streltsi* prepared to revolt. To prove the government's stability, a shaking Natalia stood on the Kremlin's famous Red Stairway, holding Peter's and Ivan's hands, but her gesture had little meaning. With further incitation the drunken guardsmen stormed into the compound and for three days murdered and looted. Peter saw his uncle and Matveev hacked to pieces and thrown over the balcony on the pikes below. Then the *streltsi* spilled out through Moscow, terrorizing and pillaging every street.

After they declared the city free of traitors, Sophia assumed command and succeeded in getting the *boyars* to accept her as regent for Peter and Ivan, reigning jointly. At the coronation, vacant-looking Ivan and bright, vivacious Peter contrasted sharply.

Sophia named her uncle, Prince Ivan Miloslavsky, as treasurer and put her married lover, the gifted Prince Vasili Golitsyn, in charge of foreign affairs. He had already served for two years under Czar Fedor, and actually for Sophia he functioned as prime minister. An obscure civil servant, Fedor Shaklovity, whom she made state secretary, was also her lover. Since the *streltsi* had thrust her into power, she realized that her position rested on their will. Thus she named a *streltsi* favorite, Prince Ivan Khovansky, as their commander even

Sophia. The Hermitage, Leningrad.

though she disliked him intensely and had once turned down his marriage proposal.

Suddenly a fresh complication arose. Many of the *streltsi* had taken up the cause of the Old Believers, who continued to protest the innovations in church ritual and drastic reform set forward some 20 years previously by the Patriarch Nikon. Conscious of their military support, the schismatics now raised their voices to a fearful pitch. Courageously Sophia decided to invite them to an open debate with the bishops. A delegation was brought before the clergy of the palace and a court group, headed by Sophia and Golitsyn. But wrangling replaced reasoned debate. When the schismatics called Nikon a heretic, Sophia cried out: "Then so were my father, Czar Alexei, and my brother, Czar Fedor, and the reigning czars are no czars, and the reigning patriarch is no patriarch, and we have no right to rule our realm."

Moved by her outburst, some *streltsi* showed their loyalty by cutting off the head of the monk who had been their spokesman. But Khovansky kept stirring up his men, and Sophia carried out her threat to take the whole court out of Moscow. She refused to return unless Khovansky came to confer with her. Against his better judgment he agreed to her demand, and outside the gates of her country palace Sophia's guards murdered him.

With the *streltsi* commander's death, Sophia returned to the Kremlin. Since Ivan was the senior czar, Peter lived with his mother in the nearby village of Preobrazhenkoe, coming to the city only to receive ambassadors. On such occasions Sophia sat behind the dual throne, hidden by a curtain, so that she could whisper to the boy rulers what to say.

"She was not prepossessing," a critical French ambassador wrote; "she is immensely fat, with a head as large as a bushel, hairs on her face, tumors on her legs." He did, however, admire her intellect. "But as far as her body is short and coarse, her mind is shrewd, unprejudiced, and full of policy. Although she has never read Machiavelli, she understands his maxims naturally." Still, some admirers described her as tall and stately.

In spite of the fact that her brothers were the nominal rulers, Sophia, who in 1686 had assumed the title of *gosudarynya* (sovereign), considered herself the autocrat of all Russia. She had decided to break precedents, but only to a certain degree. Except at church services, she wore rouge on her cheeks and went unveiled. She appeared often in public, but did not attend the great banquets in the Kremlin. From her example and through certain pieces of legislation, the position of women in Russian society improved significantly.

Her lover Golitsyn, a singularly enlightened noble who valued European practices, spoke to the receptive regent of educational reforms, religious toleration, and even the disappearance of serfdom. In spite of their mutual idealism, however, the pair achieved no great breakthroughs.

Still they could count important accomplishments. To encourage home industries, Sophia eased taxes. To bring greater security she curbed brigandage, brawling, and drunkenness. To build a better Moscow, she promoted sanitation and fire prevention measures. To bring culture to her people, she fought illiteracy. Delighted with the business of governing, she also reorganized the army, planned the first land survey, and tried to improve the graft and inertia of the entire administrative ladder. One of her admirers wrote, "And there triumphs then the great content of the nation."

Meanwhile her half brother Peter played soldiers with jolly companions at his mock fort at Pressburg, gradually molding these playmates into a distinctive, smartly uniformed military force. At the same time he learned how to be a crack sailor. He was always busy. In early adolescence he discovered the boisterous pleasures of the German Quarter in the suburbs of Moscow, and there he basked in the company of English, Dutch, Danish, and Swiss technicians, who fed his immense curiosity. When he was 17 his mother urged him to settle down and marry Evdokia Lopukhina, a *boyar*'s daughter. But after a few months his bride bored him, and he returned to his war games, boats, and lively companions.

The year of Peter's marriage, Golitsyn mounted a new effort against the Crimean khan, an ally of the Ottoman Turks and controller of the Black Sea. The khan's "scorched earth" tactics had halted a campaign in 1687. Again in 1689, when supplies ran out, Golitsyn retreated. Sophia, however, pretended that her lover had been victorious and ordered a triumphal parade and arch, greatly embarrassing him.

The spectacle disgusted Peter. Since he and Ivan were now of age and both were married, stories began to fly that it was time for Sophia to give up her regency. As plots and rumors multiplied, her supporters went out of their way to try to perpetuate her rule.

In July 1689, a clash broke out between Peter and Sophia. On a religious holiday, which also commemorated Russian deliverance from a Polish invader, she appeared in the procession and when Peter ordered her to retire to the *terem*, she paid no heed. He called for a horse and galloped away furiously.

Both sides now relied on alarming rumors. In August, Shaklovity stirred up the *streltsi* with a report that a group from Preobrazhenkoe was on its way to murder Ivan. Some *streltsi* loyal to Peter brought him exaggerated accounts that Shaklovity planned to incite the guardsmen to murder him. Still tormented by memories of 1682, Peter jumped out of bed in the middle of night and fled naked to a nearby forest. After servants brought him his clothes, he and a few friends shrewdly took refuge in the Troitsa Monastery, a national shrine. Soon his family, his companies of soldiers, and some *streltsi* joined him there.

Sophia sent the patriarch to mediate, but he sided with Peter. As fresh ultimatums came from the young czar, Sophia decided to approach him herself. A messenger ordered her carriage back, delivering Peter's warning that she would meet with harsh treatment at the monastery.

On returning to Moscow, Sophia made a moving speech to the *streltsi* and a crowd that gathered, asking that she be judged by her services and be given help. But *streltsi* companies began deserting her, and General Patrick Gordon, the English mercenary she had depended on, declared for Peter. Golitsyn fled, and Shaklovity was handed over to Peter, who ordered him executed a few days later. Golitsyn was subsequently captured and banished to the north.

Sophia refused flight and accepted Peter's counteroffer of confinement in the convent on the grounds of the Novodevichy monastery in Moscow with her sister, the Czarevna Martha. From then on Peter took complete charge in the Kremlin, allowing the weak-headed Ivan to sit as nominal co-czar until his death in 1696.

Little was heard of Sophia until the summer of 1698, when the *streltsi* rose again in revolt and falsely announced that Peter, who had been traveling abroad with his "Great Embassy," had died; Sophia, they declared, should ascend the throne. After a few days the rebellion collapsed, and Peter's troops took more than a thousand prisoners. Though reports spread that Sophia had planned the mutiny, she had given the musketeers only her encouragement.

On his return Peter began torturing and executing the prisoners. Many dead *streltsi* hung outside the windows of the nunnery where the former regent and her sister were kept under heavy guard.

After becoming a nun and taking the name Susannah, Sophia died peacefully on July 14, 1704. Religion had replaced her cunning penchant for intrigue.

Mary II
Queen of England, Scotland, and Ireland, 1689–1694

About the time the former regent Sophia entered a Russian convent, Mary II, the great-granddaughter of Mary, Queen of Scots, was crowned Queen of England. In 1688 a revolution, almost so bloodless it has been dubbed "glorious," had deposed James II, who had tried to reestablish the Catholic religion in her country. At the height of the boiling Catholic-Protestant controversy, his older daughter agreed to share the English throne with her husband, William, Stadtholder of Orange.

Mary was born April 30, 1662, at St. James's Palace in London to James, then Duke of York, and his duchess, the former Anne Hyde. The couple had met in Holland, where Anne, the witty daughter of a prominent lawyer, Edward Hyde, served as lady-in-waiting to James's sister Mary, widow of William II, Stadtholder of Orange.

After Charles I was beheaded in 1649, the Stuart sons had languished in exile in France. But when the dour Commonwealth years ended and his brother took the throne in 1660, the penniless James suddenly cut an important figure. Anne was carrying James's child when she returned to England with the Restoration and her father's ennoblement as Lord Clarendon and rise to power as Lord Chancellor. Anne wed James a week after the birth of a boy, Charles. When the baby died at four months, an already disillusioned James declared that Anne had tricked him into marriage and now dominated him.

Even so, their offspring arrived at the rate of almost one a year. After Mary came a son in 1662, a daughter, Anne, in 1665, and two more sons in 1666 and 1667.

In 1665 when the plague forced the royal family out of London, the Yorks left for the north, and Duchess Anne, taking revenge on her husband for his many infidelities, indulged in a brief flirtation herself. Once the plague was over, the Stuarts hurried home only to see London consumed by fire. Both

Mary II. National Portrait Gallery, London.

Charles II and James became highly popular for showing great personal bravery during the disaster.

The year 1667 proved tragic for the Duchess of York. Two sons died within months of each other, and her father was elbowed out of the government and sent into exile, where he later wrote his famous *History of the Rebellion and Civil Wars in England.*

Grown massively stout, the duchess, however, remained in the king's raffish circle, where she recovered her wit. Her daughter Mary looked far more graceful. The diarist Samuel Pepys wrote of the nine-year-old: "I did see the young duchesse, a little child in hanging sleeves, dance most finely, so as almost to ravish me, her ears were so good."

In 1669 Anne joined the Catholic church, well aware that all along James had been moving in her direction. Two years later she died; she had lost her last son, and Mary and Anne were her only surviving children.

Charles II also flirted with Catholicism but astutely realized that his conversion could be dangerous. To reassure his countrymen he took pains to see that his nieces were brought up as Protestants. He declared the girls wards of the state and gave them a staunchly Protestant governess, two Anglican chaplains, and their own establishment, Richmond Palace. Nonetheless the king allowed the two princesses to see their father fairly often. In 1672 James married a 15-year-old Catholic princess, Mary of Modena, and introduced her to his daughters as their "new playfellow."

Mary became fond of the Italian girl, but her closest friend was beautiful Frances Apsley, daughter of her father's treasurer. Both took part in a court performance of the masque *Calisto*, Mary playing the leading role. To Frances, older by 11 years, she wrote fanciful, effusive letters, calling her Aurelia and signing herself Mary Clorine. Gradually the fervency decreased, but even after both were married, Mary Clorine and Aurelia poured out their secrets to each other.

In 1677 Mary was introduced to her first cousin, William, who had been Stadtholder of Orange since his posthumous birth to the Princess Royal in 1650. But her first impression was so unfavorable that she burst into tears. Black-haired William was small, hawk-nosed, and hunched. Almost six feet tall, Mary, a pretty brunette, towered over him by four and a half inches and recoiled from his asthmatic wheezes.

Still, he had proved himself a formidable warrior against his great enemy, France's Louis XIV, who had twice invaded Holland. Although defeated time after time, William had doggedly kept on fighting and saved Amsterdam only by opening the dikes and flooding the land. When he arrived at the English court, he was again resisting the Sun King. Luck came with him. Charles now favored a Dutch-English alliance and willingly accepted his nephew's offer to wed Mary. The English court, however, found him sour and grumpy and frequently abstracted, for he did not try to compensate for his unprepossessing appearance by showing any good manners.

After a simple wedding ceremony in Mary's bedchamber, the bride appeared on the verge of tears. The bridegroom, on the other hand, congratulated himself on his lovely prize. A few days later Mary's stepmother, Mary of Modena, gave birth to a boy, and William stood as unhappy godfather to the little prince, destined to succeed to the English throne.

While the stadtholder waited for a good wind to bring him and Mary to Holland, an outbreak of smallpox decimated the English court. The newlyweds escaped, but on embarking ran into a storm and at the next port had to sail on separate ships. They were reunited on the Dutch coast, where coaches carried them to the palace of Honselaersdijk. Among its unusual amenities, Mary found running water in the bathroom.

The marriage turned out far better than she had expected, and she responded happily to the simplicity, cleanliness, and honesty of her new subjects. For its part the court found her uncommonly attractive and enjoyed her vivacious conversation. Her husband shared none of her charm, but she admired his devotion to duty. Since he occupied himself with state affairs most of the day, she learned to entertain him with light chatter at supper. She also had to adapt to long separations whenever he went off to his army. To her relief the war with France ended in 1678, when the treaty of Nijmegen guaranteed Franche-Comté and a number of Flemish towns to Louis. That year Mary suffered two miscarriages, and doctors told her she could not have any children.

Hiding her disappointment, she tried to learn Dutch, embroidered, encouraged her ladies to read religious tracts, and began collecting porcelain. Carefully too she watched over alterations and improvements for the summer palace at Soestdijk and the gardens at Honselaersdijk.

Back in England her uncle, Charles II, who had fallen into difficulties with Parliament, was ruling without it. Letters from London told of an intense renewal of antagonism between Catholics and Protestants. A majority of Englishmen were angry that James now openly espoused Catholicism. William came to England to confer with Charles, only to be battered by his father-in-law's sour comments.

Charles II died of a stroke in February 1685. Although a group in Parliament tried to bar James's accession, he and his wife were crowned in April. Immediately events heated up. At the time of Charles's death, William and Mary had been entertaining the Duke of Monmouth, Charles II's illegitimate son, as their house guest. Soon after James's coronation, Monmouth brought an army of 150 men to England, proclaiming his intention to seize the throne. But James defeated him at Sedgemoor and ordered his execution.

Over the next three years the king deeply disturbed Parliament by suspending laws and statutes and placing Catholics in high positions in the army and government. Over in Holland, William glumly noted his father-in-law's growing subservience to Louis XIV.

All the children of James and Mary of Modena had died. Then in 1688 the queen gave James another son, his namesake, dashing William's hopes that Mary would be heiress to the throne. Mary had been deeply suspicious that the pregnancy was contrived and had written to her sister Anne, closely questioning her about the mother-to-be's symptoms. After the baby's birth she was inclined to credit the story that a warming pan with a male child of obscure parentage inside it had been smuggled into the queen's bedchamber. Therefore she refused to recognize the new Stuart.

When James had the baby baptized a Catholic, Parliament was thrown into a panic. In October 1688, its leaders invited William of Orange, well supported by his army, to come from Holland to investigate complaints about James's questionable electoral activities, to check rumors about the birth of the king's son, and to defend Mary's claim to the crown. After the ships were calmed for several days, a "Protestant wind" finally brought William and his troops to Torbay, where supporters rushed to his side.

James made ready to face him at Salisbury, but every day his troops slipped away from him. His wife could not believe that her friendly stepdaughter would betray the king. As she wrote to Mary: "I know you to be so good that I don't believe you could have such a thought against the worst of fathers, much less perform it against the best, that has always been kind to you, and I believe has always loved you better than all the rest of his children. Besides, if you know anything of that horrid design, I am sure you could never have sent as many kind letters as you have done of late to both the king and me. You have too much sincerity."

Protesting in vain, Mary of Modena was forced to sail for France. Two days later James, disguised as a servant, fled Whitehall for the coast. But before his ship reached France, fishermen discovered his identity and returned him to England. Later his departure was officially authorized. Some people now saw him as a tragic figure in exile, a king done in by his daughters, for Anne had also passed over to the enemy. Mary did make William promise that no harm would come to her father.

Seven Whig and Tory leaders wrote to Mary, still in Holland, asking her to become queen in her own right. But she refused their offer. Her loyalty to William had survived his infidelity. In Holland he had established a mistress, Elizabeth Villiers, who although no beauty was considered an intellectual.

As soon as James left his kingdom, a convention declared the throne vacant. Another convention assembled in January 1689 to offer the crown jointly to Mary and William, who as a grandson of Charles I also had some personal claim. Parliament passed a set of conditions, the Declaration of Rights (enacted into law as the Bill of Rights), which gave it sovereign authority in the government and sole power to assess taxes and maintain a standing army in time of peace. Thus it overthrew the doctrine of the divine right of kings, so cherished by the Stuarts, and England became the first modern state to be governed by regular constitutional law. William, who had given the brusque advice "Never hold on to anything by apron strings," now demanded and received a guarantee that he would rule alone if his wife should die first.

Mary returned to England, "laughing and jolly," and shocked some observers, like the diarist John Evelyn, who thought she should have shown "some seeming reluctance, at least, of assuming her father's crown." Her admirers countered that William had commanded her to be cheerful. Actually she felt far from happy. As she wrote, "My heart is not made for a kingdom, and my inclination leads me to a retired life, so that I have need of the resignations and self-denial in the world, to bear with such a condition as I am now in. Indeed, the Prince's being made King has lessened the pain, but none of the troubles of which I am like to endure."

The long coronation ceremony in April 1689 exhausted the king. Soon his asthma worsened in Whitehall, and Mary moved him to Hampton Court, which he declared not grand enough. He wanted something on the order of Louis XIV's Versailles, and the famous architect, Sir Christopher Wren, received orders to "beautify and add some new building to that fabric." Gardens were to be laid out in the Dutch manner. Confident of his wife's exquisite taste, William left her in charge of the remodeling while he went abroad to join in the War of the League of Augsburg against Louis XIV.

Thereby he involved himself in two conflicts. Supported by the Protestants of Ulster, he was also fighting the Irish and French forces James had gathered in Ireland. At the Battle of the Boyne in 1691 he won such a decisive victory that James fled once more for France.

That same year Parliament empowered Mary to exercise rule during William's many absences on the continent while he led his troops in person in the Netherlands, where most of the land struggle of the European war took place. With William away, her love grew stronger. She wrote him that it was "a passion that cannot end with my life."

To her great relief a French invasion fleet was chased out of the English Channel. But it was the queen's unpleasant duty to order the arrest of her uncle, Henry, the Earl of Clarendon, accused of participating in a Jacobite conspiracy to restore her father. Sadly too she watched relations with her sister Anne deteriorate. Anne did not like William, who had intervened in the succession between herself and Mary. Both king and queen disliked John Churchill, the Earl of Marlborough and husband of Anne's favorite friend Sarah. Besides, Mary was jealous that Anne so easily produced children.

Religion provided a welcome escape. Devoted to the Anglican Church, Mary encouraged the appointments of such liberal bishops as Gilbert Burnet, John Tillotson, and Henry Compton. Some years before, she had sent a letter to her father on behalf of Compton, her spiritual adviser in childhood, after James sent him to the ecclesiastical court presided over by the notorious Judge Jeffreys. She received no answer, but Compton came off with an unusually light sentence.

Admittedly Mary found her chief pleasures in residences. In Kensington she supervised the building of another palace and arranged its gardens. At Hampton Court she set up a model dairy and a hothouse for rare plants. She had long collected Delft and blue ware and now spent much time arranging her pieces properly. Daniel Defoe observed: "The Queen brought the custom or humor as I may call it, of furnishing houses with China-ware ... piling their china on the tops of cabinets, escritoires, and every chimney piece to the tops of the ceilings." She also filled her palaces with the exquisite embroidery she kept producing despite frequently sore eyes. There were notable public accomplishments as well. Through a charter and funds granted by the king and queen, the College of William and Mary was founded in Williamsburg, Virginia, in 1693. By herself Mary established the Greenwich Hospital for disabled veterans.

In December 1694, during another severe smallpox epidemic, Mary fell ill and died on the 28th. William said that he had never known one single fault in her. She had, of course, almost always deferred to his political wishes.

Anne
Queen of England, Scotland, and Ireland, 1702–1707; of Great Britain and Ireland, 1707–1714

On the death of Mary II in 1694, William III became sole ruler of England. Eight years later, during a stag hunt at Hampton Court, his horse stumbled in a molehill and threw him to the ground, the fall breaking his collarbone. He had never been healthy, and complications that set in proved fatal. He was succeeded by his sister-in-law, Anne, a shy, dull semi-invalid, whose reign came to be called splendid.

The second daughter of unhappily married James Stuart and Anne Hyde, Duke and Duchess of York, she was born at St. James's Palace on February 6, 1665, just as the Great Plague broke out in London. The Yorks took their children to the north, then reappeared in London in the spring of 1666. That autumn the Great Fire scorched two-thirds of the city, but the royal residences remained safe.

Although a plump baby, Anne was frequently ill. In the belief that French doctors and climate might help her, the three-year-old princess was brought to her grandmother Henrietta Maria, widow of Charles I, at the palace of St. Germain-en-Laye near Paris. Not long after, Henrietta Maria died and Anne went to live with her aunt, Henrietta Anne, Duchess of Orleans, who was known as "Madame" at the court of Louis XIV. Poison was suspected when the stately "Madame" died suddenly in 1670 at her palace in St. Cloud.

Only a short time after Anne's return to England, she lost her mother; during her absence, two small brothers had also died. Fortunately her own health had improved in France, and at the old palace at Richmond she grew even stronger under the care of the Villiers family. Meanwhile, fearful of the Duke of York's tilt toward Catholicism, Charles II made sure that his nieces, Mary and Anne, were well grounded in Protestant doctrine by two chaplains, Drs. Edward Lake and Henry Compton.

121

Anne reacted happily when vivacious Sarah Jennings, four years her senior, joined the household as her companion. At once Sarah began to dominate the ever-admiring and docile princess. Enthusiastically the new friends took part in the masque *Calisto*, in which Princess Mary played the leading role. Observers remarked that the reserved Anne, whose eyes often watered, was not as pretty as her vivacious sister. But as a tall and curly-haired brunette with long, delicate hands, she made a good appearance. Like Mary, Anne accepted with good grace their father's new marriage to an Italian princess, Mary of Modena, but noted with dismay how his Catholic sympathies brought him increasing unpopularity. Conveniently forgetting his long service to the navy and his contributions to the victories that gave England colonies in Delaware, New Jersey, and New York, Parliament forced his resignation as Lord High Admiral.

When Mary sailed to Holland as the bride of William of Orange in 1678, Anne lay too ill with smallpox to say goodbye. The following year Sarah Jennings, now lady-in-waiting to the new Duchess of York, married John Churchill, a young lieutenant colonel attached to the Duke of York's household. So the Churchills left with the Yorks after King Charles ordered his brother to settle in Brussels. When Anne went there to visit her family, she enjoyed a happy reunion with Sarah.

In 1680 George Louis, eldest son of Duke Ernest Augustus, later the Elector of Hanover, arrived carrying special credentials because his mother, Duchess Sophia, was a granddaughter of James I. Somehow the courtship did not go well, and George returned home without proposing. A humiliated Anne gratefully accepted her father's and stepmother's invitation to stay with them in Edinburgh, at Holyrood Palace, so filled with memories of Anne's great-great grandmother, Mary Stuart.

When the family returned to London in 1682, Anne acquired a beau, the entertaining John Sheffield, twice her age. But the king frowned on her marrying him, declaring that he would look only in the royal courts for a suitable husband for his niece. After he dispatched Sheffield on a naval assignment, he showed interest in a Danish proposal for a marriage between Anne and Prince George (Jørgen), a brother of King Christian V.

In July 1683 the tall, blond and naive prince presented himself at Whitehall Palace. Not overly impressed, Charles made his famous remark that he had tried George drunk and tried him sober and found nothing in him either way. Nevertheless he speedily agreed to a marriage settlement. After their wedding at St. James's Palace, the bride and bridegroom went with the court to Windsor for the rest of the summer. Theirs had not been a passionate love affair, but Anne deeply appreciated her Danish prince's kindness and gentleness and admired his reputation as a gallant soldier. He also proved a model of marital fidelity.

Sarah Churchill continued to enrapture Anne, and at the Princess of

Denmark's request Sarah came back to her as lady-in-waiting at a new home, the Cockpit, a small residence on the side of Whitehall Palace nearest St. James's Park. Anne's first child, a daughter, was born dead in May 1684, and only Sarah could lift her spirits. The two women became closer friends than ever, and to banish any hint of inequality they chose special names, Mrs. Morley for Anne, Mrs. Freeman for Sarah.

On Anne's 20th birthday her uncle Charles lay dying of a stroke, and his courtiers worried about the crown's passing to the Duke of York. Loving James for his generosity toward her, but detesting his Catholicism, Anne had ambivalent feelings. Loyally she took part in her father's coronation shortly afterwards. She was again pregnant, and a frail daughter, Mary, was born that summer. To the court doctors her next child, Anna Sophia, arriving the next year, looked stronger and healthier.

Then Prince George suffered a serious illness through which Anne nursed him tenderly. On the heels of his recovery, their two small daughters died in quick succession. James expressed his sympathy by sending his daughter books and papers and promising to settle the crown on her if she became Catholic. Strongly influenced by Dr. Compton, Anne returned them all.

Like Anne, James's second wife, Mary of Modena, had lost all her children. She had been married for 15 years when she announced a new pregnancy, which her two stepdaughters refused to believe. Six months later Anne and George were taking the waters at Bath when John Churchill arrived on horseback with the news that a son had been born to the royal couple four weeks earlier than expected. Common gossip, he added, had it that a baby in a warming pan had been smuggled into the queen's bed. Churchill also reported that leaders who did not relish a Catholic heir were urging William of Orange, Anne's brother-in-law, to hurry to England.

On John Churchill's counsel, Anne expressed her approval in a letter to William. Once the Orange stadtholder landed with his invasion force, Prince George followed Churchill by a day in going over to him. James then ordered Sarah Churchill's arrest, and one rainy night she and Anne fled the Cockpit for Nottingham. Anne, however, was long haunted by guilt feelings at having deserted her father. A popular song ran that she and her sister "had put their father to flight and shame."

By Christmas 1688 the Glorious Revolution had ended, and the Prince and Princess of Denmark settled in London, preparing for the new reign of William and Mary. Within a month of the arrival of the Dutch troops, a Convention Parliament met to establish a new government. Meanwhile the Churchills advised Anne not to press her claim to the throne over William if Mary were to die suddenly.

Separated for several years, the sisters had grown far apart. Sarah Churchill later wrote, "On the arrival of Queen Mary in England, the Princess of Denmark went to meet her, and there was great appearance of kindness between them. But this quickly wore off, and a visible coldness ensued because Queen Mary grew weary of anybody who could not talk a great deal, and the Princess was so silent that she rarely spoke more than was necessary to answer a question."

More serious differences followed William and Mary's coronation. Anne believed she had some claims on her father's private estate and was displeased that the new king granted it away; frequently his general stinginess affronted her. She also bridled at what she considered personal insults. When not abroad, fighting in the League of Augsburg's war against France, William made fun of his brother-in-law, George, whom he regarded as a military amateur. As for Mary, she disliked Sarah Churchill intensely and soon demanded that Anne dismiss her Mrs. Freeman. But Anne stood her ground. Finally her financial dilemma was solved when Parliament came to her rescue with an allowance of £50,000 a year in addition to the £20,000 she had received in her marriage settlement.

That July she gave birth to a boy, named for a flattered King William, who granted the baby the title of Duke of Gloucester. After several miscarriages and the deaths of three infants, Anne finally rejoiced in an heir, who although somewhat sickly, gave promise of surviving. Mary had remained childless.

By 1691 the breach between Anne and George and William and Mary had perceptibly widened. Openly Anne declared her approval of a naval expedition in favor of her father and expressed grief at its failure. William had rewarded John Churchill with the title of Earl of Marlborough for his services, but suddenly suspecting him of involvement in a plot to restore James, he stripped away all his appointments. Although Marlborough was accused of high treason, the charge broke down. Anne, however, regarded his disgrace as a rebuff.

Mary continued to treat her coldly but was always kind to the little Duke of Gloucester, whom she frequently visited. When Mary died in 1694, Anne was not at her sister's bed. At first the Princess of Denmark remained aloof from the widower. Then, conscious that his wife's passing had weakened his own position, William ordered that Anne be accorded every honor and courtesy. After he reinstated Marlborough in 1695, Anne gave the king her full support. Sarah, however, referred to William as Shakespeare's monster, Caliban.

At St. James's Palace, Anne installed her own court. Only the Duke of Gloucester occupied the nursery. Since his birth she had had six more miscarriages and given birth to two more children who did not live long. In July 1700 the little duke died. Anne agreed to the Act of Settlement, which declared her father's cousin Duchess Sophia her successor. She still chafed at the humiliation she had suffered when Sophia's son George rejected her. He had succeeded his father as Elector in 1698.

With King William's death in 1702, Anne became queen and was crowned

Anne. National Portrait Gallery, London.

in April. Her many pregnancies had made her corpulent and ailing, and at the time of her coronation she suffered so much from gout that she limped, with assistance, down the aisle of Westminster Abbey.

The war with France had ended in 1697. But William had taken new alarm in 1700 when Charles II of Spain bequeathed his domains to Philip of Anjou, the grandson of Louis XIV. Louis proclaimed Philip king and declared that the Pyrenees no longer separated the two countries. Fearing the prospect of French annexation of the Spanish empire, the rulers of Austria, Prussia, England, Holland, and most of the states of the Holy Roman Empire formed a Grand

Alliance to prevent Philip from reigning in Spain and to put the Archduke Charles of Austria on the throne.

Besides championing his grandson, Louis also recognized the Young Pretender James as the English king; the deposed James had just died. Acknowledgment of the Young Pretender's rights roused the English to fighting pitch, and two weeks after Anne's coronation, England entered the War of the Spanish Succession, finding even more reasons for taking part. Holland needed defending, and the English colonies across the Atlantic requested protection because France was in the process of extending her colonial settlements.

Against France and Spain stood two great military leaders, Marlborough and Prince Eugene of Savoy. Marlborough led the English and Dutch, Prince Eugene, the German armies. Almost immediately more royal favors fell on Marlborough—a dukedom, a captain-generalship, and the Order of the Garter. Although Marlborough made all the military decisions, Prince George, described as "very fat, loving the news, the bottle, and the Queen," was named Lord High Admiral and generalissimo of the armed forces.

As Lord Treasurer, the Marlboroughs' good friend Sidney Godolphin headed Anne's first government, chiefly Tory. Sarah too was rising in the ranks. The termagant favorite continued to dominate the meek queen, even more after she became mistress of the robes and keeper of the privy purse.

The first year of the war proved disappointing for the allies. Then in 1704 at the Bavarian village of Blenheim, where Marlborough leaped from his horse to personally lead his troops, he and Prince Eugene won a smashing victory over the French. It saved Germany, but Louis did not feel ready to concede.

To honor her great commander, Anne presented him with the old park of Woodstock, near Oxford, and ordered the palace of Blenheim built there for him and Sarah. Once the foundation stone was laid in 1705, Sarah occupied herself with the construction and quarreled incessantly with its architect, Sir John Vanbrugh, and the workmen.

As the English prospered in the war, the government fell increasingly into Whig hands. Much as she loved the Marlboroughs, Anne disliked their ambitious son-in-law, the Earl of Sunderland, but after Sarah's persistent begging, she agreed to appoint him as one of her two secretaries of state along with Robert Harley.

In private, Anne always had favored the Tories because of their High Church affiliations. Now as queen she expressed her religious devotion with greater generosity. By "Queen Anne's Bounty" she granted the crown revenue from "tenths and first fruits" to help the small churches, whose clergy lived on the edge of poverty. Giving freely to charity, she also sponsored a Society for the Propagation of the Gospel in foreign lands; its members were among the first Englishmen to condemn the slave trade.

In 1706 Marlborough won the battle of Ramillies in the Netherlands, and the Whigs, the pro-war party, increased their influence. Almost since the beginning of Anne's reign, negotiations had been going on with the Scottish emissaries for an Act of Union. Since the accession of James I, son of Mary, Queen of Scots, to the English throne in 1603, England and Scotland had been governed by one sovereign, but each country had kept its own religion and own parliament. The Act of Union joined England and Wales with Scotland under the name the United Kingdom of Great Britain. It left Scottish laws and the Presbyterian Church untouched, but directed the Scots to dissolve their parliament and find representation in the British Parliament. Anne lay ill when the Whigs agreed to the final terms, but recovered enough to make a speech to Parliament. She always spoke well. A contemporary wrote: "What was most remarkable in her personal accomplishments was a clear, harmonious voice, particularly conspicuous in her graceful delivery of her speeches." The first Parliament of a united Great Britain met the following October.

As the Duchess of Marlborough spent more and more time supervising the construction of Blenheim Palace, Anne turned increasingly to Abigail Hill, whom Sarah had introduced at court. Abigail was cousin both to Sarah and to Robert Harley. Quickly Anne learned to depend on the respectful, unassuming woman for companionship and on Harley for advice. In 1707 Abigail Hill married Samuel Masham, Prince George's groom of the chamber, at a private ceremony performed in the rooms of Anne's physician, Sir John Arbuthnot. When the Duchess of Marlborough heard of the secret marriage and of Abigail's bringing Harley up the back stairs for consultation with the queen, either at St. James's Palace or at Windsor, she exploded in fury as only she could. The long friendship had begun to crack.

The next year, 1708, proved full of dramatic happenings. Harley boldly proposed himself as head of a moderate government, put in power by a third party. But his plan failed, and in February Anne dismissed him as secretary of state although he remained her secret adviser. During the spring the Young Pretender was reported to be at Dunkirk, ready to sail for Scotland, where he intended to declare himself king. But, followed by the Stuarts' usual bad luck, he came down with the measles just as the weather worsened, and he went home to St. Germain-en-Laye.

In July even better news for the English arrived. Marlborough had won another splendid victory at Oudenarde in the Netherlands, and Louis stood ready to sue for peace. Then came the disappointing report that he had backed away from the allies' terms. All this time Anne and Sarah quarreled with increasing frequency.

Anne's nerves had grown especially frazzled because of George's deteriorating health. A visit to Bath seemed to bring him improvement, but by October he was dead. His widow wrote the King of Denmark:

> I must confess to Your Majesty that the loss of such a husband, who loved
> me so dearly and devotedly, is too crushing for me to be able to bear it as I
> ought.

From then on she depended more and more on Mrs. Masham.

Marlborough won his last great victory in September 1709 at Malplaquet,
a town on the border between France and the Netherlands. With 40,000 men
lying dead or wounded within an 11-mile radius, it proved to be the bloodiest
battle of the 18th century. The duke's critics charged that knowing how short
his credit was at home, he had determined to restore it with a great victory
at whatever price.

Cries arose for his recall, and his duchess blamed Mrs. Masham. Continuing to support the war effort, a group of Whigs now asked Marlborough to
force the queen's abdication and bring the House of Hanover to England, but
loyally he refused. In 1710 the Whig government was overthrown and a Tory
government, controlled by Harley, replaced it. When Marlborough returned
to England in 1711, he found that intense peace negotiations had been going
on behind his back.

Sarah fumed even more when Anne made Samuel Masham a Tory peer.
By this time his wife had actively involved herself in plotting the
Marlboroughs' downfall. After Mrs. Morley and Mrs. Freeman had one final,
painful meeting, the famous soldier was dismissed from all his offices, and
Sarah lost her posts too. Most galling to her was Lady Masham's elevation to
keeper of the privy purse.

Anne's health had suffered, not only from her quarrels with Sarah and her
pregnancies, but from the acrid party feuds in Parliament. She had found some
relief from her tensions in the races at Newmarket, Ascot, and Epsom Downs.
She loved horses, and before her corpulence made it difficult to mount, she
was a fine rider.

Although she had no intellectual interests, her era was acquiring a splendid name, the Augustan Age, bestowed by those who wished to restore
England to political stability and classicism that had characterized the era of
the Roman Emperor Augustus. Literary leaders included Joseph Addison,
Richard Steele, and Alexander Pope, as well as Jonathan Swift, who had frequently showed up in search of an appointment. The young German musician,
George Frederick Handel, also brought luster.

It was a poet, Matthew Prior, who helped Henry St. John, Viscount Bolingbroke negotiate peace with France. The treaty gave Nova Scotia, the Hudson Bay Territory, Newfoundland, Gibraltar, and Minorca to Great Britain.
The French also agreed to expel the Young Pretender from France and to
recognize the Protestant succession in France. Although the Duke of
Marlborough had won all the great military victories, he remained in disgrace,
and he and Sarah departed for Frankfurt.

Harley had become Lord Treasurer, but the rivalry between him and Bolingbroke had grown intense. Anne herself grew to dislike Harley's heavy drinking, arrogance, and presumption, and she finally asked him to resign.

The political infighting took the last of her physical reserves, and she was extremely ill on the night of July 27, 1714, when she sat through an excessively long meeting of the privy council. It was so filled with acrimony and insults that the queen took to her bed immediately afterwards. She wanted Bolingbroke to accept Harley's post, but the privy council decided on the Duke of Shrewsbury. As her last official act, the dying queen put the wand of office into Shrewsbury's hands. The aged Duchess Sophia had died two months earlier, and Anne knew that George Louis, Elector of Hanover, would become King George I of Great Britain.

On the morning of August 1, the bells of London tolled for Queen Anne. The Stuart era had ended, and the kingdom awaited the Hanoverians.

Ulrika Eleonora
Queen of Sweden, 1718–1720

Toward its end the Great Northern War, which had lasted 21 interminable years, numbered among its casualties one of Sweden's most famous kings. The successor to the bachelor Charles XII was his dull, graceless sister, whose brief reign prepared the way for a remarkable Age of Freedom.

Born January 23, 1688, in Stockholm to Charles XI and his Danish wife, the frail Ulrika Eleonora was her mother's namesake. Since 1685 four of the young princes had died, and when doctors agreed that the new baby would survive, the ailing queen improved immediately. She had two other children, Hedvig Sophia and Charles, born in 1681 and 1682.

The romance of Ulrika's parents had played against the background of a Swedish-Danish war. Charles XI, son of the king in whose favor Queen Kristina had abdicated, began his rule in 1672. To keep his southern provinces safe, he led a bitter struggle against Denmark, his country's age-old enemy, even though he had already sought the hand of the Danish princess, Ulrika Eleonora. When her angry brother, Christian V, pressed her to break the engagement, Ulrika refused to do so. Peace negotiations finally opened in 1679, and in the following year she married Charles at a simple ceremony. In 1683 her brother Jørgen (George) became the bridegroom of Princess Anne, daughter of the Duke of York and future queen of England.

Because the dowager queen, Hedvig Eleonora of Holstein-Gottorp, suspected her daughter-in-law's Danish connections, the young wife kept away from politics and occupied herself with her children's upbringing and her charities. Like her husband, she preferred a quiet life, preferably at the castle of Carlberg. She often lay ill, but when guests came to court, she would emerge from her apartments to sit with the royal family and proudly watch as young Charles performed on horseback in an elaborate dressage show. But she died when her daughter Ulla, as the family called her, was only five. For years Ulla, her father, her sister, and her brother burst into tears when they spoke of the late queen, whose name had become a synonym for goodness, kindness, and piety. Seeking comfort in his children's company, King Charles took them for outings whenever possible. Still Ulla often felt left out and inferior to Hedvig, pert, lively, pretty, and particularly close to their brother Charles.

Even before Ulrika Eleonora's birth, Charles XI had made himself the most absolute of all Swedish monarchs. In the Parliament of 1680, the lower estates absolved him from any obligation to observe the Form of Government or to rule with the advice of the Råd (Council). The estates met only infrequently and in 1682 gave Charles full control over legislation and the possession of many of the nobles's estates. Finally in 1693, the year of the queen consort's death, Charles and his heirs were declared "responsible to none on earth for their actions, but having all the power they may ask, with which to guide and rule this kingdom like Christian kings."

Inculcating in her pupil the doctrine of absolute rule, Marta Berenson became Ulla's governess. But her influence did not extend beyond the schoolroom walls; the heart of the lonely princess went to her sympathetic lady-in-waiting, Emerentia von Düben. She needed Emerentia more than ever when Charles XI died at Eastertime in 1697. Shortly afterwards a fire broke out in the Stockholm palace, and Ulla had to watch her father's corpse being carried through the flames to a safe haven. The royal family sought refuge in another palace. For five months the queen dowager, Hedvig Eleonora, headed a regency until 15-year-old Charles, who showed promise of becoming a splendid king, assumed responsibility.

The following year, 1698, Hedvig Sophia's cousin, the jolly and high-spirited Frederick, Duke of Holstein-Gottorp, came from Germany to claim her hand. A born tease, he immediately terrified shy little Ulla by threatening to marry her to Alexei, son of the Russian czar, Peter I. Easily the young Swedish king fell in with pranks the duke and his Holstein cavaliers suggested: shooting windows to pieces, throwing furniture from the palace windows, chasing hares around the gallery. Soon gossip described their drunken hunting expeditions as episodes of decapitating sheep, dogs, and calves inside the palace.

Raucous though he might appear, Frederick won Hedvig, and Ulla dutifully played her part in the wedding ceremony held at Carlberg. Immediately afterwards, Charles, accompanied by the bride and groom and the royal family, made a progress through his country, so successful that Ulla sent enthusiastic letters back to Stockholm.

With the accession of a boy ruler, the King of Denmark, the Elector of Saxony, and the Czar of Russia considered Sweden to be at its lowest ebb and formed a coalition to seize Swedish territories around the Baltic and in Germany. But they had not reckoned with a military genius; Charles's admirers soon compared him to Alexander the Great.

Early in 1700, Saxon troops marched into Livonia but could not conquer it. Denmark attacked Holstein-Gottorp, and Charles responded by invading Denmark. Then, helped by the presence of the English and Dutch fleets, he

Ulrika Eleonora. The Swedish Institute, Stockholm.

rather quickly forced his cousin, King Frederik IV, to sign a peace. After Denmark, Charles turned his attention to the Baltic provinces, then went to the relief of the important Swedish fortress of Narva under siege by the Russians, whom he soon put to flight.

Ulrika was only 12 when her brother left Sweden for the front, and she did not see him again for 16 years. Since he had made his brother-in-law, the Duke of Holstein-Gottorp, the *generalissimus* of his German troops, Hedvig Sophia returned to Stockholm.

Charles corresponded with both sisters, always in a bantering and optimistic tone to Ulla. Soon he congratulated her on her newly acquired dignity as an aunt, for Hedvig Sophia had given birth to a son, Charles Frederick, just as her husband was leaving for Denmark.

After his sweeping victory at Narva, the Swedish king attacked Poland, where Augustus, Elector of Saxony, sat on the throne. At the beginning of this campaign, the Duke of Holstein-Gottorp was killed, and Charles wrote Ulrika:

> I hope that the Lord may comfort you in all this exceeding great sorrow of ours, and especially sister Hedvig, that she may not fret herself too sorely over this calamity, but bear it as best she can, and I hope that my dear sister and the Queen [Dowager] will do your best to comfort her.

Thereafter Hedvig carefully avoided remarriage so as not to spoil her chances of gaining the throne if her brother died in battle.

In 1706 Charles deposed Augustus, forced the Poles to accept Stanislas Leszczynski as king, and made plans to invade Russia. In the Ukraine he hoped to ally himself with Ivan Mazepa, its governor, but Mazepa was overthrown. Czar Peter had used "scorched earth" tactics, and the Russian winter took a terrible toll on the famished Swedish army.

After the battle of Poltava, in which the Russian czar whipped him soundly, Charles received the tragic news that his sister Hedvig had died of smallpox six months before. From then on the tone of his letters to his only surviving sister changed markedly. Suddenly he began treating her as a grown-up, frequently reminding her of their special status, "We who are the only ones left." Through correspondence she became his closest confidante.

Following his defeat by the Russians, Charles fled to Bender in Ottoman Bessarabia, where for four years he ruled Sweden by courier. But gloomy news kept arriving. Augustus returned to the Polish throne, the Danes invaded Skåne, and Peter moved into Finland and drove Swedish troops out of the Baltic provinces.

Meanwhile, a persistent suitor for Ulrika's hand appeared. In 1711 Frederick, Duke of Hesse, who had lost his first wife, pursued his quarry with letters, gifts, and go-betweens, far more determined than Ulrika's first suitor, the crown prince of Prussia, who had made overtures when she was 15. Ulrika had liked his portrait, but the Prussian king's envoys, fearful of any Swedish alliance, complained in letters home that the Swedish princess suffered from a too-imperious air, offensive breath, and a weak bladder. They said nothing about her looks or personality. Ulrika was still pale and stiff and had retained her shyness. She had inherited her mother's high forehead and lovely eyes and hands, but nobody considered her handsome. Her prospects, however, tantalized many suitors.

With an absent king and the ongoing war, Sweden faced new difficulties. An outbreak of the plague followed crop failures. With her grandmother and nephew, Ulrika Eleonora went to the small silver mining town of Sala to wait it out.

During his Turkish sojourn, Charles had continually badgered his hosts to attack Russia again. They had already made one successful effort at the river Pruth although they had not captured Peter. In 1713, debating future strategy, Charles quarreled with the Ottoman Sultan so bitterly that the local Turkish garrison stormed the king's residence and held him captive for a time.

Attention now focused on Ulrika. In 1713 cannons boomed throughout Stockholm as she took a seat in the privy council. At once she felt torn between her brother and the council, conscious of her loyalty to him, yet sympathizing with its desire for peace. She wrote to Charles of the need to end the war, but he appealed to their family bond and said she should cooperate with him to save Sweden. Some nobles even considered naming her regent but gave up the idea when they found little support. That year when the Swedish Senate warned Charles that he must return, he managed to escape from Turkish hands and ride on horseback across half of Europe. But he did not enter Sweden. In late 1714 he arrived at the Baltic port of Stralsund, one of the last vestiges of his territory outside Sweden and in his view the best war base.

At Stralsund he consented to Ulrika's marriage to Frederick of Hesse, having earlier advised his worried sister she could not jeopardize her succession by wedding a Catholic. The simple ceremony took place in the spring of 1715 at Stockholm Castle, with the 80-year-old queen dowager doing the honors of the festivities. When informed of the ball that highlighted them, Charles remarked smilingly to a member of his entourage: "My good sister is dancing away the crown of Sweden."

Marriage did not improve the princess's looks. She sent her brother a portrait which he rejected as "too old, too thin and worried looking." Another had to be painted for him.

From the beginning, Ulrika Eleonora, who had fallen passionately in love, let her husband dominate her and did not seem to care that he was exceedingly ambitious to become king. Almost at once he demanded that his new brother-in-law appoint him viceroy in Sweden and *generalissimus* of the Swedish army. Charles refused him the first title, but gave him the second.

Early in the new year the fort at Stralsund fell, and Charles was forced to enter Sweden. To resist a projected invasion by Russia and Denmark, he set up headquarters at Lund. It was now possible for brother and sister to meet for the first time in 16 years, at Vadstena, one of the palaces of their deceased grandmother. Charles arrived, unannounced and dripping wet. Everyone was amazed to see how much he and Ulrika resembled each other; both were tall, slim, and blonde. They embraced, and at the mention of their mother and sister, they burst into tears. Ulrika did not see him again until 1718.

That year Charles began his first invasion of Norway, still tied to Denmark in a political union; it failed, and he tried again in 1718. Not long after, a shell fragment struck him in the head and killed him. During his stay in Stralsund Charles had delegated almost dictatorial powers to a Holstein diplomat, Baron Görtz, who had remained with him at Lund. With the king's death, Görtz aligned himself with the forces supporting Ulrika's nephew, Charles Frederick of Holstein-Gottorp. Ulrika's husband was equally determined that she should have the throne, and on his orders Görtz was arrested and executed.

The disputed succession strengthened the hands of the Swedish parliamentarians, who were now ready to react against the absolute rule that Ulrika's father and brother had practiced. Because she had married a foreigner, they also questioned her hereditary right to the throne. Finally they agreed to accept her if she in turn accepted a new constitution, ruled according to the advice of Parliament, and approved all laws it passed. She could have no royal veto power. Ulrika Eleonora also had to renounce her hereditary rights and agree to being elected by the Parliament. Having been brought up under autocracy, she found it difficult to rule under any other terms. Often stubborn and proud, she quarreled frequently with Count Arvid Horn, the leader of the parliamentary forces, who finally left his post.

Much of the time she felt out of her depth, so insecure that she considered naming her husband co-ruler. Swedish law, however, did not permit a united rule like that of William III and Mary II of England. Finally on March 24, 1720, Ulrika abdicated in favor of her husband after gaining the promise that if he died she would be queen again. For his part Frederick gave up significant powers to Parliament. The so-called Era of Liberty would last 52 years until Gustavus III reintroduced absolutism.

When Ulrika abdicated, the Great Northern War still sputtered. Peace finally came in 1721, but it brought no triumph. Sweden lost all her former possessions except Finland and a few small holdings on the southern shores of the Baltic.

From then on, Ulrika Eleonora drew back from court life, devoting herself to good works and enjoying the company of her faithful Emerentia von Düben. Only once, when Frederick paid a brief visit to Hesse, did Ulrika assume power as regent. Meanwhile his love affairs became more flagrant, and in 1744 his barren wife suffered the humiliation of seeing him install in the palace his beautiful mistress, Hedvig Taube, who proceeded to bear him several children.

In 1741 Sweden went to war with Russia once more. Ulrika often prayed in her chapel for the troops in Finland. She did not see her country's painful defeat. Suffering from tuberculosis, she died on November 24, 1741. For her burial her husband ordered 512 cannon discharges, a noisy end for a quiet queen.

Catherine I (Ekaterina)
Empress of Russia, 1725–1727

But for Charles XII of Sweden, a peasant girl might never have become *Czarina* of Russia. It was Charles's war with Peter the Great that changed her destiny. Servant and camp follower, Marta Skavronska rose to power more spectacularly than any other woman in Russian history. Vulgar, practical, intensely loyal, and above all amiable, she proved to be the perfect companion in the whirlpool of Peter's life.

She was born in the Swedish province of Livonia on February 24, 1684, to Dorothea Hahn and Samuel Skavronsky, a Lithuanian gravedigger in the little town of Marienburg. Orphaned at three, Marta was separated from her brother and sisters and adopted by an aunt. Nine years later a Lutheran minister named Gluck took her into his household, where she grew up as a servant. She had just passed her 16th birthday when Czar Peter and King Charles began the Great Northern War.

Since Marta seemed to be quite free with her favors, Pastor Gluck arranged for her marriage to a Swedish dragoon named Johan Rabbe. It lasted all too briefly. Soon the Russians occupied Marienburg, Rabbe left with the Swedish garrison, and his bride returned to the Glucks. Temporarily the Glucks were allowed to go free, but Marta stayed a prisoner, working in the baggage train.

Happily for her, a protector appeared in the person of a German brigadier, who for a short time led her away from camp. Next she attracted Russian commander Field Marshal Count Boris Sheremetev and entered his household, sharing his bed whenever possible. Before long another field marshal, Alexander Menshikov, the czar's favorite, noticed the blond, deep-bosomed girl on Mme. Sheremetev's domestic staff and either bullied her protector or bought her from him. Then in 1703 the giant czar came for a visit to the Russian camp and laid covetous eyes on her. For a handsome sum Menshikov yielded up his mistress, and immediately Peter sent her away to Moscow to live in the German Quarter and be treated like a lady. But she saw little of her new lover, who moved about incessantly in the continuing war.

After she bore a boy, Paul, in 1704, Marta was received into the Russian Orthodox Church as Catherine (Ekaterina). When Peter could spend time with her, he found her an invaluable companion. She could drink glass for glass with him, and only she could calm his terrible outbursts of temper or his convulsive seizures by cradling his giant head in her arms and talking to him gently like a mother. With the birth of a second son, Peter, in 1705 their bonds grew deeper. When news arrived that his ally, the King of Poland, had gone over to the Swedes, Peter rushed off to organize his army. Catherine, however, comforted herself with pride in a new pregnancy. Her namesake was born at the end of 1706.

The Russian army had won some battles against the Swedish generals but not against Charles, who in 1707 resumed his advance. That autumn, while the czar remained at the front, both little boys, Paul and Peter, died within weeks of each other. Under such circumstances Catherine gave birth to a second daughter, Anna, early in 1708, but Peter could not visit her until she had been out of childbed for a month.

That summer Ekaterina, the elder daughter, died. Her mother, already consumed with worry over her lover, mourned alone. By the next year, however, torrential rains made fighting impossible, and Peter decided to tour southern Russia and to take his mistress with him. In the Ukraine they received word that the Swedes were on the march again, and the czar sent Catherine home to Moscow. Not until mid–July did she hear that he had won his most impressive victory, the battle of Poltava, in June. The victor came home for a short period, then left on another frenzied journey. He showed up in Moscow again in December to celebrate Poltava and the birth of a third daughter, Elizabeth.

Although Peter had contained the Swedish threat, at least for the time being, war with Turkey loomed. More confident of her hold on Peter, Catherine now made two demands, that she be allowed to go with him to the front and that their daughter Anna be recognized. An indulgent Peter gave a court dinner to name Anna as *czarevna*, then determined to grant official status to Catherine herself. During the spring of 1711, he informed the court that she was his consort and should be given all the respect due a *czarina*. Next he promised Catherine that a marriage ceremony would take place at the first opportunity.

To test her reception abroad, Peter now took her to Poland with him. She behaved properly enough and even charmed some of the Polish courtiers. Others sneered at the former peasant behind her back and repeated stories that in Livonia she had done the soldiers' laundry.

Once home, the couple did not stay there long. Charles XII had prevailed on the Turks to fight, and Catherine insisted on accompanying her lover to the Turkish border. In July they reached the river Pruth, and the Russian army entrenched itself on its shores, only to be suddenly surrounded by Turks and

Tartars. For some hours Catherine sat in a carriage in camp, then—unable to bear the screams any longer—stepped out and began to tend the wounded. The battle raged July 9–12, when the victorious Turks finally agreed to terms. By surrendering the fort of Azov, Peter was allowed to march his surviving troops home. Beyond caring for the wounded and comforting her husband, Catherine seems to have played only a minor role in the battle. But Peter fostered the legend that she had bought off the Turks with her jewels and those of other women in camp.

True to his promise, he married Catherine at the beginning of 1712. Johan Rabbe was officially declared to have been killed in 1702. Peter's nine-year marriage to Evdokia Lopukina had been dissolved when she entered a nunnery in 1698. At the time of her wedding, Catherine was heavily pregnant, and a few weeks later a daughter, Maria (or Natalia), was born.

That year, still hating memories of the bloody Kremlin, Peter declared his new city, St. Petersburg, the official capital of Russia. He had begun building it in 1703 on the Neva river to face the West, which gave him most of his ideas for reform. While he kept a watchful eye on construction, he and Catherine often lived at the Dutch-style Little House. But by 1712 the architect Domenico Trezzini had completed a simple two-story palace, also Dutch style, in the Summer Gardens, laid out by Peter to follow French and Dutch models. The palace interior boasted paneling, silk hangings, and tapestries, which appeared in Russia for the first time. Meanwhile Menshikov, now a prince and still Peter's favorite, built a splendid baroque palace, which the czar borrowed when important visitors required entertainment on the grandest scale. Although Catherine enjoyed her new palace, she had to endure months of separation from her husband, never free for long of the Swedish war. Frequently she grew bored and restless, and her ladies-in-waiting learned to cope with her increasingly irregular hours.

Peter won an important naval victory over the Swedes at Hangö in 1714, the year Catherine gave him another daughter, Margareta. He now honored his wife with a new order of chivalry, the Order of St. Catherine the Martyr, its motto, "Through Love and Fidelity," recognizing her years of devotion.

The next spring brought a storm of grief. Within weeks of each other, the youngest daughters, Maria (Natalia) and Margareta, died. But in October 1715, to his father's great rejoicing, a boy, Peter's namesake, arrived. His parents called him Petrushka. While still celebrating the birth of a son, Peter fell seriously ill, and Catherine worried endlessly about what might happen to her and the children if he died. Then suddenly he recovered, and she was radiant once more, absorbed in a new project. In 1714, after his victory at Hangö, Peter had ordered Alexandre Leblond, a French architect, to come to St. Petersburg to design a summer palace at Peterhof to rival Versailles. He himself had drawn the preliminary sketches. By 1725 the main work would be completed—palaces, Upper and Lower Parks, and innumerable fountains.

Leaving Petrushka in the care of nurses, Catherine set out with the czar on a grand tour of Europe at the outset of 1716. One year later, still on tour, she gave birth in Wessel to another son, Paul, who died within 24 hours. To Peter's great wrath the French court would not receive her, and the English court would not even accept the czar because of his wife. The Prussian court, however, gave the couple a warm reception.

After their return, still smarting from the snubs, Peter invited another Frenchman, Jean Marc Nattier, to St. Petersburg to paint his wife's portrait. Providing a flattering mirror, Nattier made Catherine look suitably elegant. Not long after he finished his successful canvas, a family tragedy broke. Peter accused his and Evdokia's rebellious son, Alexei, of subversive intrigues, and in 1718 the young heir was tortured to death by his father's order or possibly by his father's own hand. Following her usual pattern of birth after death, Catherine bore one more daughter, another Natalia. Meanwhile she and Peter had had one of their infrequent quarrels over her favorite attendant, Mary Hamilton. The young woman had killed her illegitimate child at birth. Catherine pleaded for her life, but Peter ordered Mary's execution.

To add to her unhappiness, the spring of 1719 brought Petrushka's death. Of all Catherine and Peter's numerous brood, only three little girls, Anna, Elizabeth, and Natalia had survived.

The war with Sweden, which had occupied the czar for 21 years, finally came to an end with most favorable terms for the Russians. But Peter was still caught up with military matters. He took Catherine with him on an expedition designed to snatch control of the trade routes to the Orient. After scant success, he turned back. Because of this arduous trip, he suffered another severe illness through which his wife nursed him. On recovering, he continued to work furiously on his reforms as though he were racing against time. His moods became blacker, and only his "amiable Katinka" could deal with him. As her influence increased, she used it to save from death her old lover, Menshikov, who had been accused of taking money from the state coffers.

Catherine's last child, Peter, born in 1723, died at birth. By 1724, Czar Peter had decided to crown her empress, in full regalia. At her coronation in May, she wore a Byzantine crown covered with almost 3,000 jewels. Overwhelmed, the corpulent woman with blackened hair tried to smother the czar's hands with kisses, but he irritably pushed her away.

Not long after her crowning, Catherine was accused of having entered into a liaison with her chamberlain, Wilhelm Mons, the brother of Anna Mons, Peter's mistress during his roistering youth in the German Quarter. Mons was further charged with peculation. Nobody could prove the intimacy, but an intensely jealous Peter ordered him tortured and beheaded. In a final blow he drove Catherine in a closed carriage past Mons's remains.

By the age of 40, Catherine had lost much of her physical attractiveness. The visiting Margravine of Bayreuth had written in 1723:

The Czarina was short and huddled up, very much tanned, and quite devoid of dignity or grace. The very sight of her proved her low birth. She was muffled up in her clothes like a German comedy waitress. Her gown had been bought in an old clothes shop; it was very old-fashioned, covered with heavy silver embroidery and with dirt. . . . She had a dozen orders, and as many portraits of saints and relics, fastened all along the facings of her dress, so that when she walked, she jangled like a mule.

A less snobbish critic noted:

There was nothing unpleasant about her manners, and anyone who remembers the princess's origin would have been disposed to think them good. It might fairly be said that if this princess had not all the charms of her sex, she had all the gentleness.

Yet another writer told of a common face, turned-up nose, "goggle eyes, an opulent bust, and all the general appearance of a servant girl in a German inn."

Still, she had to be considered a presumptive ruler. In 1722 Peter had signed an Act of Succession, giving the reigning autocrat the authority to choose his successor, but he did not use this privilege. When, faithfully attended by Catherine, he died of strangury at the beginning of 1725, the dynasty consisted of his widow, their three daughters, Alexei's son Peter, and two daughters of the czar's dim-witted half brother, Ivan. Catherine and Anna had become the Duchesses of Mecklenburg and Courland. Then within weeks of Peter's burial, the *czarina* lost her daughter, Natalia.

Several members of the old aristocracy wanted to name young Peter emperor. Menshikov, back in power, pushed Catherine's candidacy, and his cohorts courted the military. Finally the most elite units of the army settled the matter by declaring for Catherine. Their move set a precedent, for twice more within the century the guards would place an empress on the throne.

Less than a month after Peter's death, his widow accepted the title of Autocrat of all the Russias. Impetuous, ruthless, determined, Peter had had enormous goals — building fleets and armies, raising money to support them, turning old Muscovy into modern Russia, fundamentally changing all of Russian life. Although she promised to follow in his footsteps, Catherine did not have his vision.

Yet she began showing a quality singularly absent from his nature — compassion. With Menshikov at the helm, she reduced taxes, freed commerce of irksome restrictions, and introduced measures to ease the hardships of the common folk. As her foreign minister she picked Andrei Ostermann, and she told him she wanted peace. More than once she said, "We need a long rest from war," or blurted, "Wars are so damned expensive!" Still she did carry out Peter's wish of founding an Academy of Sciences in St. Petersburg, and she

Catherine I. The Hermitage, Leningrad.

encouraged another of his projects, Captain Vitus Bering's voyage to explore the northeast passage between Asia and America.

Perhaps her most important step was to create a Supreme Privy Council, consisting of Menshikov, Ostermann, and five other important men in her administration. Peter had delegated authority to the Senate and Synod. Catherine, on the other hand, gave her new council the right to inspect all proposals on domestic and foreign affairs submitted to the throne. In essence she made herself a puppet ruler. During her first year as empress regnant, her daughter Anna married Charles Frederick, Duke of Holstein-Gottorp. But Catherine refused to interrupt her period of mourning for her husband.

During the celebration she dined alone and called on the wedding party only to drink a cup of wine with the bride and groom.

Natalia and Peter, children of the murdered Alexei, were brought to live in back rooms at the court, and Catherine and her daughter treated them with great kindness. By the Act of Succession the empress had the privilege of naming her successor, and she chose young Peter. Also at court she provided for members of her long-lost family after locating them in Livonia.

Meanwhile she prepared to enjoy her luxurious and boisterous pleasures to the fullest. Her entertainments were invariably extravagant, and Catherine, beset by fears and her own sense of inadequacy, drank too much. Soon her life became totally undisciplined, her hours so irregular that she often dined at three in the morning.

With her body taxed by overindulgence and possibly venereal disease, Catherine fell gravely ill in January 1727 and died on May 17. In her will she kept her promise of leaving her throne to her 12-year-old stepgrandson, Peter. She thought she had assured a long male succession. No Russian would have believed that within three years a widow, Anna Ivanovna, from an obscure Baltic duchy would wear the imperial crown.

Anna Ivanovna
Empress of Russia, 1730–1740

Anna Ivanovna came to her throne only because young Peter II, successor to Catherine I, died of smallpox on his scheduled wedding day at the Kremlin in 1730. To follow him, eight nobles, who formed the Supreme Privy Council, first brought forward the name of Catherine and Peter the Great's daughter Elizabeth and then that of her nephew Peter, baby son of her sister, the late Duchess Anna of Holstein-Gottorp. Next Prince Dmitry Golitsyn proposed a candidate who he fondly imagined would be willing to rule with limited authority, Anna, Duchess of Courland and younger daughter of Ivan V. Swayed by Golitsyn's arguments, the Council chose her.

The fourth daughter of Praskovya Saltykova and the feeble-minded Ivan, co-czar with his half brother Peter, Anna was born February 8, 1693. Since Ivan spent most of his time in prayer and fasting, court gossip attributed paternity to one of the gentlemen of the bedchamber.

Although given to extravagant expressions of charity, Czarina Praskovya fully indulged in pleasures of the table and neglected her children. Ivan died in 1696, and three-year-old Anna and her two sisters, Catherine and Praskovya, found themselves controlled by Czar Peter from then on. Much of the year Praskovya and her daughters lived at Ismailov Palace three miles from Moscow. There the girls' education and training in social graces were superficial. Disliked by those close to her, Anna endured a scarred childhood and grew up self-willed, spiteful, and suspicious, frequently quarreling with her domineering mother.

In 1711 Peter gave her in marriage to Friedrich Wilhelm, the young Duke of Courland. His small Baltic duchy was a vassal fief of Poland, and various nations continually competed for its control. Peter had eagerly offered Russian protection. Everything seemed propitious, but after a splendid wedding in Moscow, the bridegroom, who had overindulged in food and drink, died on the way to Mitau, his capital. The disconsolate bride returned to her mother.

The marriage contract had promised Anna an annual pension of 40,000 roubles and a residence in Mitau. When the new duke, Ferdinand, refused to pay the young widow, Russian troops arrived and Ferdinand fled to Danzig. In the spring of 1712, Czar Peter decided to send his niece back to Mitau to encourage the formation of a pro-Russian party among the Courland gentry. Anna's mother and sisters accompanied her as far as Riga, the last staging post on the road to Mitau.

For the next four years while Russian agents pressed Anna's claims with the Courlanders, she remained alone in Riga, going to St. Petersburg and Ismailov Palace whenever possible. On one of those trips she attended the wedding of her sister Catherine to the Duke of Mecklenburg. Finally in 1717, sour and apprehensive, Anna arrived in her duchy.

Life in Mitau proved to be generally dull and without luxury. Often she successfully implored Czar Peter for money so that at least she could set a good table. Less generous, her mother cut her off completely when told of Anna's having an affair with the Russian ambassador, Count Peter Bestuzhev. Only on her deathbed in 1723 did Praskovya forgive the duchess. Anna then formed a more open alliance with a handsome German adventurer, Count Ernst Buhren, who proceeded to marry a woman not given to jealousy.

In 1726, more inspired by ambition than by love, a suitor arrived in Courland in the person of the dashing Count Maurice de Saxe, a natural son of the King of Saxony. Deeply attracted, Anna nominated him as duke-elect. But Prince Alexander Menshikov arrived from Russia to declare that Maurice's illegitimate birth made him unacceptable. Menshikov had 300 dragoons in tow and did not hide his own ambition to become Duke of Courland. But Anna complained of his bullying ways, and Catherine I, Czar Peter's successor, recalled him.

Meanwhile the Polish Diet declared Courland united with Poland and nullified Maurice's election as duke. For a time he blockaded himself in Mitau, then left to travel through Europe enlisting troops. When he returned Anna had become disillusioned by his many love affairs, and she realized he was a political liability. After the Empress Catherine's death, Menshikov sent an army of 8,000 to Mitau. Maurice, who had gathered only 500 soldiers around himself, fled for his life.

Under the regime of Peter II, which banished Menshikov, Anna's financial position remained difficult. Her dream of fat years and revenge, however, came true far earlier than expected. On Peter's sudden death in January 1730 and her acceptance by the Supreme Privy Council, messengers sped to Mitau with a Points of Government (*Punkti*), written by Prince Golitsyn to increase the council's power. The document declared that the empress would have to govern through a new and larger Privy Council and that on her own she would not be able to declare peace or war, impose new taxes, give away or confiscate state land, or condemn a subject to death. Eager to escape from her drab little court, Anna willingly signed the paper.

Almost immediately on arriving in Moscow, she ripped up the *Punkti*,

Anna Ivanovna. The Hermitage, Leningrad.

knowing she had the support of the Preabrazhenkoe guards and the im-
perialists, led by Baron Andrei Ostermann, who had feigned illness to avoid
putting his name to the restrictions. Thus Anna firmly rejected the idea of a
constitutional monarchy, akin to the British and Swedish models. Her
audacious behavior stunned the Privy Council into silence, and the swarthy
amazon with a deep voice and perpetual frown was crowned *czarina* of all the
Russias in May. Observers thought that her double chins and sausage-like
ringlets made her look every inch a dominating empress. As time passed, they
noted approvingly that she paid scrupulous attention to the details of public
business.

The Buhrens had accompanied her to Moscow, and once on the throne
she created her beloved Ernst grand chamberlain and gave him a Russian court
besides. To reflect his new eminence, Buhren took the name of some old
French warrior dukes, Biron. Soon other Baltic Germans clogged the court
and took over the army and navy. By tearing up the *Punkti*, Anna quickly
established herself as an autocrat and used her power to reward her favorites
lavishly.

For two years she divided her time between the old palace in the Kremlin
and her childhood home at Ismailov. Then she had a new palace, the Annenhof, constructed within the Kremlin walls and ordered a second Annenhof
built in a park outside the city. In 1733 she removed the court to St. Petersburg.
Again she enjoyed the companionship of her sister Catherine, the Duchess of
Mecklenburg, who had found her husband intolerable and had returned to
Russia with her young daughter. Catherine died later that year. The grieving
empress promptly adopted her niece, whom the Russian Orthodox Church
received as Anna Leopoldovna.

Once the mourning was over, the empress moved between her ornate new
Winter Palace and Peterhof, her summer residence. The royal parks were
stocked with imported animals that enabled her to indulge a passion for hunting so intense that she often shot at birds from the palace windows.

The year was further darkened by a grave famine and Russian involvement
in the War of the Polish Succession (1733–1735). When the Polish throne
became vacant, Russia aligned herself with Austria and supported the
pro–Austrian Augustus III of Saxony over the French-backed and
pro–Swedish candidate, Stanislas Leszczynski, father-in-law of Louis XV. Russian troops drove Stanislas out of Warsaw, and with French support he set up
a court at Danzig. Because of widespread famine, Russia could hardly afford
to be involved, but did send its troops to capture Danzig the following summer.
The peace established Augustus in Poland and gave Lorraine to Stanislas.

To make up for her long years of deprivation in Mitau, Anna demanded
luxury and indulged her taste for gilded salons. To have her court reflect some
aura of culture, she also patronized the arts, welcoming operatic and theatrical
companies and popularizing ballet.

But foreigners noted that she always combined sumptuousness with squalor and that she preferred bizarre pleasures. Dwarfs and jesters entertained her as did the "little Persian and Lesghian girls" she requested. Amusements reached the height of crudity—brawls among members of her entourage, mocking ceremonies, humiliating tricks forced on the Russian nobles. To pay for her gratifications and wars, she taxed the peasantry relentlessly.

The Austrian alliance also involved Russia in a prolonged war with Turkey (1735-1739). Messengers brought word of splendid successes, then of heavy losses. Peace settlement attempts failed because the Turks refused to make concessions, and the empress demanded glittering prizes. Meanwhile fires, unprecedented in number and scale, blazed in Moscow, St. Petersburg, and various towns. But Anna remained indifferent to the flames outside.

The war put a great strain on the exchequer, and she looked for a man to redress matters. She thought she had found him in Artemus Volynski, who took a seat on the Privy Council as Biron's protege. Volynski, however, soon schemed to displace both his mentor and Ostermann.

Meanwhile the war did not go any better. Finally, after another inconclusive campaign, General Burkhard von Münnich won the battle of Stavechany. But this victory came too late because Austria had already made a separate peace with Turkey. Ostermann had no other option than to do the same. Ceding all conquests except Azov, he saw to it that Turkey recognized part of the Caucasus as a Russian sphere of influence.

The Turkish war over, there were more intrigues. Volynski called for reforms, which on his terms meant the dismissal of all foreigners. Advised of his plotting, Biron brought about the would-be usurper's downfall and ultimately his execution. Among the papers Volynski neglected to burn was one commenting on Giovanna II of Naples:

> Weak, foolish, and dissolute. She made her reign one long scandal, which reduced the kingdom to the lowest depths. Her perpetual intrigues and political incapacity made Naples a prey to anarchy and foreign invasion, destroying all sense of patriotism and loyalty both among the nobles and the people.

Volynski had scrawled in the margin, "She! She! This is she!"

The bitter winter of 1739-40 brought an unbelievable display of Anna Ivanovna's strain of barbarism. She had long made a practice of degrading to the level of mountebanks and fools the noblemen who displeased her. Her most unfortunate victim, for having converted to Roman Catholicism, was Prince Mikhail Golitsyn, whom she made court jester with the principal duty of sitting on a nest in a basket and cackling like a hen. After he lost his wife, Anna demanded that he marry one of her Kalmuck or Mongolian serving women. Following a wild parade, bride and bridegroom were shoved into an elaborately constructed ice palace, stripped naked, and left inside all night on a bed of ice. Amazingly, they survived.

Always highly suspicious, Anna and Biron invoked strict censorship, and Biron used Courland soldiers for his police activities. He had set up a court of secret police to bring to trial those whom he or the empress considered subversive, and during Anna's reign he deported more than 20,000 to Siberia.

In one sop to the nobility she established the corps of cadets in St. Petersburg, making it possible for young aristocrats to gain easy preferment. By so doing, she flew in the face of Peter the Great's previous attempts not to favor them.

About this time Anna chose Prince Anton of Brunswick-Wolfenbüttel-Bevern as a suitable husband for her niece, Anna Leopoldovna, and in 1739 staged their wedding with great extravagance. To the empress's joy, Anna Leopoldovna gave birth to a boy, Ivan, in August 1740.

Meanwhile, continuing its pro–Austrian stance, Russia had approved the Pragmatic Sanction issued by the Holy Roman Emperor, Karl VI, to provide for the succession of his daughter, Maria Theresa, as sovereign of Austria. Russian involvement in the War of the Austrian Succession, however, would be forestalled only by Anna's death and a sudden war with Sweden.

Widely despised and hated outside royal circles, the *Czarina* Anna succumbed to a painful kidney ulcer on October 28 that year. Wishing to maintain her father's line of succession, she had chosen her grand-nephew, the baby Ivan, as her heir. As a last gesture, she had appointed Biron regent for what she expected would be a long minority.

The empress was little mourned. There were no tears; rather, her subjects sighed with relief.

Maria Theresa (Maria Theresia)
Archduchess of Austria, Queen of Hungary and Bohemia, 1740–1780

In contrast to the barren Russian Empress Anna, Maria Theresa of Austria produced 16 children, 10 of whom survived to adulthood. Thus it seemed natural for her to call herself "general and mother" of her country.

From birth her rule was assured. When the lovely Elizabeth Christina of Brunswick-Wolfenbüttel bore a daughter at the Hofburg in Vienna on May 13, 1717, her husband, Karl VI, the Holy Roman Emperor, reigned as Hapsburg sovereign—Archduke of Austria and King of Hungary and Bohemia. (His great-grandson, Franz II, the last Holy Roman Emperor, first held the title of Emperor of Austria.) Karl had already promulgated the Pragmatic Sanction, which flouted the Salic law and decreed that a female descendant could succeed to the Hapsburg throne. But it precluded a woman from becoming the Holy Roman Empress, except as consort. To gain their acceptance of the Pragmatic Sanction, Karl for years made substantial concessions and extravagant gifts to various European rulers, thereby exhausting his treasury.

Growing up with a younger sister, Maria Anna, in the baroque magnificence of Vienna, Maria Theresa was supervised by a succession of governesses, then passed on to tutors, one of whom encouraged her considerable musical talent. From one or the other she picked up Latin, Italian, and Spanish, but showed most proficiency in French.

Prince Eugene of Savoy, the great military leader, urged Karl to find as son-in-law some powerful prince who could protect his daughter's dominions, but the indulgent father allowed her to marry for love. Her choice fell on Duke Francis Stephen of Lorraine. To gain her hand, however, he renounced his hereditary rights to Lorraine, which France demanded as its price for recognizing the Pragmatic Sanction. In compensation he received a promise that he would succeed to the grand dukedom of Tuscany.

The couple was married in 1736 in a ceremony of exceptional splendor. Guests described the bridegroom, called Franz Stephan in Austria, as a "pretty

Frenchman" and the bride as "a pink and white, golden-haired Dresden shepherdess." The following year the last Medici in Tuscany died, and Franz Stephan left with his wife for Florence, where they stayed until 1739 and he demonstrated his financial acumen.

When her father died in 1740, Maria Theresa, pregnant with her fourth child, assumed her heritage and soon named her husband co-regent. From the outset she refused to be cowed by difficulties within and without. The public treasury was still empty, the army neglected, and popular discontent at its height. Their promises to the contrary, Austria's neighbors were plotting to repudiate the Pragmatic Sanction and divide Maria Theresa's inheritance among themselves. Prussia wanted Silesia, Austria's most prosperous province; Spain kept looking covetously at Austrian possessions in Italy; Bavaria and Saxony claimed the Hapsburg succession; and France supported Bavaria's further claims to a portion of the Hapsburg lands.

At this juncture Frederick II of Prussia, newly come to his throne, cynically offered to support the young woman against her enemies if she turned Silesia over to him. When she refused his bid, his troops marched into Silesia at the end of 1740, Bavaria and France joined the attack, and the War of the Austrian Succession began. In her plight Maria Theresa looked to England, Austria's traditional ally, but Robert Walpole, the prime minister, turned aside. Next she appealed to the Hungarian Diet in Pressburg and made such a winning impression that it speedily raised a contingent of 29,000 men.

Meanwhile, Charles Albert of Bavaria was elected Holy Roman Emperor and with German and French troops captured Prague. But the Austrians were saved when Frederick refused to join the Bavarians for fear of French hegemony. After he signed a secret treaty with Austria, Maria Theresa's troops threw the Bavarians out of Bohemia. Quickly, however, Frederick returned to the attack and so badly defeated the Austrian army under Franz Stephan's brother, Charles of Lorraine, that Maria Theresa agreed to negotiate. In the resultant Peace of Berlin, Austria renounced its claim to Silesia.

The next year proved more successful for the archduchess. Sardinia came in as a fresh ally, and the French conceded Bohemia. Now Maria Theresa could be crowned Queen of Hungary and Bohemia. The Austrians began to pile up victories, and Bavaria expelled Emperor Charles Albert. He died in 1745, and his successor in Bavaria agreed to recognize the Pragmatic Sanction and give his vote to Maria Theresa's husband in the election of a new Holy Roman Emperor.

Then her old enemy, the Prussian Frederick, turned up again and invaded Bohemia. After several routs of her army, the Austrian archduchess signed the Peace of Dresden, confirming the status quo. For his part Frederick agreed to support Franz Stephan, thereby assuring his election.

When the Holy Roman Emperor was crowned in Frankfurt in 1745, the royal couple charmed an onlooker:

Maria Theresa. The Embassy of Austria, Washington, D.C.

When her husband returned to the cathedral and presented himself as it were in the guise of Charlemagne, he raised both hands as if jokingly to show her the Imperial orb, the scepter, and the wondrous gloves; and then provoked her to endless laughter, to the great joy and edification of the assembled people, who had thus been honored with this spectacle of the good and natural marital relations existing between the most exalted couple in Christendom.

Hostilities dragged on for three more years with no decisive victory on either side. New negotiations culminated in the Peace of Aix-la-Chapelle in 1748, by which Austria ceded some Italian territory to Spain and confirmed Frederick's possession of Silesia.

During the war years, Maria Theresa continued to bear children and supervise their education. At court she practiced austerity, but allowed celebrations at certain times, especially after a military victory. She herself liked to dance and play cards.

Gradually Maria Theresa replaced many of her father's over-aged and indecisive ministers with younger and more brilliant men. As she wrote in a subsequent memorandum: "The chief concern of a sovereign is the choice of his advisers." To one of her ministers she wrote:

What you cannot get voluntarily, you must drag from the people by force. You will say I am cruel. I am. But I know that I can make good a hundredfold all the suffering I must now inflict in order to save my country.

Count Frederick William Haugwitz, a Silesian, supported many of the reforms she enacted in order to strengthen Austria so that it might recover Silesia. The Haugwitz program was based on centralization. Thereby Bohemia and Austria were placed under an enlarged central administration, separate from the judiciary. Thus the provincial parliaments, dominated by the nobles and holding most of the purse strings, lost much of their authority. At the same time landowners saw their tax exemptions abolished, but they were allowed to keep forced labor. As the army underwent thorough reorganization and modernization, Haugwitz encouraged industry in the provinces so that they could contribute more generously to the military. The exception was Hungary, whose nobles stood in determined opposition. In still another area, Maria Theresa's personal physician, the Dutch-born Gerhard van Swieten, carried through drastic changes at the universities, and textbooks became available for the first time.

Carrying his more or less empty title of Holy Roman Emperor with dignity, Franz Stephan did not participate in his wife's political decisions. But she let him advise her on money matters, and only his astuteness made many of her reforms possible.

Haugwitz, however, found himself continually undercut by Wenzel Anton von Kaunitz, who became state chancellor in 1753. Kaunitz and his ruler

forged a new alliance with Saxony, Sweden, Russia, and France in order to sur-
round Frederick of Prussia with an inviolable coalition. In retaliation, Prussia
and England then became allies. Some years later Maria Theresa wrote of
Frederick, the "Prussian fox": "I did not hate him, but then I also felt no sympathy for him because he himself never showed any. I always abhorred his
devious nature." Two other women played important roles in this diplomatic
revolution—the Russian Empress Elizabeth and the Marquise de Pompadour,
for the prudish archduchess had not held herself above asking for help from
Louis XV's exquisite mistress.

In 1756, the year Maria Theresa gave birth to her last child, the undaunted
Frederick launched the Seven Years War. She welcomed it, however, as a
chance to recover Silesia. Initially Frederick won so many brilliant victories
that he gained his sobriquet, "the Great." But then his luck turned, and his
defeat by the Russian army at Kunersdorf in 1759 led to a series of Prussian
disasters over the next few years. Only unexpected events in St. Petersburg
saved him. In 1762 Empress Elizabeth died and her pro–Prussian nephew and
heir, Peter III, pulled Russia from the west, leaving a great hole in the alliance.
By 1762 Frederick's position seemed hopeless.

That year Leopold Mozart brought his prodigy son Wolfgang to Schön-
brunn Palace. The boy played to an appreciative audience; all Maria Theresa's
children were musical. (She herself often delighted guests by singing at elegant
evening musicales.) After his performance six-year-old Wolfgang slipped on the
waxed floor only to be picked up by seven-year-old Maria Antonia (Marie Antoinette), whom he impulsively offered to marry.

History has idealized Maria Theresa's maternal role. As head of state she
was too preoccupied to devote much time to her children, but she gave detailed
instructions for their training and provided individual governesses or tutors.
The little archdukes and archduchesses kept to themselves except at carnival
time when they could attend fancy dress parties for children of the nobility.

In 1763 the Seven Years War ended with the Peace of Hubertusburg, which
confirmed Frederick's possession of Silesia. During this second war of her reign,
Maria Theresa had developed the habit of governing autocratically. Convinced of her God-given majesty, she nevertheless once drew a circle around
a coffee stain on a state paper and sweetly apologized.

Just a year later, while the royal family gathered in Innsbruck to celebrate
the wedding of the young archduke Leopold to Maria Louisa of Spain, Franz
Stephan died suddenly of a stroke. His distraught widow considered shutting
herself up in a convent and leaving the government to her eldest son Joseph.
She returned to public life only because Kaunitz and her other advisers begged
her to do so. From then on, dressed always in black and wearing a widow's veil,
the Hapsburg sovereign refused to appear at any frivolous entertainments. As
she became more religious, her detractors said her piety bordered on fanaticism

and bigotry, pointing out that when she touched on topics like Calvinism and Jewry, her voice carried a steely undertone.

On his father's death, Joseph was named co-regent and subsequently Holy Roman Emperor. The ambitious young man wanted to share in the governing, but his mother allowed him only to take care of army reform and to share foreign policy duties with Kaunitz. For the next 15 years mother and son, thoroughly self-opinionated, were locked in continuous struggle, Joseph, a disciple of the Enlightenment representing progressive forces, Maria Theresa reactionary ones.

For the Austrian ruler, the trying decade of the 1760s recalled the 1740s, when three of her daughters had died in infancy. Between 1761 and 1767 she lost two more daughters and a son in adolescence. Especially troubling was her violent quarrel with Joseph after his attempt to acquire Bavaria led to the War of the Bavarian Succession against Prussia in 1767–1768. When Joseph lost his nerve, his mother forced herself to negotiate new terms. Thanks to Kaunitz, the peace turned out to be advantageous, for Austria gained the southern portion of Bavaria.

Along with death, the decade brought weddings, Maria Theresa having assigned her daughters specific places in a dynastic scheme. Maria Amalia became the wife of Ferdinand of Parma, Maria Carolina was wed to Ferdinand of Bourbon-Naples-Sicily, and Maria Antonia to the French dauphin who became Louis XVI. Only her mother's favorite, Maria Christina, was free to marry the husband of her choice, Prince Albert of Saxe-Teschen.

Reform on all fronts had become a way of life. Maria Theresa pushed forward a new penal code to standardize judicial proceedings and punishments, a new public debt policy and poor law, and a prospectus for compulsory primary education. But her zeal had its darker side. As the Catholic church retreated more and more from secular affairs, she decided that the state must control the country's intellectual life. Thus she instituted government censorship.

In 1772 Joseph and Kaunitz pressured her into the first partition of Poland. When she bewailed it as immoral, foreign courts labeled her performance "lachrymose hypocrisy." In the disposition of spoils Austria received Galicia; Russia, under Empress Catherine II, seized "White Russia"; and Prussia took West Prussia except for the cities of Danzig and Thon.

To all her children, long after they were grown, Maria Theresa sent endless letters of rebuke. She also insisted on having a say in the upbringing of her numerous grandchildren. She was, however, keenly aware of her own shortcomings: "In matters of the church, religion, and the law, in bringing up my children and maintaining my dignity," she wrote, "I am now aware of sins. But I do accuse myself for many covert flaws. I am guilty before God for the wars I waged because of excessive ambition. I am also guilty of envy, wrath, flabbiness, and sloth. I am guilty of having neglected the holy confession, offending my neighbors, with words, and of the lack of loving kindness."

Grown immensely stout and suffering from rheumatism by 1780, she began complaining she lacked the strength to govern. Toward winter while out hunting pheasants, she caught a bad cold and rapidly sickened. On November 29 she died in Joseph's arms in her birthplace, the Hofburg. She had occupied her throne for 40 years.

Joseph Sonnenfels, a leading literary light, gave the memorial oration, emphasizing her impact:

> When [she] ascended the throne, the monarchy had lost its influence abroad and its vitality at home; its talents lacked encouragement and alacrity; agriculture was paralyzed by oppression and destitution; trade was negligible; the finances of the state were disordered and in disrepute. At her death she handed on a nation which enjoys an improved constitution in its westernmost regions, is open to every form of improvement and once more occupies that vital position within the European system which its greatness, the overall fertility of its lands, and the gifts of its inhabitants should always have earned it among the great powers.

In the 20th century, the cardinal who served briefly as Pope John Paul I, addressed her: "Yet in spite of everything, of all the sovereigns of your age you emerged as the least ugly, the conductor of a great nation who never claimed to be able to play all the instruments."

Elizabeth (Elizaveta)
Empress of Russia, 1741–1762

Maria Theresa's father declared her his successor; Elizabeth Petrovna's did not. In 1727 and 1730, following the deaths of her mother, Catherine I, and of Peter II, she showed little interest in asserting her right to rule. Only the events of 1740 and 1741, the death of Anna Ivanovna and the accession of a baby czar, forced her to stage a coup d'etat.

A sturdy, well-formed child, Elizabeth was born to Catherine at Kolomonskoye Palace on December 29, 1709, just as Czar Peter I arrived home in Moscow to celebrate his great victory over the Swedes at Poltava. Two years later Elizabeth appeared as a bridesmaid at her parents' wedding. Early on, the lively girl showed promise of great beauty and even greater sensuality, happily posing at eight for a nude portrait as Venus. Naturally lazy and self-indulgent, she avoided study and never knew, for instance, that England was an island.

But she did acquire fluency in French because Peter had ambitious marriage plans for her. He chose as her bridegroom Louis XV, but the French court turned up its nose at the daughter of a peasant and camp follower. Some years before, it had decisively snubbed Catherine herself. Elizabeth, however, accepted the slight good-naturedly and ever after closely copied French fashions and manners.

The year 1725 ushered in a swirl of events. Peter died, Catherine became empress, Elizabeth's second surviving sister Natalia also died, and her elder sister Anna married the Duke of Holstein-Gottorp, who offered a kinsman, Karl, the Prince Bishop of Lübeck, as a willing suitor for Elizabeth. Both she and her mother liked the young man, and Catherine announced the engagement. Unfortunately he died of smallpox before any wedding could be arranged.

The next year the *czarevna* lost her mother and was deprived of her sister's company, the Duke of Holstein-Gottorp having proved so troublesome that he was asked to take Anna to Kiel. She died there some 12 months later after giving birth to a son, Karl Peter Ulrich. But Elizabeth was not the kind to feel lonely or to mope. At the country estates her mother left her, she enjoyed herself, dancing expertly, hunting and hawking, riding hard, and passing through a score of lovers – guardsmen, pages, or ostlers.

Fair-haired and sparkling, she frequently served as the enchanting companion of her half nephew, Peter II, and certain eminences at court urged marriage. But in 1730, with Peter's unexpected death and the accession of the surly Anna Ivanovna, who bitterly resented her cousin's magnetism and beauty, Elizabeth met a thinly veiled hostility she had never known before. When secret police began to meddle in her private affairs, the countryside, where the peasants enjoyed romping with her, was a happy escape. She had by now taken her most devoted lover, Alexei Razumovsky, a handsome Ukranian with a splendid singing voice. Like the peasants, he would always be a welcome antidote to the tense and mistrustful men and women at court.

When Anna Ivanovna died in 1740, leaving her throne to her grandnephew Ivan, Russia found itself with a baby czar and Anna's hated lover, Ernst Biron, as regent. Biron tried briefly to ingratiate himself with Elizabeth against Ivan's parents. Then a military conspiracy ousted him and banished him to Siberia. Ivan's mother, Anna Leopoldovna, replaced him as regent, but did not care for the business of governing. When war broke out with Sweden in 1741, the regent seemed more preoccupied with new coiffures for her court ladies than with military matters.

Anna Leopoldovna, her inconsequential husband Anton, her Saxon lover, and her lady-in-waiting, Julie Mengden, whom she adored, quickly earned the name of "the Brunswick Quartet" and were roundly despised. Well aware of her own unpopularity, Anna Leopoldovna regularly invited Elizabeth to the palace for gossip sessions, but feared the *czarevna*'s intentions and her popularity among the guards. Again secret agents shadowed Peter the Great's only surviving daughter. She also suffered the humiliation of having to beg for money from Anna Leopoldovna and waiting a long time for any advance.

As the unpopularity of the Brunswick Quartet increased, and as rumors flew that Anna Leopoldovna intended to declare herself empress, Elizabeth's friends urged her to make a bid for power. Finally when Anna threatened to place her in a nunnery, Elizabeth heeded Razumovsky and her advisers, Mikhail Vorontsov, her physician Armand Lestocq, and the Shuvalov brothers, Peter and Alexander. The most influential voice, however, belonged to the French ambassador, the Marquis de la Chetardie, who wanted to reverse Russia's pro–Austrian, anti–French policy.

One snowy December night in 1741, Elizabeth, tall and full-figured in her mailed cuirass, went to the barracks of the Preobrazhenskoe Guards. "I have decided to save Russia from our German torturers," she announced dramatically, and the grenadiers gave her their rousing oath of allegiance.

After sending couriers off to the other barracks with urgent messages calling on their support, Elizabeth moved on to the Winter Palace, where she gained entrance with nerve-tingling words to the sentries: "You know whose daughter I am. You know that by right the crown belongs to me." Inside the palace Elizabeth ordered Anna Leopoldovna taken into custody along with the other members of the Brunswick Quartet. After exacting a plea that no harm would come to young Ivan, the ex-regent and her husband submitted to imprisonment in the fort at Dunemünde.

With the military solidly behind her, Elizabeth saw no reason to delay her coronation and in a sumptuous sleigh traveled to Moscow for the ceremony. Nobody seemed to mind that she had violated Peter the Great's Act of Succession.

First she generously gave titles and money to all those who had helped bring her to power. Then she abolished the Privy Council and restored the Senate as the chief governing body as it had been in her father's day. Its power turned out to be only nominal since Elizabeth let her private chancery rule for her. Andrei Ostermann, in office since the reign of Catherine I, had been locked up, but she commuted his death sentence and that of Marshal Münnich, who had backed Anna Leopoldovna. As soon as they were banished, Biron returned from exile to live on one of his Russian estates.

The new empress personally detested her vice-chancellor, Alexei Bestuzhev-Ryumin, but found him indispensable in the conduct of foreign policy and therefore gave him her complete confidence. Since he showed himself pro–Austrian, pro–British, and anti–Prussian, her friend and supporter, de la Chetardie, lost his gamble.

The French ambassador lost on a second front as well. He wanted the empress to end the war with Sweden, France's ally, by ceding back all Russian gains, but stubbornly she refused. The Russian troops were ultimately victorious and won a portion of Finland. Soon the two friends broke completely. Spies brought to Elizabeth's attention a document in which de la Chetardie suggested that her coup had weakened Russia and that therefore his government should encourage the Turks to attack. She expressed outrage, and the marquis hastily retreated to Paris.

That same year Elizabeth entered into a morganatic marriage with Razumovsky. Legend has it that she bore him several children either stillborn or dead within a few days. Three months after her accession she brought her orphaned nephew, Karl Peter Ulrich, from Holstein and declared him her heir so that the Romanov succession would be preserved. He was made a member of the Russian Orthodox Church and given the title of Grand Duke Peter. Unfortunately, the son of her beloved sister proved to be a boor and a weakling.

For all his faults, Elizabeth doted on him at first. In 1744 she arranged for him to marry a little German princess in the following year. Sophia of Anhalt-Zerbst (Catherine the Great) remembered long after:

ЕЛИСАВЕТА   ПЕРВАЯ
Императрица   *Самодержица*
Всерос-   *синская*

Elizabeth. The Hermitage, Leningrad.

[T]he Empress had a fancy to have all men appear at the court all dressed as women and the women as men, wearing masks. . . . The only woman who looked really well and compelling as a man was the Empress herself. As she was tall and powerful, male attire suited her. She had the handsomest leg I have ever seen on any man, and her feet were admirably proportioned. She dressed to perfection, and everything she did had the same special grace whether she was dressed as a man or as a woman. One felt inclined to look at her and turn away with regret because nothing could replace her.

The same year as Peter's wedding, 1745, Razumovsky persuaded Elizabeth to make a state visit to the Ukraine. It proved to be a great success, and she always called her stay in Kiev the two happiest weeks in her life. In gratitude she made Alexei a grand marshal and his brother the hetman (governor) of the Ukraine.

Never interested in assuming a dominant role in government, she let her favorites control most state offices. Thus the country's financial situation deteriorated, and the gentry acquired broad privileges at the expense of the peasants and serfs, now more downtrodden than ever. She also did away with one of her father's most cherished reforms, giving members of the lower classes the opportunity to acquire hereditary noble status by service to the state.

In 1748 Russia formally allied itself with Austria. To seal the novel friendship, Elizabeth was named godmother to Maria Theresa's newborn son. Drawn late into the War of the Austrian Succession, the Russian army approached the Rhine, a move so upsetting to the French-Prussian allies that they speedily concluded the Treaty of Aix-la-Chapelle.

Even as her soldiers marched, the sensuous but pious Elizabeth busied herself with splendid court activities and church celebrations. Although she had 15,000 gowns in her wardrobe and liked to wear diamonds and black feathers in her hair, she had the common touch and was never happier than when standing as godmother to a guardsman's baby.

With her constant craving for carnal pleasures, she needed a steady flow of lovers whom an understanding Razumovsky graciously accepted. They were always handsome young men, usually nobodies. Only the intellectual Ivan Shuvalov, a cousin of her advisers, the Shuvalov brothers, proved an exception. To anger the Shuvalovs, Bestuzhev pushed forward an especially good-looking and even younger lover, Nikita Beketov, a cadet.

In addition to his passionate nature, Elizabeth had inherited her father's interest in architecture; she wanted to transform St. Petersburg into the most beautiful of cities. At enormous expense the architect Bartolomo Rastrelli began building an extravagant Winter Palace to replace the old one, enlarged Peterhof, filled the city with other baroque palaces and public buildings, and reconstructed the country house at Tsarkoe Selo for fetes, masquerades, balls, and banquets. Elizabeth herself never lived to see the completed Winter Palace.

In 1744 the savant, Mikhail Lomontsov, had trumpeted, "Now . . . comes the age of gold." Since then he had given a quickening impulse to Russian scientific scholarship and belles lettres. In 1755 he and his friend, Ivan Shuvalov, Elizabeth's lover, established the first Russian university. Two years later the *czarina* founded the Academy of Fine Arts. Opera, ballet, theater, and the basic arts also thrived in the opulent and elegant atmosphere.

Meanwhile in 1756, Bestuzhev pressed on Elizabeth a new military alliance with England, which to his horror tied itself to Prussia. He continued in office but lost much of his power to a consortium of ministers. Elizabeth's hatred of Frederick II had not changed; when told he had threatened to restore the imprisoned Ivan VI to the throne, she decided the time had come to act. Against Prussia and England, Russia formed an alliance with France, Austria, Sweden, and Saxony and thus was drawn into the Seven Years War. The empress avidly followed battle reports, rejoicing when the Russians won two major victories at Gross Jagersdorf (1757) and Kunersdorf (1759). But when they suffered embarrassing retreats and grim defeats, the news seriously affected her health. In 1760 they entered Berlin.

A special blow fell on her in 1759. Bestuzhev's enemies accused him of treason, but the kind-hearted Elizabeth again chose banishment for him rather than death. Six years earlier she had tried to declare capital punishment illegal, but her decree had never been promulgated.

After recovering from a grave illness in 1757, Elizabeth began to lead a most irregular life, growing moody and unhappy and drinking as vigorously as her mother before her. Constantly she fretted about her heir and his wife, but showed excessive fondness for their son Paul, of whom she took complete and unfortunate charge. Then she sickened again, refused all medication, and died on January 5, 1762, a glass of cherry brandy at her lips.

True daughter of Peter the Great, this ebullient autocrat had faithfully followed his vision of Westernizing Russia and shaping it into a great power.

Catherine II (Ekaterina)
Empress of Russia, 1762–1796

Elizabeth had carried out her coup without bloodshed; Catherine II complicated hers with murder, the victim being her husband, Peter III, Elizabeth's designated successor.

At the beginning, however, Catherine's horizons seemed decidedly limited. The only daughter of Prince Christian Augustus of Anhalt-Zerbst and his wife, Johanna Elizabeth of Holstein-Gottorp, she was born in Stettin on May 2, 1729. Christian Augustus, who ruled only an eighth part of the small principality of Anhalt, served the King of Prussia as a field marshal.

In his obscure German court Sophia (Figchen), much brighter than her brother, received a fine education from a French governess, Babette Cardel, who helped her master French and German and taught her to write well. (Years later, when the famous Empress of Russia was corresponding with Voltaire, who dubbed her "le Grand," she signed herself "Mlle. Cardel's pupil.")

In 1744 a wider world beckoned. After searching for a consort for her nephew and heir Peter, Elizabeth of Russia finally decided on the little princess of Anhalt-Zerbst. A sentimental reason motivated her: She had once been engaged to the girl's uncle, Karl, the Prince Bishop of Lübeck, who had died shortly before the wedding.

Toward the end of the year the girl arrived with her light-headed mother in icy St. Petersburg, carrying only three simple gowns, a few shifts, a dozen handkerchiefs, and six pairs of hose in her trousseau. After a brief stay, Sophia and Johanna rode in the empress's own sleigh to Moscow to meet the magnificent Elizabeth and the sulky Peter. From this time on the young German princess lived in splendor.

Following two months of instruction, she was baptized into the Russian Orthodox faith and renamed Catherine for Elizabeth's mother. When Peter had recovered from smallpox, the wedding was celebrated with great pomp in the summer of 1745. As quickly as possible, the young grand duchess shed all her German skin, setting out to learn the Russian language, showing devotion to church and state, and ingratiating herself with important aristocrats. Years afterward, she recalled that she had made a threefold resolution, "to please her husband, Elizabeth, and the nation."

Catherine had never really cared for her mother and sighed with relief when Johanna left the court under a cloud of suspicion that she had acted as the King of Prussia's agent and conspired with the French ambassador, the Marquis de la Chetardie. The young bride did not care for her husband either. They were a singularly mismatched pair. He was neurotic, indolent, and childlike, constantly amusing himself with toy soldiers or a puppet theater; she was ambitious and clearheaded, always working to improve herself. With dismay, Elizabeth's vice-chancellor, Bestuzhev, noted that the grand duchess avidly read Greek historians and contemporary French and German philosophers.

He appointed a vigilant husband-and-wife team, the Choglokovs, to oversee the royal couple; Catherine hated their tyranny and felt terribly isolated, for Elizabeth, who had once seemed fond of her, grew suspicious and distant. In addition to boring her, Peter often humiliated her. Early in their marriage Catherine decided he was incapable of acting like a sovereign and looked on herself as really suited to the role.

When after seven years she failed to produce an heir, rumor ran that Peter had some physical disability rendering him impotent. Meanwhile Catherine had taken lovers, first Sergei Saltykov ("as handsome as the dawn"), who jilted her, and then the Pole, Stanislas Poniatowski.

At length surgery removed Peter's impediment, and in 1754 after miscarrying twice, Catherine gave birth to an heir, Paul. Although the court generally accepted him as Peter's son, his mother hinted much later in her memoirs that Saltykov was the father. Still, in temperament and interests, Paul would always resemble Peter. The grand duchess, however, saw little of her son because Elizabeth assumed complete charge over him. Within a couple of years Catherine bore Poniatowski a daughter, Anna, acknowledged as a Romanov princess but dead before her second birthday.

Peter had his own romantic interests. With growing sexual appetite, Catherine picked as her next favorite Grigory Orlov, who stayed with her for 12 years although he did not exclusively occupy her bed. She was carrying Orlov's child when Elizabeth died at the beginning of 1762. The baby boy, born that spring, was brought up at court. (After becoming emperor, his brother Paul gave him the title of Count Alexei Bobrinsky.) By Orlov again, Catherine subsequently had two daughters whom a rich woman in St. Petersburg reared as her own nieces.

Catherine was not happy over Peter's accession, and his first moves thoroughly frightened her. Since 1757 Russia had been involved in the Seven Years War, and Elizabeth had grown obsessed with the idea of destroying Prussian power. Peter, on the other hand, was a fanatical admirer of Frederick the

Great, and almost immediately on becoming emperor he withdrew the Russian armies from the battlefront. That June he concluded a separate peace treaty by which Prussia recovered all the lands it had lost.

At first Peter showed some interest in governing and issued a sweeping manifesto that statutorily freed the gentry from every form of military and other service except in the event of war. He also took steps toward a draft calling for freedom for the serfs. But he went out of his way to offend the court, the church, and the guards, whose regiments he tried to break up. His preparations for a campaign against Denmark to aid the duchy of Holstein in recovering Schleswig were considered absurd.

Always acting like a true Russian while her German husband showed contempt for the country, Catherine quietly encouraged her supporters, primarily her lover Grigory Orlov and his four brothers, to weave the threads of conspiracy. When Peter proposed divorcing his wife and marrying his mistress, Countess Elizabeth Vorontsova, who often wore the imperial diamonds and rubies, Catherine decided on action. Other advisers spoke of putting the seven-year-old Paul on the throne with his mother as regent, but she rejected the plan.

Her memoirs describe what happened:

> On the 28th of June at six in the morning, Alexei Orlov came into my room, woke me, and said very calmly, "It is time for you to get up; everything is ready to proclaim you." I did not hesitate . . . dressed as quickly as possible without making a toilette, and got into the carriage he had brought. . . . We got out at the barracks of the Ismaylovsky regiment. . . . The soldiers arrived, kissed me, embraced my feet, my hands, my clothes; two carried up a priest with a cross, and they began to take their oath.
>
> After I resumed my seat in the carriage, the priest with the cross went in front of us and we went on to the Semyonovsky, which met us shouting "Vivat!" So the procession, swollen by the regiments of the guards, went with drums and Vivats!
>
> I alighted at Kazan Cathedral. Then the Preobrazhensky Regiment arrived, also shouting "Vivat!" and saying, "Forgive us for being the last to come . . . some of our officers tried to arrest us." . . . The Horse Guards then came, led by their officers in such frenzy of joy as I have never seen before, weeping and shouting that the country was free at last.
>
> I went to the Winter Palace to take the measures necessary for success. There we had a consultation, and it was resolved that I should go at the head of the army to Peterhof.

Dressing herself in a guard's uniform, Catherine then set out to confront her husband from whom she had endured many public insults during almost 17 years of marriage. After signing an act of abdication, he removed himself to his estate at Ropsha. Eight days later, Catherine received a message that he had died there. The true story never came to light, but Alexei Orlov was presumed one of the assailants who either choked Peter or beat him to death.

Another version was that the czar had perished in a drunken brawl with his guards.

In October that year Catherine traveled to Moscow for her coronation at the Uspensky Cathedral within the Kremlin. The stunning pageantry over, she dismissed Elizabeth's last chancellor, Vorontsov, saying "I must rule in my own fashion." At this stage she characterized herself: "If I may venture to be frank, I would say about myself that I was every inch a gentleman with a mind much more male than female; but together with this I was anything but masculine and combined, with the mind and temperament of a man, the attractions of a lovable woman."

Another death, closely following Peter's, also relieved Catherine's anxiety. Many Russians considered the ousted Czar Ivan VI, whom Elizabeth had imprisoned since babyhood, as the rightful sovereign. Catherine was not unhappy to hear that the 22-year-old youth, who had led a tortured existence, had been murdered by his jailer following an attempt to rescue him from his secret cell in the castle of Schlussenburg.

Triumphant at last, she began her reign with exuberant gusto. Many saw her as a ruler of tremendous energy and intellectual curiosity, who often worked 15 hours a day. Almost at once she began to replace the impoverished treasury by following a plan, proposed by Peter the Great, to secularize the entire property of the clergy, who owned one-third of the land along with its serfs.

Beyond the treasury a second urgent task involved preserving friendly relations with Prussia's and Russia's traditional allies, France and Austria. Eventually Catherine would play diplomat to the hilt.

As though 1762 had not offered enough drama, she ordered a show of force to assure the election of her former lover Poniatowski to the Polish throne. He did not want to leave Russia, but Catherine packed him off despite his plea, "Do not make me king. Only let me come back to you."

Still influenced by the French philosophers she read and corresponded with so avidly, she considered herself an enlightened autocrat. In 1767 she summoned a legislative commission of all social classes, the serfs excluded, to frame a constitution and recodify the laws. She spent a year and a half drafting an elaborate *Nakaz* (Instruction), much of it derived from Montesquieu's *Esprit des Lois* and Beccaria's *Of Punishment and Crime*. To her great disappointment, her commission found it unpalatable, and months dragged on in tedious debate.

In 1768, as war with Turkey threatened, she prorogued the commission. Disillusioned with her attempts to bring about domestic reform, she had decided to push her foreign policy to dreams of national grandeur. The Turkish sultan, alarmed by her interference in the Polish state, let an incident near the border flame into war. Alexei Orlov inflicted a sweeping defeat on the entire Turkish navy at the Bay of Cesme in 1770, but the victory did not bring peace.

On the heels of war and a terrible plague in Moscow, the Pugachev rebellion broke out in the Ural regions. In 1773 Emilian Pugachev, a former officer, gathered support throughout southeastern Russia when he proclaimed himself to be Peter III, escaped from Ropsha before Catherine's officers could kill him. His followers murdered landowners and burned down houses with such fervor that he felt powerful enough to march on Russia with his Cossack troops. Fortunately for Catherine the Turkish war ended, and she used the returned soldiers against the uprising. It was overthrown, and Pugachev publicly beheaded. By the treaty of Kuchuk-Kainardje, ending the Turkish war, the Crimea gained independence, and Catherine was ceded Azov and several strongholds north of the Black Sea.

Catherine's liberalism ended with the Pugachev rebellion. As a young grand duchess, she had dreamed of emancipating the serfs. But as empress she came to see how much she depended on the owners of the huge estates. To strengthen their positions she made the condition of the serfs even more deplorable and extended serfdom to the Ukraine.

She had never felt close to her son Paul, who during his early childhood had been the exclusive property of the Empress Elizabeth. In 1762 he was old enough to understand what had happened to his father, and the tragedy at Ropsha always lay like a shadow between him and the Empress Catherine. In 1773, however, she let him choose his bride, Nathalie of Hesse-Darmstadt. When the Grand Duchess Nathalie died in childbed in 1776, mother and son briefly drew together in grief. But while taking note of the new intimacy, diplomats knew that the grand duke's political views were anathema to Catherine.

During the temporary reconciliation she chose his second wife, Princess Sophia Augusta of Württemburg (Marie Fedorovna). In 1777 Catherine rejoiced over her first grandson, Alexander, and then again in 1779 over a second, Constantine. With her customary determination she took charge of both boys' upbringing, even writing a sensible *Elementary Instruction*.

In 1774 the empress had selected a new chief lover. With the exception of Orlov, all her previous entanglements had been affairs of the flesh, but in the one-eyed Grigory Potemkin she met a man who was more than her intellectual match. In her transports of love, Catherine bestowed extravagant names on him—golden pheasant, peacock, dearest pigeon, wolf-bird, tiger, lion of the jungle, my darling like no king on earth. The hot affair lasted only two years, but as prime minister he remained at her side until his death in 1791.

Despite his excesses and spells of lethargy, the astute Potemkin guided her to a comprehensive reform of the structure of local governments that resulted in a rigid bureaucratic system, operating within units of local government and fitting Catherine's requirements for autocracy. Increasingly now she allied herself with the nobles and in 1785 signed a charter confirming and codifying privileges they had gained since the death of Peter the Great.

She was still so sexually active that a disapproving Maria Theresa called her a harlot. After the affair with Potemkin ended, he obligingly selected most of her lovers, who as she aged became younger and younger. She herself wrote, "God is my judge that I did not take them out of looseness, to which I have no inclination. If fate had given me a husband whom I could have loved, I should have remained always true to him. The fact is that my heart would not willingly remain one hour without love." As long as the nobodies gratified her, she saw to their schooling and showered them with titles, estates, and money. When one of them, Alexander Lanskoy, died of angina in 1784, the empress mourned him for months.

During her reign, St. Petersburg had grown more visually splendid than ever. As palaces and public buildings sprang up, neoclassic architecture, much of it designed by Giacomo Quadrenghi, replaced Bartolomeo Rastrelli's baroque style from Elizabeth's day. For the Winter Palace, Catherine requested the addition of a special wing, the Hermitage, where she could meet with savants and a select band of friends. She also enlarged the summer palaces, Peterhof and Tsarkoe Selo, where for her pleasure Charles Cameron created Pompeian interiors. Two palaces reflected her most famous love affairs. For Orlov the empress had summoned Antonio Rinaldi to design the Marble Palace. As her special gift to Potemkin she asked Ivan Starov to build the Tauride Palace, which boasted 30 hothouse rooms. In the last year of his life Potemkin staged there in her honor a banquet considered one of the most extravagant evenings in Russian history.

Catherine's ambitious plans for general education had foundered when she was diverted by the Turkish war and the Pugachev rebellion, but she was proud of having established early in her reign the Smolny Institute, a superior academy for daughters of the nobility. She gave new life to the Academy of Sciences by appointing Princess Catherine Dashkova as director in 1782.

She also brought about an upsurge in printing and publishing. She herself acted as publisher of and chief contributor to a literary magazine inspired by Addison and Steele's *Spectator*. Moreover, she carried on an extensive correspondence, usually in French, and wrote her memoirs, a Russian history, fairy tales, comedies and historical dramas.

With Potemkin's blessing, Catherine began an impressive art collection and sent her agent, Baron Frederick Melchior Grimm, around Europe buying up collections as well as the libraries of her famous correspondents Voltaire and Diderot. He succeeded so well that she ordered a special gallery, the Little Hermitage, added to the Winter Palace. Her own creative urges she expressed in cameo-making, engraving, painting, and sculpture.

Potemkin's annexation of the Crimea in 1787 led to his stage-managing a triumphal tour for the *czarina* personally to take possession of that territory. To impress her and the Austrian ruler Joseph II, who accompanied her, Potemkin created fake villages along the Volga. Dreams of reviving the

Catherine II. The Hermitage, Leningrad.

Byzantine empire in the Balkans under Russian sponsorship, however, had soured.

The annexation brought another declaration of war from Turkey. Artfully Catherine persuaded John Paul Jones, the American naval hero, to serve as admiral in her Black Sea fleet. But Russian officers made Jones's position difficult, and rather quickly he decided to leave Russia. After signing as Russia's ally, Austria pulled back in 1791 following terrific losses; Russia held out until 1792. Then, by the treaty of Jassy, Catherine retained the Crimea and won a large area on the Black Sea coast.

One segment of her vision of empire had revolved around Poland, and her interference there resulted in some of the ugliest chapters of her life. At the beginning of her reign she had exerted power on the Polish state to restore rights to the Orthodox and religious minorities. When armed conflict broke out, Russian forces put it down. After she had settled Poniatowski on the Polish throne, Austria and Prussia hurried to conclude an agreement with Russia whereby none of the three would acquire Polish territory to the exclusion of the others. Then they proceeded to carve up part of the country. In the First Partition of 1772, Poland lost nearly one-third of its territory, and Catherine gained a large stretch of White Russia.

Almost 20 years later the liberal nobles in Poland set forth a new constitution, and their conservative opponents appealed to Catherine. Russia and Prussia invaded Poland in 1792, and the Second Partition, in which Russia acquired still more slices of territory in White Russia and the Ukraine, reduced Poland to less than one-third its original size.

The Second Partition inspired Taudeusz Kosciuszko's insurgence, and again Russian and Prussian troops invaded Poland, the Russians virtually massacring the defenders of Warsaw. With Austria, Prussia and Russia sharing the remaining territory; Catherine took formal possession of Courland and the leftover stretch of Lithuanian territory. Poniatowski remained king until this final partition.

Catherine had grown increasingly conservative as she aged, and in her last years she reacted with horror to the French Revolution. At 62 she took her last lover, the insolent young Platon Zubov, a 22-year-old cavalry officer, who proved to be a mischief maker. But she worked as hard as ever at her administrative activity. "Papers, papers, papers," she told her faithful correspondent Grimm, "in my study nine tables are covered with them, and still they come."

She had little to do with her erratic son Paul, who always resented his father's murder. Still she delighted in supervising the education of her grandchildren and great-grandchildren and playing blindman's bluff with them. Each year she felt more and more that Paul was too unstable to succeed her, and her favor fell on Alexander, his eldest son. But before she could declare him her successor, she suffered a stroke and died on November 17, 1796.

Four years before, she had prepared her epitaph, which concluded:

> On the throne of Russia she wanted to do what was good for her country and tried to bring happiness, liberty, and prosperity to her subjects.
> She forgave easily and hated no one. She was tolerant, understanding and of happy disposition. She had a republican spirit and a kind heart.
> She was sociable by nature.
> She made many friends.
> She took pleasure in her work.
> She loved the arts.

Historians have never agreed whether she was a great empress but a bad woman or an extraordinary female but a poor sovereign.

Maria I
Queen of Portugal, 1777–1816

Like Juana of Castile, Maria of Portugal has gone down in history as another mad queen. But unlike that unfortunate daughter of Ferdinand and Isabella, Maria ruled for 11 good years before suffering a mental collapse.

Of the House of Braganza, she was born in Lisbon on December 17, 1734, the eldest daughter of José Emmanuel, son of the reigning king, and Mariana Victoria, daughter of Philip V of Spain. Her inheritance was hardly propitious, for almost all her mother's relatives suffered from religious mania, melancholy, and persecution complexes.

Maria's grandfather, João V, "raised a chain of costly churches and sired a multitude of natural children." Gold flowing into Portugal from the colony of Brazil allowed him to indulge his passionate devotion to art. With three sisters, Ana, Francisca, and Benedita, Maria grew up in a city he had enriched with magnificent buildings, sculpture, and paintings. But as an adolescent, the infanta watched him sink into deep melancholy and turn his government over to incompetent advisers who failed to cope with a bankrupt treasury. With João's death in 1750, she came closer to the throne and gained the title of Princess of Brazil.

Indolent and reluctant to bear the burdens of statecraft, José, the new king, filled his time with shooting, cards, the theater, and concerts. Supreme authority he entrusted to Sebastião José de Carvalho e Melo, later the Marquis of Pombal, who quickly began acting like a dictator. The queen, Mariana Victoria, disliked him intensely as did most of his countrymen.

A terrible earthquake shattered Lisbon on All Saint's Day, November 1, 1755. Followed by fire and a tidal wave, it killed 30,000 persons. But it brought Pombal a temporary surge in popularity when he issued a crisp order, "Bury the dead and relieve the living." The royal family had been at Belém, where the three shocks and several aftershocks proved comparatively mild. Still the tragedy affected the king so strongly that for a long time he refused to enter any of his surviving palaces, preferring to live in a tent and later in a wooden palace.

Three years after the earthquake, an attempted assassination threw new fear into the Braganzas. One evening, as José returned by coach from an assignation with the younger Marchioness of Távora, her husband and several in-laws, all known opponents of Pombal, fell on the king, but were repulsed by his guard. Pombal imprisoned the would-be assailants and ordered several put to death. When he heard of possible Jesuit participation in the plot, he banned the order from Portugal.

Pombal's reign of terror followed. His measures had become increasingly oppressive, and his adversaries were arrested, tortured, and frequently killed. To Maria's horror, he also attacked the church, which he despised because it challenged his reforms.

Lisbon was still being rebuilt in an austere style under Pombal's strong but stern direction when the 26-year-old princess married her 42-year-old uncle Pedro, another son of João V, in 1760. Pedro had inherited the suburban palace of Queluz in 1747, had torn it down, and had begun constructing a pink miniature Versailles, which would not be complete until 1794. The Queluz gardens became noted for their topiary, statues, and fountains. There he and Maria lived and brought up their children. Only three of the seven survived their early years—José, born in 1761, João, in 1767, and Maria Ana Victoria, in 1768. One boy was stillborn in 1762; the first João died in infancy the following year. A two-year-old girl, Maria Clementina, died in 1776, an infant daughter, Maria Isabel, a year later.

When Pombal saw many of his enemies moving in Maria and Pedro's circle, he arranged to have their eldest son, José, educated by his adherents. He also sought to introduce the Salic law, declaring that a female could not inherit the throne. But as rumors spread that Maria might be excluded by her son José, so did talk of a "Braganza curse," based on the story that after King José had whipped a mendicant friar, the man had warned, "No firstborn son of the House of Braganza shall live to rule."

On hearing about the Salic law, Maria appealed to her father, who then surprisingly sought Pombal's advice. The dictator reacted by banishing one of his protégés who had been preparing the case against the Princess of Brazil.

By 1777 José lay gravely ill, and his wife assumed the regency. In his testament he asked his daughter "to govern with peace and justice, pay his debts, protect his faithful servants, and protect those guilty of crimes against the state whom she considered worthy of clemency."

Before he died, he wanted to see his oldest grandson married. In a curious ceremony the 16-year-old José, Prince of Beira, was wedded to his mother's sister, Benedita, 14 years her nephew's senior.

Maria, the first queen regnant of Portugal, inherited the throne in March 1777. Although given the courtesy title of king (*el rei*), Pedro chiefly concerned himself with prayers and masses. Encouraged by her vindictive mother, Maria first acted to rid the government of Pombal. Legal proceedings were brought

Maria I (Portugal). Museu Nacional do Coches, Lisbon.

against him, but because of his advanced age the queen spared his life and banished him to one of his estates.

Quickly prison gates swung open, freeing many of Pombal's enemies. Somewhat against her inclination, Maria also pardoned those Távoras, who had been behind bars for almost 20 years. Deeply loyal to her father's memory, she still resented the assassination attempt, but Pombal's foes now had the upper hand. Nonetheless, the intendant of police remained in office. The queen's confessor, the jovial Fr. Ignacio de São Caetano, also had ties to the old regime, having sat on Pombal's board of censorship. Maria chose the Marquis of Angeja as her chief minister.

Angeja abandoned many of Pombal's trading ventures and monopolies and cut back expenditures everywhere. Even the royal bull fights were suspended. Maria won praise for deeply involving herself in the changes. Of her husband a contemporary noted: "He is liberal in his aims, talks much in precepts of goodness and justice, but as he has no knowledge of mankind or business, he is easily governed, right or wrong, by those immediately about him, especially if they belong to the church." The same observer described Queen Maria as more "circumspect in what she says, more prudent, more enlightened in her opinions."

She loved Pedro deeply and suffered intense grief at his death in 1786. Royal festivities were banned, and state receptions resembled religious ceremonies. Two years later, the Braganza curse story was revived when the heir, José, died of smallpox, quickly followed by his 20-year-old sister, Maria Ana, who in 1785 had been married to a son of Charles III of Spain. That same tragic year saw the passing of the queen's confessor and her chief minister, Angeja.

The weight of bereavements proved too much for Maria, who earlier had borne the deaths of four young children. Talk of a coming revolution in France further disturbed her. Now her mind began to give way. As her fits of melancholy and recurring nightmares increased, the idea that she was headed for hell possessed her more and more. William Beckford, the young English author, reported: "Queen Maria, fancying herself damned for all eternity, therefore on the strength of its being all over with her, eats barley and oyster stew Fridays and Saturdays and indulges in conversation of a rather unchaste nature." Dr. Francis Willis, who had treated George III of England, was summoned, but he could do nothing. One February night in 1792 Maria threw a fit, and her only surviving son, 25-year-old João, took over as acting regent. He was named Prince Regent in 1799.

Queluz had been designed for gaiety, joy, and enchantments. But the atmosphere became oppressive when the queen's quarters resounded with her demented cries. After a visit to the pretty palace, Beckford wrote:

> The most agonizing shrieks—shrieks such as I hardly conceived possible—inflicted on me a sensation of horror such as I had never felt before. The queen, herself, whose apartment was only two doors off from the chambers where we were sitting, uttered those dreadful sounds, "Ai Jesous. Ai Jesous!" did she exclaim again and again in the utterances of agony.

Beckford escaped the gloom by raking through the box hedges of the garden with João's young, tomboyish wife, Carlota, daughter of Charles IV of Spain. Again in 1795 Beckford told of Maria's being "dropped in the sea and scrubbed for very little purpose."

While his mother sat in her twilight world, Dom João, benevolent and conscientious, worked hard to keep Portugal from being swept up by the revolutionary winds blowing in from France. As a first step he joined in the war against the revolutionaries who had decapitated Louis XVI and Marie Antoinette. Then, after Spain made a separate peace in 1795, Portugal drew closer to Britain. It proved a prescient move. In 1796, despite his wife's Spanish ties, João felt threatened by a Spanish invasion; obligingly the British sent a 6000 man-force to keep the Spaniards at bay.

By 1807, however, Napoleon demanded that Portugal join in the Continental Blockade against England. Portugal refused, and while he fought his European campaigns he slackened his pressure. But after his victories in Austria, Prussia, and Russia, he overran Portugal in 1807.

The artillery of the French General Junot could be heard over the hills that November day when the royal family fled in a driving rain, Maria sure that the French soldiers were on their way to murder her. João took with him all the royal art treasures and gold so that 36 ships, escorted by eight British men-of-war, were waiting to transport the Braganzas and the entire court to sanctuary in Brazil. The British were left to defend Portugal, and Sir Arthur Wellesley, later Duke of Wellington, used the country as his base for operations that drove the French from Spain.

The voyage lasted 52 days. Carlota, whose shrewishness and profligacy had made her highly unpopular, complained incessantly about stinking water and crowded quarters. The entire court suffered from storms and seasickness. When the ships landed at Bahia, the inhabitants welcomed the Braganzas warmly. But Maria, terrified of Negroes prancing around her sedan chair, screamed that she was in hell with devils pursuing her.

The climate in Bahia proved too hot, and a month later the royal party and their courtiers settled in Rio de Janeiro. A rich planter offered his new suburban estate of São Christavão, as a palace. There the royal family settled in except for Queen Maria, who was confined to an old convent of the Carmelites. João and his children enjoyed the exotic new environment, but Carlota constantly complained of thunderstorms, lurking tropical diseases, and limited housing and transportation.

Meanwhile the Prince Regent worked hard. After listening to a request from Count da Ponte, governor of Bahia, João threw open Brazilian ports to world trade and ended Portuguese restrictions and monopolies. He went on to encourage industry and a free press, to invite immigration, to authorize a national bank, military academy, and medical school, and to establish a national art museum and library. In December 1815, he designated the Portuguese dominions as the "United Kingdom of Portugal, Brazil, and the Algarve."

The next year he started building a royal palace on the outskirts of the city. About the same time he invited European men of science and culture to join a National Institute. So occupied, he had little time or perhaps inclination to mourn for his mother. The old queen had died on March 20 after 24 years of almost total insanity. Once she had ruled wisely and benignly.

Maria II (Maria da Glória)
Queen of Portugal,
1826–1828; 1834–1853

Maria da Glória did not come easily to her throne, gaining it only after civil war and her father's ultimate sacrifice. Once crowned, she found she had entered a topsy-turvy world of politics.

She was born April 4, 1819, in Rio de Janeiro, the eldest child of Dom Pedro, heir to JoãoVI of Portugal, and Maria Leopoldina, daughter of Emperor Franz I of Austria. João had been king since 1816, when he succeeded his mother, mad old Maria I, for whom the baby princess was named. Reluctant to leave Brazil, where the royal family had lived since 1807, he delayed returning to Lisbon. Some years before, he had designated the Portuguese dominions as the United Kingdom of Portugal, Brazil, and the Algarve.

In 1820 a revolt broke out in Lisbon, and its leaders disavowed the British regency and summoned the Cortes, which had not met for more than a century. Their republic lasted only 90 days. To save his throne, João sailed to Portugal in the spring of 1821, leaving his son Pedro as regent in Brazil. Meanwhile, to Maria da Glória's delight, the scholarly but athletic Leopoldina began to fill the royal nursery. An heir was born in 1821, but died early in 1822. Januaria arrived the same year, Paula in 1823.

Leopoldina's pregnancies coincided with the first steps toward an independent Brazil. Even before João reached Lisbon, the Cortes, wishing to restore Brazil to its former colonial status, began to undo many of the reforms he had instituted there. When the legislators ordered Dom Pedro to come to Lisbon to complete his political education, he refused, formed a ministry, and convoked a legislative assembly. On September 7, sitting on horseback beside a little stream, the Ipiranga, Pedro flourished his sword and uttered his famous *Grito* (Cry), "Independence or death!"

Lord Cochrane, a British naval officer in Pedro's service, forced the Portuguese garrisons to withdraw, and that December, three-year-old Maria watched her father crowned Emperor of Brazil. João supported Pedro, but the

177

Cortes did not recognize Brazilian independence until 1825. João then obligingly legitimized his son's title by declaring himself Emperor of Brazil and immediately abdicating in his favor.

At the time of Ipiranga, Pedro, notorious for many love affairs, had begun
a liaison with the beautiful Domatila de Castro Cantel e Melho. Domatila,
whose marriage was soon conveniently dissolved, gave Pedro a daughter, Isabel
Maria, in 1824, the same year the gentle empress bore him another daughter,
Francesca. Next Domatila demanded a title, that of Viscountess of Castro and
a post as court attendant to Leopoldina. Again, within a year, both women
were pregnant by the handsome Pedro. Triumphantly Leopoldina produced
the Prince Imperial, a second Pedro. Domatila also had a son, but he lived only
three months.

Recovering quickly, she insisted on accompanying the emperor and empress on a pleasure cruise to northern Bahia. Of the royal children, only Maria
da Glória came along. As Pedro openly flaunted his mistress on board, the Empress Leopoldina tried to resign herself. Finally her patience wore thin, and at
the end of the journey she demanded that Pedro immediately send Domatila
away from the royal palace. He agreed, but gave the young woman a new title,
Marqueza of Sanchez, and a new home.

In Lisbon, in 1822, João had been forced to sign a radical constitution,
which proclaimed the "sovereignty of the people" and established a one-house
legislature. He was opposed by the absolutists, led by his smoldering, Spanish-
born queen, Carlota Joaquina, and her favorite son, Miguel, who wanted the
traditional Cortes and no constitution at all.

With João's death in March 1826, Pedro accepted his inheritance and announced his intention of conferring on Portugal a constitution like the one he
had promoted in Brazil. The document, which returned executive authority
to the king and established a two-house legislature, was prepared and signed
in April, but did not reach Lisbon until July. Pedro never foresaw how much
his Charter would contribute to his daughter's political problems.

Once the Charter was off his desk in Rio de Janeiro, he announced his intention to give up the Portuguese throne in favor of Maria da Glória. His condition was that she become betrothed to his brother Miguel, who in turn
would have to accept the Charter. Miguel was scheduled to become regent in
1827; until then, the regency would be headed by Pedro's sister, Maria Isabel.

Almost as soon as Pedro had proclaimed his conditional abdication,
Domatila demanded that her eldest daughter be legitimized. Her lover did
more; he elevated Isabel Maria to regal rank as the Duchess of Goyaz. The girl
began to share meals, lessons, and playtime hours with her half sisters at the
palace, but the small princesses took their revenge by pulling the invader's hair.

When the emperor called Leopoldina to task, she responded by falling ill
and suffering a miscarriage. Infection set in, and soon she lay on her death bed.
Toward the last she dictated a letter to her sister, Marie Louise, Napoleon's

second wife: "For almost four years, as you already know, dearest sister, I have been reduced—by a monstrous temptress—to the deepest humiliation, for I am utterly forgotten by my adored husband."

Grief fell most heavily on the intelligent, emotional Maria da Glória, who had been so close to her mother. To compound Maria's sorrow, Domatila continued to bring Isabel Maria to the nursery. Almost every day the Duchess of Goyaz and the small princesses engaged in a stormy exchange of fisticuffs.

In the summer of 1827 the royal favorite gave birth to a girl named Maria Isabel, who soon died. Still Domatila continued to hope that Pedro would marry her. Public opinion, however, clamored for a consort of royal blood.

By now talk had reached Rio de Janeiro that in Lisbon the regent Miguel was fitting the crown to his own head. Pedro decided to send his eldest daughter to Europe before her uncle could win too many supporters. As her escort he picked the Marquis of Barbacena, who had already been delegated to find a royal bride. Just as the frigate *Imperatrix* docked at Gibraltar, messages arrived that Miguel had enthroned himself in the palace of Queluz. It was decided that Maria da Glória could expect only the worst from him and therefore must be left in England for a time.

Waiting to be received at the British court, which had been deluged with angry protests from Miguel, the Brazilian visitor settled down in a country cottage at Laleham. Barbacena wrote Pedro that she continued to enjoy excellent health: "She is taller, less fat, and therefore more beautiful and elegant. Her teeth, which had been gray, crooked, and twisted, are now being straightened. . . ." Barbacena further described lessons in French, English, geography, history, architecture, drawing, painting, and needlework. But Maria da Glória had to wait months to be received by George IV.

Barbacena's long quest for an imperial bride finally succeeded. He informed Pedro that he was returning with the former Empress Josephine's granddaughter, 17-year-old Princess Amelia of Bavaria, whose father, the late Eugene de Beauharnais, had been made Prince of Leuchtenberg by his stepfather, Napoleon. Maria da Glória was on board the *Imperatrix* when the pink-cheeked and lively Amelia arrived with Barbacena in October 1829. On deck, stepdaughter and stepmother, separated by only seven years, stood hand in hand. One week after Pedro and Amelia's wedding, Domatila gave birth to her last child sired by Pedro. But he refused to give the baby boy a suitable credential because he had promised his new wife fidelity. So the indomitable mistress moved on to new conquests.

The emperor fell in love with his young bride, whose pink gowns were so copied by her female subjects that Rio de Janeiro bloomed with soft color. His children were delighted with her too. Pedro, however, misinterpreted her generosity. He wanted Domatila's daughter to join the family, but Amelia demanded that the girl be dispatched immediately to her mother in São Paulo. Domatila sent the Duchess of Goyaz to a Parisian convent.

In 1831 as his relations with Brazilian political leaders became increasingly strained, Pedro decided to recover the Portuguese throne for his daughter. He willingly abdicated as emperor, leaving the Brazilian throne to his young son, Pedro II, and a regency. He and Amelia went aboard a British man-of-war, taking Maria da Glória with them.

The order to sail, however, was delayed, and the royal trio was transferred to a smaller cruiser, the *Volage*, scheduled to depart in a week. While they waited, Maria da Glória could be seen running back and forth on deck with a black goat. The Empress Amelia seized the opportunity to write a letter in which she referred to the imperial children left behind as "orphans of the state" and urged that they be made official wards of the nation.

Finally the *Volage* sailed. But just as it reached the breakers, the British envoy, who had chartered a fast tug, climbed up the rope ladder to insist that Maria da Glória could not leave. Since the Court of St. James recognized King Miguel, Maria da Glória's presence on a British warship was a diplomatic affront. The princess went back to the palace for two weeks and then started out again, under an assumed name, on board a French merchantman.

Pedro met his daughter in Paris and left her in his wife's care. In the spring of 1832 he went to the Azores to launch an invasion of Portugal. Before leaving, he asked Maria to embroider a silken banner showing the Braganza crest and her own cipher so that the "Queen's Army" could hold it aloft while storming to victory.

In July Pedro's expedition left the Azores for Portugal. Having taken over a large fishing fleet, they sailed into Oporto. The garrison fled, the city capitulated without a shot, and Maria da Glória's flag was raised. But soon Pedro's men had to fortify themselves against attacks by the powerful Miguelite army. So began the War of the Two Brothers, the bloodiest civil war in Portugal's history. Pedro vainly begged Viscount Palmerston, the British Foreign Secretary, for aid.

Miguel appeared to have overwhelming support and to be winning the war. But then in 1833, Pedro's fleet, under a mercenary British-born commander, defeated the Miguelite fleet, and his forces captured Lisbon. He now sent for Maria da Glória and her stepmother, who boarded a Portuguese man-of-war at Le Havre. In Lisbon, delirious crowds welcomed them, and plumed horses brought the gilded royal coach to the palace of Queluz, where Maria da Glória held her first audience.

By this time Pedro was very ill. Campaign hardships had brought on a tubercular cough and a kidney ailment. At his wife's insistence he left for a Swiss cure and before departing placed the diadem on his daughter's head.

With the Miguelites still in control of most of the country, the war was far from over. When Pedro returned to Lisbon, he claimed to have been helped by the Alpine air, but he had obviously lost his vigor. To add to the gloom, word came that Maria's sister Paula had died in São Paulo.

The spring of 1834 produced welcome news; Pedro's army inflicted a decisive defeat on Miguel at the Battle of Asserceira. In May, Miguel capitulated in the Convention of Evora-Monte and was permanently banished.

On the first anniversary of the siege of Oporto, Maria invited her father to accompany her on a visit to the heroic place. But during their stay Pedro began to cough up blood, and he was rushed to Lisbon. From his bed at Queluz Palace, Pedro disbanded the regency and named his daughter sole ruler. By law 15-year-old Maria was a minor, but a special decree declared that she had attained her majority; her advisers affirmed that she showed a seriousness and maturity beyond her years.

Pedro died in September 1834. The next year Maria da Glória married her stepmother's brother, Prince August of Leuchtenberg, but he died of angina shortly after reaching Lisbon. A new marriage was speedily arranged, the matchmaker being King Leopold of the Belgians. He chose his Catholic nephew, Ferdinand of Saxe-Coburg-Gotha, a first cousin of Prince Albert, who a few years later married Britain's Queen Victoria. As Victoria was to become enamored of Albert, so Maria fell deeply in love with 18-year-old Ferdinand, blond and clean-shaven. In many respects he resembled Albert, especially in his sense of duty and love of painting and music. Unlike Victoria, Maria made her husband king consort.

Young Ferdinand felt prepared for his role. His Uncle Leopold had written down for him "everything he ought to know about the organization of government," and he had with him a tutor, Dietz, who participated freely in Portuguese politics.

Plump, pretty, and docile in her domestic life, Maria was to bear her husband 11 children, two of whom were to become kings of Portugal. (Indeed, some historians have speculated that her frequent pregnancies contributed to the tumult of her reign.) Ferdinand had ambitious educational plans for his sons and daughters: Pedro (1837), Luis (1838), João (1842), Ferdinand (1846), Augusto (1847), Maria Ana (1843), and Antonia (1845). A daughter Maria, a son Leopoldo, and a daughter Maria da Glória were stillborn in 1840, 1849, and 1851.

As the country slowly recovered from the civil war, Maria da Glória found herself a prey to contending factions. The army had learned to make and unmake governments; liberals hated the church. Above all, supporters of the constitution of 1822 and the Chartists continued as enemies. (The absolutist cause had been quashed with Miguel's departure and Carlota Joaquina's death in 1830.)

The Duke of Palmela headed Maria's first ministry but before long was succeeded by his rival, the Duke of Saldanha, Pedro's victorious general. Saldanha would return time and time again, dominating her reign more than any other political figure.

Suddenly in 1836, revolt flared. Encouraged by events in Spain, where the

Maria II (Maria da Glória). Museu Nacional de Arte Antiga, Lisbon.

constitution of 1812 had been restored, Portuguese radicals, led by Manuel da Silva Passos, demanded a restoration of the 1822 constitution and carried Oporto in the election. When their deputies arrived in Lisbon, they found support from the National Guard and from demonstrators in the streets. Passos then came to power in the September Revolution.

Maria and Ferdinand viewed the agitation for the radical constitution as a threat to the throne. After the king consort appealed to the British ambassador, the couple left the Necessidades Palace for Belém, expecting to board a British warship. Ferdinand's uncle, Leopold of Belgium, meanwhile con-

sidered sending a relief expedition. Populace and army feared Belgian intervention, and the government gave way to a junta headed by the more moderate
Sá da Bandeira. He warned Maria that asking for foreign help was a risky
business, and she went back to Lisbon.

The Septembrists surprised the court by writing a new constitution which
did not include the hateful doctrine of the "sovereignty of the people." Nor did
it advocate a return to a unicameral legislature. But it did replace life peers with
an elected senate. The new penal code and administrative changes did not
please the Chartists. Saldanha and the Duke of Terceira gathered an army and
tried to restore the Charter, but were defeated. From London, Lord
Palmerston told Maria, "We will not interfere." and suggested that she work
with the radicals. Ferdinand was far more upset than his wife at the British
answer, and the British ambassador remarked: "He has more bottom, though
not as flashy."

Sá da Bandeira's government fell in April 1839. It had begun negotiations
to restore relations with the Holy See, which Pedro had antagonized by con-
fiscating church property. When in 1841 the government agreed to recognize
the bishops appointed by Miguel, the schism began to heal. A year later Pope
Gregory XVI gave Maria da Glória the Order of the Golden Rose. Meanwhile,
in 1840 her brother had begun his reign as Emperor Pedro II of Brazil.

In 1842 a young radical, António Bernardo da Costa Cabral, joined the
Chartists and on becoming minister of finance, forced the resignation of his colleagues. The new government of the Duke of Terceira restored Pedro's Charter, and Costa Cabral became minister of the interior, his brother minister of
justice. The Costa Cabrals' reforms led to another uprising beginning in 1845.

It was given the pseudonymous name of Maria da Fonte because of the
prominent part played by women. For sanitation reasons a government decree
forbade further burials in churches or on church grounds and instead established public cemeteries away from towns and villages. To peasants, priests, and
especially women, the dead seemed condemned to damnation. From north of
Lisbon, the rebellion spread rapidly as Costa Cabral's opponents joined the in-
surgents. Another junta was set up, and the rebels swept close to Lisbon. In May
1845 Maria da Glória had to dismiss Costa Cabral. Palmela, again in power,
canceled the cemetery order, and the rebellion subsided.

After calling for elections, Maria's veteran adviser, Saldanha, helped unite
the Chartists with the former followers of Costa Cabral. Such acts infuriated
the Septembrists, who issued a manifesto once more demanding the "sovereignty of the nation." After Saldanha went out to obtain the support of the garrison, Maria asked him to form a government and restore the status quo.

The angry Septembrists set up a junta in Oporto and demanded her
dismissal. Thereupon Maria assumed full power and made Ferdinand
commander-in-chief of the army. But the rebels steadily gained ground. Costa
Cabral, now minister to Spain, encouraged the Spanish to move troops to the

frontier. From London Queen Victoria sent a mediator, who got Maria to agree to a complete amnesty for the radicals and the formation of a new government devoid of Chartists or Septembrists. But the Oporto junta made new demands, and the negotiations ceased. An Anglo-Spanish naval division then blockaded Oporto, and Spanish troops crossed the frontier at several points. In June 1847, the junta capitulated.

Saldanha resigned and was replaced by a group of his friends, who announced free elections to bring him back to power. In December 1847 he returned and stayed until June 1849, when Costa Cabral ousted him. Saldanha tried to stage a revolution but was unsuccessful until the Oporto garrison threw him its support. He entered Lisbon, tossed out Costa Cabral, and once more headed the government. In 1851 and 1852, realizing the need for "regeneration," he introduced several modifications to the Charter.

The queen usually helped Saldanha in his political maneuvering. Though far different from her grandmother, Carlota Joaquina, in appearance and personality, she had inherited a penchant for intrigue. But Maria's motives were purer; she was devoted to upholding her father's Charter.

Political misfortunes aside, Ferdinand took pleasure in encouraging the arts. Spurred by his interest, a National Theater was built in Lisbon, and great monuments were restored. For himself and his beloved queen he transformed an old monastery into a spectacular Arab-Gothic-Renaissance palace, Pena, on top of Sintra's highest hill.

He also avidly followed the construction of Portugal's first railway. As he and Maria participated in the opening ceremony, an observer described the scene:

> The earth being turned with a handsomely ornamental wheelbarrow, with gilded mounting, the queen returned to her box, attended as before, amidst discharges of rockets, accompanied by the most animating martial music. The king conversed with Mr. Hislop and Mr. Valentine, the English engineers, expressing his hope to the former that he would use every exertion to carry out his desired undertaking. The queen then partook of refreshments; ices and pastry were liberally provided.

Six months later, on November 15, 1853, at the age of only 34, Maria died after delivering her 11th child, a stillborn son, Eugenio. Her 10th child had died at birth the preceding February. History would remember the reign of this Brazilian-born monarch as almost two decades of political turbulence.

Maria Cristina (1)
Regent of Spain, 1833–1840

In 1828 a Braganza princess, Maria-Francisca, an aunt of Maria da Glória of Portugal, was fiercely determined to be Queen of Spain. Married to the austere Don Carlos de Bourbon, brother of the prematurely aging and childless widower, Ferdinand VII, she thought her chances excellent. But she reckoned without her sister-in-law, Carlota, wife of the king's second brother, Don Francisco de Paula. When the Council of Castile petitioned the king to marry for the fourth time "for the sake of the nation," Carlota produced a small portrait of her sister, Maria Cristina. It had the desired effect. Carlota and Maria Cristina happened to be Francisco's and Ferdinand's nieces, but, as with his brother, such consanguinity made little difference to the gouty king, who sent an emissary to Naples to ask for the young woman's hand.

Maria Cristina was born April 27, 1806, in Portici, to Francis I, King of the Two Sicilies, and Maria Isabella, fifth daughter of Charles IV of Spain. In the midst of a large family — seven brothers and seven sisters eventually — she grew up fun-loving and warm-blooded. That inveterate traveler, the Countess of Blessington, warmly approved of her looks: "Her features are small and neatly finished, her eyes expressive, her teeth beautiful, and her smile full of fascination. Her complexion is of a pale, clear olive, which, if less brilliant than the Irish roses and lilies of our English ladies, is not without its charm."

Maria Cristina willingly accepted Ferdinand's offer of marriage and from Naples made a triumphal journey to Madrid. Shortly before Christmas, 1829, the wedding came off with great glitter; among the spectators Maria-Francisca stood stony-faced, Carlota exultant.

The birth of the royal couple's daughter, Isabella, on October 10, 1830, revived Maria-Francisca and Don Carlos' expectations, for they pinned their hopes on the Salic law, introduced in 1713, forbidding female succession to the Spanish throne. Few knew that in 1789, Ferdinand's father, Charles IV, had declared a Pragmatic Sanction, allowing a woman's rule according to old Spanish tradition. In 1830 Ferdinand revealed this secret law, but the Carlists, supporters of Don Carlos, refused to recognize it.

Not long after the birth of his second daughter, Luisa, in 1832, Ferdinand injured his head in a carriage accident while en route to the family's summer palace of La Granja. Maria Cristina nursed him devotedly, but after a couple of months the doctors told her he was dying. The queen consulted Francisco Calomarde, one of the king's reactionary advisers, who warned that a blood bath would follow Isabella's placement on the throne. Maria-Francisca and her widowed sister, the Princess of Beira, sounded even more baleful. "All these Portuguese princesses," wrote a Spanish duchess "are demons either in politics or in love, and sometimes in both." A frightened Maria Cristina roused Ferdinand from his sick bed to declare the Pragmatic Sanction invalid and to make Don Carlos his legal heir. But he ordered the signed document kept secret until his death.

After Ferdinand lapsed into a deep coma, the doctors pronounced him dead. But when officials began preparing his body for burial, they discovered he was alive. Thereupon the volatile Carlota descended on La Granja, scolded her sister for spineless behavior, and tore Ferdinand's decree to shreds.

During her husband's convalescence, Maria Cristina was appointed regent. In the summer of 1833, Ferdinand felt strong enough to stage a great ceremony so that the Cortes could swear allegiance to his daughter. But by September he died of apoplexy. For all his insensitivity he had been perceptive enough to note, "Spain is a bottle of beer, and I am the cork. Without me it will all go off in froth."

With her infant daughter proclaimed queen, Maria Cristina became regent again. From the moment of entering Spain she had been courted by the liberals, who ranged from right to left in the political spectrum, and now her only hope lay in aligning herself with them.

Her husband had tarried with them briefly when, after Napoleon's final exile, he had returned from imprisonment in France and agreed to support a forward-looking constitution. Almost as quickly he revoked it and restored authority to the old conservative and regressive institutions. For 19 years with this backward king, Spain had sunk into an oppressive lethargy.

An alliance with the liberals forced Maria Cristina into a broad liberalization program, also undertaken to spite Don Carlos, the archetype of absolutism. When a new ministry succeeded Calomarde's, it reopened universities, dismissed reactionary generals and officials, and offered amnesty to many political prisoners. In high dudgeon Carlos and his family took off to Portugal.

But his supporters continued troublesome. Whereas England, France, and the south and central part of Spain recognized the tiny queen, Russia, Austria, the pope, and Spain's traditionalist north declared for Carlos, now openly called Carlos V of Spain. Revolts in the north followed an uprising in Talvera in favor of Don Carlos. So began the First Carlist War.

Meanwhile Maria Cristina, "very handsome and beaming with goodness,"

Maria Cristina (1). Prado, Madrid.

as an English visitor observed, had given her heart to a young corporal in the guards. According to the most frequently cited story, one afternoon on a drive to La Granja she borrowed a handkerchief from a soldier to stanch a minor nosebleed. When she leaned out of her carriage window and returned it, she suddenly noticed its owner, the darkly handsome Corporal Muñoz, who dramatically raised it to his lips. She made arrangements for future meetings, and only three months after Ferdinand's death, the pair was secretly married.

In 1834 Don Carlos fled from Portugal with his brother-in-law, Miguel, when Maria da Glória was proclaimed queen in Lisbon. He and his family sailed for England, but one week after they arrived, he left the country with a false passport and returned to Spain to meet Maria Cristina's slowly advancing forces.

That autumn the queen regent bore Muñoz's first child, a son, Agosto, a confinement so easy that ten days later she was reviewing her troops. She and Muñoz would have three more children: another son, Fernando, and two daughters, Amparo and Mulagros. In spite of the war, Maria Cristina settled down to a happy life at her country palaces. Then suddenly Carlota declared her sister unfit to bring up children and demanded custody of her two nieces. Maria Cristina, however, sent her accuser packing. She could not easily dismiss the press. Lampoons against the corporal began to appear so frequently that for a time Muñoz had to drop out of sight.

Maria Cristina's sympathies lay entirely with the more conservative liberals. But her first prime minister proved too conservative for the more radical liberals, and she was forced into appointing one of them, only to see him fall. After she had installed a conservative once more, the radical liberals took up the cry, "Long live the constitution of 1812!" A mutiny in the garrison at La Granja suddenly erupted, threatening Muñoz's life. To save him, the queen regent signed a decree restoring the constitution Ferdinand had revoked 15 years earlier.

By 1835 the First Carlist War, fought chiefly on the Carlist side by mountain guerrillas, had become almost monotonous, every victory succeeded by a defeat. Carlists and Cristinos seemed incapable of winning or losing, and Don Carlos decided to make a spectacular march on Madrid. Dashing his hopes, the city did not rise up, and he retreated.

The following year his wife, Maria-Francisca, died and in 1838 he married his even more formidable sister-in-law, the Princess of Beira, whose passion for intrigue led to dissension at his headquarters.

When a reconciliation took place between the queen regent's General Baldomero Espartero and Carlos's General Rafael Maroto at a deserted farm at Vergara, they threw themselves into each other's arms, and their soldiers followed suit. So the treaty that ended the war came to be called "Abrazo de Vergara" (Embrace of Vergara). It was widely rumored, however, that Maria

Cristina had bribed the Carlist general with huge amounts of money. She had earlier won many Carlists to her side by a clever maneuver. At the suggestion of Juan Mendezabal, her prime minister, she had confiscated the still enormous land holdings of the church and put them up for sale to many Carlists, who profited from attractive prices.

After the Carlist war, generals took charge of Spanish politics, and for the rest of Isabella's reign they would remain dominant, providing the military arm for the *moderatos*, as the upper middle class oligarchy was now known, and conversely for the *progressivos*, the lower strata of the urban middle class. Unreservedly the *moderatos* supported the crown. The restored constitution had been revised in 1837, reflecting a *moderato* trend, and the postwar election for the Cortes returned a *moderato* majority, which hurried to introduce a bill to strip the more radical municipalities of the independence granted them by the constitution. Maria Cristina again sided with the *moderatos*, but set out to win General Espartero's support. The hero of Vergara and his army favored the *progressivos*. Noting that his entry into Barcelona was far more triumphant than her own, she took his advice not to sign the Muncipal Bill. Then, goaded by her conservative liberal ministers, she signed it after all.

Barcelona reacted by revolting. Espartero refused to disperse the crowds until the queen regent revoked her decree and dismissed her *moderato* ministry. But when more radical politicians were installed, she suddenly turned stubborn and declared that a riot would not force changes in the Municipal Bill. As ministry quickly succeeded ministry, Madrid led a procession of cities proclaiming their independence. Swallowing her pride, Maria Cristina asked Espartero to form a new government. Once he had taken his oath, she announced her decision to abdicate and leave her daughters in his charge. In October 1840 she bade a tearful goodbye to Isabella and Luisa and with Muñoz and their children boarded ship for France.

In Paris the French king, Louis Philippe, ordered her received with military honors and installed her in the Palais Royal. Dispatching a florid message to Madrid, Maria Cristina pleaded with her former subjects to love her daughters and respect her memory. But a few months later she had a change of heart and dictated a second letter declaring she remained queen regent. An unsympathetic Espartero countered that in the first manifesto she had forfeited her royal right.

She moved on to Rome for another purpose. Because of their secret ceremony, she was not married to Muñoz in the eyes of the church, and now she discreetly appealed to Pope Gregory XVI for dispensation. When he granted it, she took pains to see that the Spanish government still considered her a widow. With her return to Paris, she carefully cultivated the friendship of the French king and his chief minister, Louis Guizot.

By the fall of 1842, she fell into political hot water once more. A junta had been established in her name in northern Spain, and General Diego de Leon hatched a plot to carry off the girl queen to the junta, hold her hostage, and demand her mother's return. The plot failed, and the Spanish ambassador insisted on Maria Cristina's expulsion from France. But her cultivation of Guizot paid off, and he refused. She lay ill in Paris when Queen Isabella II was declared legally of age in 1843. Espartero had left the country, driven out by one of the periodic revolts and General Ramon Narvaez's march on Madrid.

Don Salustiano Olozaga, the ambassador who had asked for the queen mother's expulsion from France, now became head of a *progressivo* government in Spain. When he fled from charges that he had fraudulently obtained the queen's signature on a document, the *moderatos*, led by Narvaez, came back to power. They called for the return of their heroine, Maria Cristina.

Once over the border, she received a tumultuous welcome, and on an open plain near the palace of Aranjuez, she staged a happy reunion with her royal daughters in 1844. As soon as possible, Maria Cristina urged Isabella to make Muñoz the Duke of Riansares, a grandee of the first class. In addition a royal decree legitimized their marriage. Then the couple, who had lived together for 20 years, was properly married in the royal chapel by the Bishop of Cordova. The bride had grown stout, but remained as animated as ever. Washington Irving described her "queenly grace and dignity, mixed with the most gracious affability; she surpasses any sovereign I have ever seen."

Now she began to think about Isabella's marriage. Don Carlos, her erstwhile enemy, had offered his son, the Count of Montemolin. For a time Maria Cristina even considered her much younger brother, Count Trapani of Naples. But finally she chose her effeminate nephew, Francisco de Asis, son of her quarrelsome sister Carlota, who had recently died. At the same time the queen mother arranged for the marriage of her second daughter Luisa to Louis Philippe's son, the Duke of Montpensier.

Although celebrated with pomp, Isabella's marriage in 1847 failed from the beginning; within a few weeks she had taken a handsome military lover. In disgust Maria Cristina left with Muñoz for France and from Paris wrote the young queen: "I never offended a husband Providence destined for me and only when I was free from all bonds of duty did I allow my heart to cherish a love which is made lawful before God." Shortly she was summoned to Madrid to effect a reconciliation between the 16-year-old queen and king consort.

The *moderatos* remained in power from 1844 to 1854. Even though they produced a still more conservative constitution, they could not stabilize their rule or prevent military risings by the *progressivos*. In this period the even more radical Democratic Party developed. It was prepared, however, to support the monarchy if its members gained government offices.

Ever since her return to Spain, Maria Cristina had been making money, speculating on the exchange, using railway contracts to feather her own nest, even helping herself from the public treasury. People called her *la ladrona*—the thief, and even her niece Josefa warned Isabella about the regent's "insatiable greed for gold."

As the years passed, the acquisitiveness increased, along with public grumbling. By the summer of 1854, rebellion had broken out. With the capital in an uproar over Leopoldo O'Donnell's attempt to overthrow the ministry, a mob surged toward the queen mother's house. When shouts rang out, "Death to Cristina! Death to the thief!" the crowd surged through her palace, smashing glass and china, flinging gilded furniture over the balconies, and burning paintings while the boldest women helped themselves to her lavish wardrobe and paraded on the balconies.

To restore order, Isabella asked the long-absent Espartero to return. But she realized that to keep her throne, she could not let her mother stay in the country. Again the two women said a tearful farewell, and one early morning Muñoz and his wife left by carriage; Maria Cristina never returned to Spain. Some 16 years later in Paris she watched her daughter sign a decree of abdication.

Maria Cristina and her devoted Muñoz lived quietly in their final exile. He died in La Havre in 1873, she five years later on August 23. She had found her greatest fulfillment, not as queen regent, but simply as Muñoz's wife.

Isabella II (Isabel)
Queen of Spain, 1833–1870

Maria Cristina's older daughter lost not only her throne; she lost her reputation. In the eyes of most Europeans, Isabella II thoroughly disgraced herself. Aside from her questionable morals, however, she was brave and generous to a fault, and the common people of Spain never stopped loving her.

The first child of Ferdinand VII and Maria Cristina was born October 10, 1830, in the Palacio Real in Madrid and was christened Maria Isabella. Her sister Luisa arrived two years later. In 1833 Ferdinand appeared to be dying. Goaded by his frightened wife, he revoked the Pragmatic Sanction, which would have allowed his daughter to rule, and declared his brother Carlos his heir. But his wife's strong-willed sister Carlota tore up the royal decree and saved the throne for Isabella. When Ferdinand temporarily recovered, he arranged for the Cortes to declare allegiance to his tiny daughter, who nibbled sugar plums during the tedious ceremony.

Following her father's death some months later, Isabella was proclaimed queen under her mother's regency. But the supporters of Don Carlos declared him king instead, and the First Carlist War broke out. Meanwhile that December Isabella gained a stepfather when Maria Cristina secretly married Corporal Fernando Muñoz. Enveloping her daughter, the regent's happiness spread through the various palaces the family occupied. The battles taking place to the north seemed far distant, until the royal army came under the command of Baldomaro Espartero, who in brilliant campaigns over the next few years steadily reduced the enemy and forced the Carlists to surrender in 1839. Caught in unceasing factional struggles, Maria Cristina gave up her regency in 1840 and left with Muñoz and their children for Paris.

The new regent, General Espartero, appointed a governess, the Countess Espoz y Mena, for Isabella and Luisa, but they never learned their lessons well. The little queen, plump and untidy, could be capricious and stubborn on the one hand, lively and charming on the other.

Soon after her mother's departure, Isabella suffered through what she later called "that awful night" of October 8, 1841. As she and Luisa were beginning a music lesson in the Palacio Real, shots suddenly shattered a window. General Diego de Leon's forces were attacking the palace guard in an attempt to kidnap the queen and bring her to a junta that clamored for Maria Cristina's return. Just in time, General Espartero's troops arrived to restore order, and by morning the danger had passed.

From then on Espartero felt it wise to appear with Isabella as often as possible. In 1843 he allowed her to open the new Cortes, and observers carefully noted the contrast between clumsy Isabella and graceful Luisa. The next year author-envoy Washington Irving, seeing Isabella on her 14th birthday when she had to receive long lines of diplomats, was more favorably impressed. "She acquitted herself," he wrote, "with wonderful propriety and self-expression." He even thought she looked "quite handsome."

In the fall of 1843, political tempers flared. Barcelona, always quick to revolt, did so once more. Other cities also established juntas, and two successive ministries resigned. At this point, Isabella, running to fat and plagued by eczema, was declared legally of age and set on the throne.

The former ambassador to France, Salustiano Olozaga, who had tangled with Maria Cristina in Paris, became prime minister in a liberal government. He counted, however, implacable enemies among the conservatives surrounding the queen, among them General Ramon Maria Narvaez. They were bent on getting rid of him, and Isabella involved herself in their shady business. Trying to help her power base, Olozaga prepared a document dissolving the Cortes and came to the queen for her signature. After writing her name, Isabella with customary affability offered him a box of chocolates for his daughter.

The next morning he was dismissed, accused of having obtained the queen's signature by force. At a public inquiry a statement from the queen charged that the former prime minister had locked her in the room and laid hands on her, compelling her to sign. Olozaga countered that the room had no locks or bolts, that the queen's signature looked anything but shaky, and that she would not have offered him candy if she had been threatened. Still he would not accuse her of lying. At length proceedings were dropped, but he left for Portugal.

With Narvaez and the moderates heading the government, Maria Cristina triumphantly returned to Spain. In a dramatic scene on the open plain near the castle of Aranjuez, Isabella flung herself into her mother's arms, bridging a separation of three years. Plump and sensual looking, the queen at 16 was considered ripe for marriage. Maria Cristina now busied herself with finding suitable husbands for both her daughters. The "Spanish marriages" even brought Queen Victoria and Prince Albert to Paris for discussions with King Louis Philippe. There agreement was reached that Luisa would not become a bride until Isabella had wed and produced an heir. Louis Philippe and Victoria concurred that the best candidate would be a non–French Bourbon prince.

Isabella herself had no say. Encouraged from abroad, Maria Cristina

Isabella II. Print Collection, Miriam & Ira D. Wallach Division of Art, Prints and Photographs, The New York Public Library, Astor, Lenox and Tilden Foundations.

settled on small and mincing Francisco de Asis, the son of her sister Carlota and Francisco de Paula, Ferdinand VII's younger brother, thus Isabella's cousin in a double sense. At the same time, forgetting the proviso that Luisa should wait, Maria Cristina netted Louis Philippe's son, the handsome Duke of Montpensier, as her daughter's bridegroom. Queen Victoria, who had favored a Coburg prince, exploded: "The settlement of the Queen of Spain's marriage, coupled with Montpensier, is infamous, and we must remonstrate." But she did little more than complain.

The double wedding was celebrated in October 1846, with both Isabella and Francisco bursting into tears at the altar. The bridegroom, an observer reported, looked like a young girl "dressed up as a general." Years later Isabella quipped, "What shall I say of a man who on his wedding night wore more lace than I?" Disappointing though he appeared, Francisco was given the title of king consort.

Almost immediately Isabella took a lover, General Francisco Serrano, and threw the king consort out of her bedroom.

Distraught over her daughter's adultery, Maria Cristina left with Muñoz for Paris. On tiring of Serrano, Isabella fixed her attention on a young opera tenor. Narvaez reacted by packing him off and calling for her mother to return and help him arrange a reconciliation between Isabella and her husband, mostly for the sake of appearances. Maria Cristina obliged.

For all the stories about her adultery, the thick-lipped, overpassionate young queen, whose lovely eyes and attractive voice added to her charm, enjoyed immense popularity. Sweetly smiling and unfailingly generous, she could be seen peeling off her bracelets and throwing them to beggars in the streets. To the daughters of her ministers and generals she often gave huge dowries.

The queen and the king consort shared only one belief, absolute certainty that a nun, Sor Patrocinio, who displayed the stigmata on her hands, gave them divinely inspired counsel. Francisco, as governor of the palace, took Sor Patrocinio's advice to get rid of the dictatorial Narvaez, and Isabella agreed to the scheme. It was a bloodless coup; an official gazette merely announced that Narvaez and his ministers had been replaced. Moving swiftly, Narvaez put down the "lightning ministry" and removed the king from his governor's post. During the revolt Isabella's new lover, the Marquis of Bedmar, feared for his life because Francisco had threatened to have all his wife's paramours hanged from her balcony. On Narvaez's return he roundly scolded Isabella, who refused to brook any interference in her private life or to dismiss her lover. Maria Cristina intervened in the quarrel, and in the end Bedmar left the palace.

Isabella's first child, a boy, was born in July 1850. Nobody knew with certainty the identity of the father. Within hours, however, the baby died. In early 1852 a daughter, her mother's namesake, arrived. Gossips called her La Aranuela, for the queen had acquired a fresh lover, a young officer named José Ruiz de Arana.

A few weeks later on her way back to the Palacio Real from the royal chapel, where she had given thanks for her safe delivery, Isabella was stabbed by Martin Merino, a Franciscan priest who had officiated at mass. The metal embroidery on her gown and her whalebone corset, however, prevented a serious injury. Still the priest was garroted and his body burned. Because of the assassination attempt, Sor Patrocinio moved into the palace, and Isabella prayed constantly and donated large sums to the church.

As her religious fervor grew, so did her lechery. Lover followed lover, her preference running to musicians and soldiers. Her third child, a girl, arrived in January 1854. The baby died three days later, father again unknown. Oblivious of the gossip in Madrid about her behavior, Isabella whiled away that summer at La Granja Palace. Soon her subjects found new grounds for complaint, accusing Maria Cristina of insufferable greed and the administration of corruption.

Since Isabella's *moderato* ministers, representing the upper middle class oligarchy, had long ignored the constitution, General Leopoldo O'Donnell's *pronunciemiento* called for the return of a constitutional regime. Fearlessly, Isabella drove back to Madrid, hoping to present herself to her troops. But her ministers held her back; they preferred to declare a state of siege as Madrid rose in revolt. In the turmoil the queen believed that Espartero alone could save her. At her request he dutifully returned from Portugal, but demanded that she reform her private life and that Maria Cristina be expelled to France. Again Isabella bade her mother goodbye.

To great rejoicing, she gave birth to a son, Alfonso, in 1857. Again questions arose about the father, who may have been a young army lieutenant or an American dental assistant named McKeon. But King Francisco swallowed his pride and gave the boy the title of Prince of the Asturias. Nor was he considered the father of Pilar, Paz, and Eulalia, Isabella's three daughters born between 1861 and 1864.

Isabella's uncle, Don Carlos, for whom the First Carlist War was fought, died in 1855. In 1860 his son, the Count of Montemolin, encouraged by his stepmother, the Princess of Beira, decided to try for the throne. A landing force came ashore on the coast of Valencia and marched inland. But when told the purpose of the expedition, the soldiers balked. Although Montemolin had counted on a simultaneous uprising in Madrid, it never materialized. When the leaders were captured he begged for mercy, which Isabella granted in exchange for his promise to renounce all plans to take the throne. Thereupon his brother Juan became the Carlist pretender. Abruptly Montemolin canceled his repudiation, and Carlist supporters grew confused by the rivalries between their two "kings." The matter was settled, however, by Montemolin's unexpected death early the next year.

After the Montemolin affair, O'Donnell turned his attention to overseas adventures and won extravagant praise for a punitive expedition against Morocco. Then, trying to revive old glories, he sent troops to Mexico, South America, and Indochina.

Meanwhile the queen had paid a visit to Napoleon III and the Empress Eugénie at Biarritz, where observers described her as looking like a giant India rubber ball. Nonetheless Eugénie approved of her and commended her "très grand air."

In spite of innumerable love affairs, Isabella had remained a loyal daughter of the church, and like Giovanna I of Naples and Maria da Glória of Portugal, she was awarded the Golden Rose, the papal prize for queenly virtue. Her husband reaped no honors at all. When Francisco visited Paris some time later, Princess Metternich called him "the most insignificant creature imaginable." Still, his political meddlings in France led the government in Madrid to resign in protest. About this time Isabella chose a singularly curious lover, a fat, middle-aged traveling player named Carlos Marfori. Unlike his predecessors, he determined to play a part in public affairs. To all appearances, the queen showed more interest in him than in her children. She could be affectionate enough, but devoted little time to them. The king, who had probably fathered none of them, kept away from them as much as possible. Of all her brood, Isabella's favorite was Alfonso, but visitors complained that she forced him to study too much religion.

For a long time the Duke of Montpensier, Isabella's brother-in-law, had wanted the throne, if not for himself, at least for his wife Luisa. In 1866 he allied himself with General Juan Prim, who after an abortive revolt against the queen had fled to France and England. In exile Prim kept plotting revolution and asked Montpensier for financial help. The cards seemed stacked against Isabella—the scandal of her private life affronted her subjects, and she suffered blame for the misdeeds of the various political factions. In Spain, General Serrano, Isabella's erstwhile lover, had entered the conspiracy. A dedicated follower of Montpensier, he sent an emissary to Luisa saying that if the throne were to be vacated, it would be offered to her.

The government learned of the intrigues, and Serrano and the Duke and Duchess of Montpensier were sent to that favorite land of exile, Portugal. But Prim kept on the move. Encouraged by several earlier uprisings, he proposed that the Carlists join his liberals in a revolution. But the alliance proved impossible.

In September 1868 Admiral Juan Bautista Topete, a follower of Montpensier, issued a proclamation declaring Luisa Queen of Spain. Although not enthusiastic about the plan, Prim agreed to a revolution. The question of a future sovereign, he told the admiral, must be decided by the Cortes.

The revolutionaries landed at Cadiz and drew up a manifesto intended to unite all the queen's opponents. As the rebellion gathered support, Serrano, who had returned to Spain, marched on Madrid.

Isabella was staying at San Sebastian, a seaside resort to the north, when she heard of Admiral Topete's declaration. Showing her customary bravery she wanted to enter Madrid, but her close circle at court begged her not to come. With the resignation of the prime minister, Gonzalo Brabo, a military dictatorship under Manuel Concha took over, and troops were sent against Serrano. Again Isabella determined to return, but Concha repeatedly warned that Marfori must not accompany her. Equally stubborn, Isabella would not start without her favorite in tow.

Late in September 1868 she received word that Madrid had risen against her and that Serrano's troops had been victorious. Although Pope Pius IX advised her not to abdicate, she realized she would have to leave the country. When her train neared the frontier, tears choked her words, "I thought I had struck deeper roots in this land."

Gratefully Isabella accepted Napoleon III's offer of the ancient castle of Pau as a temporary home. Later she moved to Paris, buying the house of a ruined Russian gambler which she renamed the Palais de Castille. Marfori, Sor Patrocinio, Isabella's children, and her confessor, Father Claret, lived there with her while Francisco moved to a little villa outside the city. Her daughters were educated in a convent; her son enrolled at a Parisian college. As usual, she saw little of them although sometimes she played cards with them or drove with them through the Bois de Bologne.

Soon she went to Rome to call on the pope and discuss the problem of the family vendettas. The thought bothered her that the Carlist branch had more claims than she to the Spanish throne, and on her return to Paris, she met secretly with the new Carlist pretender, Carlos VII. But they accomplished no more than a cordial stroll. By 1870 several of Isabella's counselors persuaded her to abdicate. On June 25, with her mother present, she signed the decree of abdication in favor of her son, Alfonso. At this ceremony her good humor struck all observers. One month later, France and Prussia were at war.

When the Second French Empire collapsed after losing the war in 1871, Isabella moved to Geneva. She enrolled Alfonso at a college in Vienna; later he was sent to the Military College at Sandhurst, England. But like many former crowned heads, Isabella finally returned to Paris, which continued to wear a royal look.

In Spain, Serrano became regent and, disregarding Isabella's decree, sent Prim around Europe looking for a new king. The envoy found a likely candidate in Amadeo of Savoy, the son of King Victor Emmanuel II of Italy. But the day Amadeo arrived in Madrid, Prim was assassinated.

Spanish politics proved to be as labyrinthine as ever, and within two years Amadeo and his queen left for Portugal. In Paris, Isabella kept herself informed of the continuing turbulence. A rump parliament proclaimed a federal republic, and the Carlists took to arms in the Second Carlist War. At first they seemed successful while the situation in Madrid deteriorated. In eight months the First Republic (1873–1874) had four presidents, none of whom could find a prime minister able to hold a government together. Then as cities and provinces declared their autonomy, the army stepped in.

By the end of 1874 the Carlists were losing, and a brigadier's *pronunciemiento* invited 18-year-old Alfonso to accept the Spanish crown. Early in the new year delirious crowds welcomed him back to Madrid. With his Sandhurst training, he proved himself an effective soldier, and within a year he had ended the Carlist war.

Now Isabella and her recently widowed daughter, Isabel, could return too.

But because she had frittered away much of her fortune, she began quarreling with the treasury over her pension. At the same time she interfered in religious matters to such an extent that the prime minister decided to move her to the Escorial Palace. There she fumed over the announcement that her son planned to marry her niece Mercedes, the Duke of Montpensier's daughter. She left for Paris in a huff and refused to attend the wedding in January 1877.

It was a real love match. But a few months later the darkly lovely Mercedes died of gastric fever. Two more deaths in the family soon followed, that of Maria Cristina in 1878 and of Isabella's daughter Pilar in 1879. Like her brother, Pilar was tubercular.

Meanwhile Spanish officials had been hunting for a successor to Mercedes. Isabella approved of the final choice, the Archduchess Maria Cristina of Hapsburg, a second cousin of the Emperor of Austria, Franz Joseph. She also liked Prince Ludwig Ferdinand of Bavaria, who married her daughter Paz in 1883 and brought her to the Nymphenburg Palace near Munich. But the ex-queen often sighed over her rebellious daughter, Eulalia. The same year Paz married, Eulalia became the wife of the Duke of Montpensier's son, Antoine, mostly because she so admired the father.

In his 12 years on the throne, Alfonso proved to be a much better ruler than his mother. He died of tuberculosis in the latter part of 1885; six months later his young widow gave birth to a son, Alfonso XIII, and became regent for him. On Alfonso XII's death, one of Isabella's ex-ministers claimed that her abdication had never been formally publicized and that therefore she should resume her rights as queen. Putting aside old differences, she and her brother-in-law, Montpensier, began to conspire against the regency of Alfonso's widow. When the government heard of Isabella's plotting, she was ordered to return to Paris. But she was allowed back when her little grandson fell seriously ill. As he began to recover, she wrote to her daughter Paz, "It is a perfect miracle that he is alive."

Mostly she lived in Paris, remaining on distant terms with her husband, whom she met only on their birthdays. If their carriages passed on the street, the ex-queen would acknowledge him by lowering her head into her capacious chins, and the diminutive Francisco would stand up and bow stiffly.

All Isabella's children, whoever their fathers, looked like true Spanish Bourbons. Each grew up to be respected and loved, especially the Infanta Isabel, her eldest daughter. By contrast, Isabella's life continued to be disreputable. Constant partying went on at the Palais de Castille; its bespangled chatelaine dyed her hair many colors, finally ending up with a red wig. Her figure meanwhile grew increasingly porcine, but the lovers kept coming. Most unpopular with her retinue was a certain Haltmann, who acted as her secretary-general and treasurer. In 1890 she met Queen Victoria for the first time. The two women had lunch together in Biarritz, but the topic of Victoria's hand in Isabella's marriage plans long before never came up.

During the Spanish-American War Isabella's usually robust health began to fail, and she seldom left Paris for Madrid. In the spring of 1904, the ex–Empress Eugénie came visiting at the Palais de Castille. Although fighting influenza, Isabella insisted on standing in a draughty doorway to receive her guest and later to show her out. "Disowned monarchs," she declared, "are sensitive to want of attention."

After this exposure her cough worsened, and she grew weaker by the day. On April 9, surrounded by her daughters, Isabel, Eulalia, and Paz, she received extreme unction. To her son-in-law, Prince Ludwig, she spoke her last words: "Take my hand and pull my right arm as hard as you can! There is something very strange in my chest. I think I am going to faint." Nobody had expected her to apologize for a wayward life. In her own fashion, in and out of power, she had thoroughly enjoyed herself.

Victoria
Queen of the United Kingdom of Great Britain and Ireland, 1837–1901; Empress of India, 1876–1901

"Plump as a partridge" was how Edward, Duke of Kent, described the girl born to him and his German wife, Mary Victoria, on May 24, 1819, at Kensington Palace in London. Named Alexandrina Victoria, she clearly owed her existence to her late cousin, Charlotte.

Her grandfather, George III, was still King of England, but because his mind had been deranged by porphyria, his profligate son George ruled in his place. The Prince Regent's only child, Charlotte, wife of Leopold of Saxe-Coburg-Gotha, had died in childbirth in 1817; her baby was stillborn. The tragedy had driven Charlotte's bachelor uncles into hasty marriages in order to produce legitimate heirs. In hopes of supplying a replacement for Charlotte, Kent had given up his French mistress and married when he was past 50. His bride was Leopold's sister, widow of a German princeling. The same year that Victoria was born, the wives of Edward's two youngest brothers also gave them children.

When his daughter was eight months old, the heretofore robust Duke of Kent died suddenly of pneumonia, followed a few days later by George III. For a time the widowed duchess thought of returning to her familiar German setting, but her daughter's position as third in line to the throne made her decide to stay in England.

The new king, George IV, had never been fond of his brother Edward and was reluctant to contribute much to the duchess's income. Fortunately her brother, the dandified Leopold, who remained in England after Charlotte's death, provided financial assistance.

A high-spirited child, Victoria had as her constant companion her half sister, Fedora, her senior by ten years. A German governess, Louisa Lehzen, supervised both girls. Life in a grace-and-favor apartment at Kensington Palace stayed simple and quiet because the Duchess of Kent, carefully watching her budget and battling the animosity of her royal in-laws, admitted only a narrow circle.

The heir to the throne, Frederick, Duke of York, another of Victoria's uncles, died in 1827, a few days before George IV. Thereupon, William, Duke of Clarence, became king. Since all his ten children were illegitimate, Victoria was heiress presumptive.

The next year Leopold left for Brussels to sit on the throne of the newly created kingdom of the Belgians. In his place the Duchess of Kent began to rely more and more on John Conroy, the Irish comptroller of her household. He agreed with her that Victoria should be strictly guarded and kept fairly secluded at Kensington Palace.

Visiting tutors were brought in to augment Fraülein Lehzen's lessons, and the princess received a good grounding in English, French, and German. By herself she chose to read history prodigiously. She also took music and drawing lessons. In 1830 Fraülein Lehzen slipped into one of her pupil's history books a paper showing the family tree. Pondering her significance, Victoria made her famous declaration, "I will be good."

Bluff William IV was never a popular king, and his opposition to the Reform Bill of 1832 brought him new enemies. Openly now the Duchess of Kent, who had assumed an air of great self-importance, courted his political rivals. That summer she took Victoria on a tour through the English provinces that William derisively called a "progress." But it proved so successful that over the new few years the duchess set out on similar journeys. Breaking the solitude of Kensington Palace, the trips enthralled the little girl and led her to begin a journal which she conscientiously kept for the rest of her life.

After the gritty Conroy arranged for Fedora's marriage to a German prince, Victoria endured even more loneliness. As he became increasingly dictatorial, she developed a deep antipathy toward him, a feeling shared by Fraülein Lehzen. Because of Conroy, Victoria quarreled frequently with her mother.

In the summer of 1836, her handsome cousins, Ernest and Albert, the sons of Mary Victoria's eldest brother, arrived in London from Saxe-Coburg-Gotha on a visit planned by their Uncle Leopold. Their cousin Ferdinand had just married Maria da Glória, Queen of Portugal, who was exactly Victoria's age, 17. The English princess found the young men perfectly to her taste. Blue-eyed and fair-haired, but not especially pretty, she stood less than five feet tall. Still she radiated a high-mindedness that impressed the German guests.

By this time relations between King William and his sister-in-law had worsened almost to the breaking point. At a public birthday party in his honor, the king prayed that he would live nine months longer until Victoria gained her majority. If he did, her mother would never be regent. Conroy, who dreamed of glory under a regency, was infuriated and began to spread rumors of Victoria's emotional instability and need for guardians. The princess had indeed been the center of intrigue and conflict over the past four years, but the government knew that she was not unfit to rule.

King William received his wish. When Victoria celebrated her 18th birthday, he was still alive, but dying. So Conroy stepped up his campaign. When, however, he wrote that the princess "must be coerced," even the Duchess of Kent became apprehensive and asked him to desist.

On the morning of June 20, 1837, she awoke her daughter with the news that the king had died. In a dressing gown, with her hair flowing down her back, the small, regal figure walked alone into a room where the Archbishop of Canterbury and the Lord Chamberlain were waiting to kneel to her and kiss her hand. That day she met her first council. With great relish she wrote in her journal that she had undertaken her initial duties "quite alone." She had also just told her mother that they would no longer share a bedroom.

Her splendid coronation at Westminster one year later so exceeded all previous ceremonial displays that the Turkish ambassador complained, "All this for a woman!" But the diminutive queen impressed onlookers with her natural dignity and self-possession. About her worthiness to rule she suffered no doubt. The public showed an intense interest in her love of riding, novel reading, Italian opera, theater, and dogs, particularly spaniels.

As mistress of the newly completed Buckingham Palace and other royal residences, Victoria continued to shun her mother save in private. As her closest confidante she accepted Fraülein Lehzen, whom she created a baroness. Conroy stayed on, but the queen forbade him access to her private rooms. At the beginning of 1839, when Lady Flora Hastings, the Duchess of Kent's lady-in-waiting, appeared with a swollen stomach, Victoria quickly believed the rumor that the young woman was pregnant by Conroy. Gossip flew about and made Lady Flora's life miserable. A few months later she died, and the postmortem revealed a tumor. The whole affair damaged court and queen and caused Conroy to leave royal service.

On her accession, Victoria had found a mentor in her graying prime minister, the worldly and cynical Lord Melbourne, a Whig. Enchanted by the serious young girl, he gave her a thorough political education, filled her with social gossip, and became a constant companion; frequently they rode horseback together in Hyde Park. She was in fact so devoted to Melbourne that she refused to dismiss him when the Tories gained a majority in the House of Commons in 1839. But to Victoria's dismay, Sir Robert Peel was obliged to take Melbourne's post. Her reaction, known as the Bedchamber Plot, was to set aside the precedent which decreed dismissal of a queen regnant's ladies of the bedchamber once a government changed. Peel resigned, and Melbourne returned, to stay in power until 1841.

Since his nephews' visit to London in 1836, King Leopold had been working tirelessly to arrange a marriage between Albert and Victoria. When the

Victoria. National Portrait Gallery, London.

prince arrived again in the autumn of 1839, Victoria wrote in her journal, "It is with some emotion that I beheld Albert—who is *beautiful*." After an engagement of a few months, they were married in February 1840. Even as the wedding took place, the British were fighting in China; their victory in the Opium War (1839–1842) brought Hong Kong to a growing empire. Also in 1840 Upper and Lower Canada were united and given self-government.

Sweet domesticity would always be Victoria's chief interest. She did not enjoy pregnancy, but between 1840 and 1857 gave birth to Victoria, the Princess Royal (Empress of Germany); Albert Edward, the Prince of Wales (Edward VII); Alice (Grand Duchess of Hesse); Alfred (Duke of Edinburgh); Helena (Princess Christian of Schleswig-Holstein); Louise (Duchess of Argyll); Arthur (Duke of Connaught); Leopold (Duke of Albany); and Beatrice (Princess Henry of Battenberg). With motherhood, Victoria's feelings toward her own mother softened, and the Duchess of Kent delighted in being a fond grandmother.

The serious-minded and methodical Albert, so stiff and guarded in his public manner, did not intend to be a subordinate partner. Quickly the "darling dearest husband" dismissed the jealous Baroness Lehzen. But he himself remained under the influence of his former tutor, Baron Stockmar, the writer of voluminous memoranda. As Melbourne had done, Albert explained state business to her and emphasized the duties of a constitutional monarch. During the day they sat at adjoining tables and worked on household accounts as well. Politics aside, Albert turned his interests to the development of industry and the encouragement of science, becoming chief promoter of the Great Exhibition of 1851, the world's first international fair, designed to show the progress mankind had made in the 19th century as well as to promote the idea of peace and industry. But even as the Crystal Palace glimmered in its expanse of steel and airy elegance, journalists and writers, among them Charles Dickens, were pointing out some of the seamier aspects of industrialization.

The marriage was proving an unqualified success. "Politics (provided my Country is safe)," Victoria wrote, "must take only second place." A stern but loving father, Prince Albert also made himself a demanding teacher of his royal brood. Osborne House, built in the 1840s on the Isle of Wight, became a favorite retreat. The family always spent Christmas at Windsor Castle, which the prince filled with enormous, decorated fir trees according to an old German custom. Soon all proper English households had their holiday trees.

Queen Victoria grew to admire Peel when he came back into the government. But Albert distrusted his successor, Lord John Russell. On the other hand, he and the queen thoroughly approved of Lord Derby, who followed Russell. Frequently they tangled with Lord Palmerston, the longtime foreign secretary. In 1846 Victoria had been angry at his interference in the marriage plans she was making for Queen Isabella II of Spain. In 1851 she stormed over his approval of the coup d'etat which made Prince Louis Napoleon the

Emperor Napoleon III of France, and Palmerston resigned. Later, however, she became friendly with the emperor and his empress, Eugénie.

In the Crimean War, which broke out in 1853, Britain sided with the Turks against Russia. The British government's mismanagement of the campaigns resulted in the return of Palmerston as prime minister, the only man the nation would trust. Victoria found him more agreeable in this post and gave him credit for winning the war. Palmerston fell, however, and Lord John Russell enjoyed a brief second administration only to find Palmerston waiting in the wings once more. This time Victoria and Albert opposed his resurgence because they feared his and Russell's foreign policy. Nonetheless Palmerston's popularity won him his old post back.

During this period, Balmoral Castle, which would become another favorite family vacation spot, was being erected in the Scottish Highlands, largely following Albert's designs. At Balmoral, which suffered—Lord Clarendon said—from "tartanitis," the queen greatly admired the simple, blunt Highlanders.

In 1857 the Sepoy Mutiny resulted in the abolishment of the East India Company and the transfer of India to government control. At the same time the overworked Albert received the title of prince consort. The following year the 17-year-old Princess Royal, Victoria (Vicky), was married to Crown Prince Frederick of Prussia.

The most difficult of Victoria and Albert's offspring was Albert Edward ("Bertie"), the playboy Prince of Wales. Famous for her prudery, his mother always believed that "Bertie's fall" was at least partially responsible for his father's death. After writing "with a heavy heart" about rumors of his son's brief involvement with a free-spirited young actress, Albert received Bertie's confession and forgave him. Still he felt impelled to go to Cambridge in November 1861 to talk to the young man. He returned physically exhausted and ill. Typhoid was diagnosed, and in mid–December the prince consort died at the age of 42.

Overwhelmed by grief, Victoria secluded herself for a long time and never stopped wearing her widow's weeds. (Later in life, however, she habitually put on her head a little white cap with ruching and veil.) As she wrote in her journal, she was "a person who has to cling to someone in order to find peace and comfort."

The errant Bertie married lovely Princess Alexandra of Denmark in 1863. Because of family ties, Victoria turned her back on her daughter-in-law and supported Prussia in its war with Denmark over Schleswig (1864). Unlike many of her ministers, she had upheld Russia's brutal suppression of Poland's national uprising in 1863. During the Seven Weeks War between Prussia and Austria in 1866, she continued her pro–Prussian sympathies.

As often as possible she came to Balmoral, where she took her tea laced with whiskey rather than milk. There John Brown, the most colorful of the ghillies (hunting and fishing guides), became her "devoted attendant and friend." Visitors to the Scottish castle were almost shocked at his rough, curt ways with the queen. But Sir Henry Posonby, her indispensable secretary, and others saw Brown as immensely useful because better than anyone else he could persuade her to do things that might be against her will. She called him "the perfection of a servant" and added, "He thinks of everything."

In 1868 Victoria became especially close to her new prime minister, the flamboyant Benjamin Disraeli. Fondly she called him "Dizzy." She completely disliked his successor, William Gladstone, with whom Disraeli played a game of political-musical chairs for several years. Disraeli, who gibed that Gladstone treated her "like a public department," flattered her outrageously. The queen's relations with later prime ministers like Lord Rosebery and Lord Salisbury were often strained, but not as severely as with Gladstone. At times, in confrontations with him, the queen threatened to set aside her crown and sail to Australia.

Her second son Alfred had married a daughter of Czar Alexander II. When Marie Alexandrovna insisted on being addressed as "imperial highness" rather than "royal highness," Victoria declared her own wish to be called Empress of India. She was so proclaimed in 1876.

Helped by the Rothschild banking family, Disraeli had already bought the majority of the Suez Canal shares from the bankrupt Khedive of Egypt. The canal, opened in 1869, proved to be the world's most lucrative waterway. British intervention in an antiforeign uprising led to the establishment of a protectorate over Egypt in 1882, the year after Disraeli's death.

Along with the expanding empire, Victoria's reign was notable for deft adaptation to social and political change; notably reform of the land system, improved labor conditions, and expansion of the franchise. Education was made compulsory, local government democratized, and slavery abolished in the colonies. The achievements, to be sure, were made possible by her ministers. Victoria could only warn, advise, or encourage them, which she often did in a capricious and demanding way.

In literature, the field was crowded. Victoria's own favorite was Alfred, Lord Tennyson. She approved of women novelists, but abhorred "this mad folly of women's rights." Overwhelming change swirled about her, and before her death, men envisioned space travel.

The indefatigable Posonby died in 1895, and his son Frederick became assistant private secretary. The younger Posonby was instrumental in revealing the true origins of an Indian servant whom the queen made her Indian secretary or Munshi. Bearded and turbaned, Munshi often offered his arm to the little old woman, who usually hobbled on a cane. He had claimed to be the son of a surgeon general in the Indian Army, but Posonby declared that he was a low-caste Hindu. Finally the queen-empress agreed to have him "put in his proper place."

Victoria Regina celebrated her Golden Jubilee in 1887, her Diamond Jubilee, with its special imperial flavor, ten years later. A great many royal and serene highnesses (whom she called "the royal mob") had to be accommodated at Buckingham Palace and Windsor Castle. Royal prestige had never been higher. One of her grandsons was Emperor of Germany, one of her grand-daughters the Empress of Russia. Other grandchildren would occupy the thrones of Norway, Greece, and Spain.

In 1897 six miles of London streets were bedecked with flowers, and the queen, a small, dumpy figure in elaborate black moire and bonnet with ostrich feathers, acknowledged the cheers as she rode in an open carriage at the end of a long procession of carriages of state, mounted cavalry, and foot soldiers in the varied uniforms of Britain's far-flung empire—Canada, India, Australia, Trinidad, Borneo, Jamaica, Nigeria, Hong Kong, Singapore, and Sierra Leone. (Soon thereafter Britain added South Africa to that empire upon the successful conclusion of the Boer War.) She was at the height of her popularity, an endur-ing symbol of British power. That evening the 78-year-old queen wrote in her journal, "No one, I believe, has met with such an ovation as was given to me . . . the crowds were quite indescribable and their enthusiasm truly marvelous and deeply touching. The cheering was quite deafening, and every face seemed to be filled with much joy."

Having outlived three of her children, the queen died at Osborne House on January 22, 1901. An observer said that her last moments "were like a great three-decker ship sinking. She kept on rallying and then sinking." Like Elizabeth I, she gave her name to an age.

Maria Cristina (2)
Regent of Spain, 1886–1902

Isabella II's daughter-in-law became queen regent in 1886 for her tiny son, Alfonso XIII. The second Maria Cristina was as unlike the former queen as could be: slender, dignified, erudite, and virtuous. Lacking wit and sparkle, she also seemed far different from the first Maria Cristina. She looked like a true Hapsburg with the firm family jaw and the confident regality of the Austrian court.

Born at Gross Seelowitz in Moravia on July 21, 1858, she was the daughter of Archduke Karl Ludwig Ferdinand and the exceptionally beautiful Archduchess Elizabeth. Maria Cristina grew up with three brothers, Frederick, Karl Stephan, and Eugen Ferdinand, all close to her in age. Her only sister, Eleanor, had died in infancy. The Archduke Karl was a cousin of Emperor Franz Joseph, and Maria Cristina learned to pay exemplary attention to court ceremonies and rigorous protocol.

This highly eligible Catholic princess easily caught the attention of former Queen Isabella's widowed daughter, Isabel, who was looking for a second wife for her brother, Alfonso XII. Lovable, extremely pious, and always respected, she had acted as the king's hostess before and during his first marriage. In the summer of 1879 she arranged for the young man and woman to come to the resort of Arachon near Bordeaux. They did not meet as complete strangers, having become acquainted at court when Alfonso was a student in Vienna.

At Arachon, Alfonso did not cut a dashing figure. He carried his arm in a sling after a carriage accident, and he was prone to moods of dejection after the recent deaths of his wife Mercedes and his sister Pilar. Maria Cristina's warm sympathy and skillful piano playing soothed his nerves, but the Spanish king did not fall in love. His heart still belonged to Mercedes although he was not blind to the charm of the Archduchess Elizabeth, who chaperoned her daughter. As he wrote to one of his sisters, "The mother attracts me enormously, but it is the daughter whom I have to marry."

Alfonso knew his duty, and within a week he and Maria Cristina developed sufficient closeness to become engaged. Their wedding followed in

Maria Cristina (2). Print Collection, Newark Public Library, Newark, N.J.

November. Having inherited some of his mother's sensuality, the bridegroom did not wait long to find distractions beyond his bedchamber. The small, handsome king's infidelity deeply wounded Maria Cristina, who had fallen deeply in love. Usually she kept her emotions under tight control. But one day she did slap a courtier as he prepared to introduce his sovereign to an attractive young singer.

The new queen became the mother of two daughters, Mercedes in 1880, and Maria Teresa in 1882. She was again pregnant in November 1885 when Alfonso showed alarming signs of the tuberculosis that had killed his sister Pilar. To regain his strength he settled briefly at a palace on the outskirts of Madrid. When his mother, his wife, and his aunt, the Duchess of Montpensier, visited him one afternoon, he insisted on arising from bed and driving out with them in an open cabriolet. The mountain air proved too cold and raw for him, and two days later his legs would not support him. Death came quickly. Briefly Mercedes was heiress apparent, but on a May morning in 1886 a 21-gun salute resounded through Madrid for a posthumous heir, King Alfonso XIII.

On Alfonso XII's death, various factions had begun struggling for control of the regency, supporters of his sister Isabel putting her name forward and relatives of the long dead Carlota, the first Maria Cristina's sister, setting forth their claims. Even Maria Cristina's mother-in-law had plotted with the Duke of Montpensier to regain her throne.

A serious illness of the baby king reunited the family which finally accepted Maria Cristina as regent. Even with her new responsibility, she remained a careful mother, spending much time with her children. At San Sebastian she built a holiday castle called Miramar so that an open-air regimen and much exposure to salt water could improve Alfonso's health.

As had been the practice during her husband's reign, a prearranged transfer of power by the leaders of the conservative and liberal parties insured domestic calm. Sometimes, however, Maria Cristina complained that this policy led to inertia. Meanwhile she carefully saved her money and turned it over to an Austrian uncle for prudent investment.

Within a few years troubles overseas beset her. A civil war erupted in the Spanish island of Cuba and brutally, though unsuccessfully, the mother country tried to stamp out the rebellion. The United States, which supported the rebels, warned the Madrid government that unless more civilized methods were used, it would intervene. President Grover Cleveland also told Maria Cristina she must make concessions to the Cubans, but she felt offering any would indicate weakness on her part.

In 1898 President William McKinley sent the United States cruiser *Maine* to Cuba to protect Americans on the island. On February 15 it exploded and blew up in Havana harbor, killing 270 sailors on board. Nobody ever pinpointed the exact cause, but Americans clamored for war. Although Spain agreed to all of McKinley's demands, he urged American intervention. With a disclaimer of any intention of annexing Cuba, Congress declared war in April.

The United States fleet blockaded Havana at once and forced Admiral Cervira to put out to sea where his fleet was destroyed. Further foreshadowing the war's outcome, Admiral George Dewey then demolished the Spanish squadron in Manila Bay. American troops invaded Cuba and at El Caney and San Juan Hill soundly whipped Spanish forces there. In less than three months the defeat had been swift and terrible, and Maria Cristina had no choice but to sign the humiliating Treaty of Paris in late 1898. Spain granted Cuba its independence and ceded Puerto Rico, Guam, and the Philippines to the United States, receiving $20,000,000 for them. Blame fell on the queen regent, who with her customary self-control accepted responsibility.

In her unpopularity the Carlists, still loyal to their dream of setting a Carlist pretender on the throne of Spain and thereby achieving absolute autocracy, saw their chance. Over the past 60 years they had met defeat in many uprisings, but now the time seemed especially opportune. By letter the Carlist pretender, Don Carlos VII, began conspiring with General Valeriano Weyler, the "butcher" of Cuba, to foment a rebellion. But Don Carlos's formidable second wife, the Princess Bertha de Rohan, prevented a meeting between the two men. The new Carlist war began without Don Carlos, but in the absence of an effective leader, it quickly ended.

On the heels of this war, Maria Cristina faced new problems with the announcement of the forthcoming marriage of her older daughter Mercedes to Prince Charles of Bourbon. The father, the Count of Caserta, had once been a general in the Carlist army. Spaniards immediately began asking why the son of a notorious Carlist leader should be taken into the royal family just as a Carlist revolt had been quashed.

The Cortes debated the engagement, Jesuits were attacked, students demonstrated. Soon open revolt flared in Madrid, Seville, and Granada. But Maria Cristina refused to cancel the marriage plans. On the wedding day the palace was barricaded, and troops were put on alert throughout Madrid. Recognizing a fait accompli, the protesters withdrew.

Deciding she would give advice if asked but would never interfere in politics, Maria Cristina gracefully stepped down as regent when Alfonso XIII assumed his full rights as king on his 16th birthday in 1902. His mother's careful regimen had made him a handsome boy bursting with good health and energy. He was an avid sportsman and hunter, but carried not a trace of her cultural and intellectual interests.

Shortly afterwards, Maria Cristina's daughter Mercedes died in childbirth, leaving a son, who was heir to the throne until Alfonso had a wife and children. Spain did not wait long for the king's wedding. In May 1906 he married Victoria Eugenia (Ena), daughter of the Prince and Princess of Battenberg. After the ceremony a bomb was thrown at the royal coach carrying the bride and bridegroom. Although men and horses lay scattered across the road, Alfonso and Ena were somehow spared.

The king never enjoyed his mother's luck in seeing politicians of opposing parties regularly exchange office. In the first four years he went through 14 ministerial crises. As clearly defined parties began breaking up into little groups, the king assumed command during each change of government and consequently began acting like an autocratic Carlist.

Not only defeat abroad but poverty at home caused unrest. Anarchists and union leaders aligned themselves to protest the hardships of the Spanish lower classes. An uprising led by an anarchist named Francisco Ferrer was put down in Barcelona in 1909, but the revolutionary movement kept growing as bombs proliferated. Five attempts were made against Alfonso's life.

Meanwhile Maria Cristina had become a grandmother. Queen Ena gave Alfonso a son in 1907. In time she would produce three more sons and two daughters. Unfortunately through her mother's mother, Queen Victoria, she was a carrier of hemophilia. Two boys suffered from the disease; another was a deaf mute. The fourth, Juan, became the father of the present King of Spain, Juan Carlos.

When World War I broke out, the queen mother and the queen had relatives on opposite sides but never discussed their sympathies. Since Spain remained neutral, Alfonso was free to help prisoners of war and to locate soldiers missing in action. Maria Cristina took particular pride in his humanitarian efforts.

In 1912 Spain had established a protectorate over part of Morocco. Nine years later the Riffian tribes inflicted a crushing defeat on the king's troops, and blame was heaped on him as it had been on his mother during the Spanish-American War. He and his government were also considered liable for the troubles of farmers and industrial workers. Feelings ran so high that Alfonso agreed to let General Miguel Primo de Rivera make himself dictator after a bloodless revolution. On declaring martial law, Rivera conveniently postponed any return to constitutional government. During his Directory, Spain with French help gained control over Morocco once more, and Alfonso paid a conqueror's visit.

During all those turbulent years of her son's reign, Maria Cristina, spry, vigorous, and still somewhat starchy in public, lived in complete harmony with him and his family. The nation was shocked when she died suddenly on February 6, 1929, of angina pectoris. The evening before, she had attended a film showing in the palace and had looked forward to helping Queen Ena receive Denmark's King Christian X and Queen Alexandrine in the morning.

One year later Alfonso and the army forced Rivera out. In 1931 elections confirmed the popular demand for a republican government. Alfonso refused to abdicate, but he and his family left Spain for good. Five years later a civil war erupted that turned out to be far bloodier than the Carlist wars of the 19th century.

It would have been difficult for Maria Cristina to accept her son's departure. "I believe he will do," she once said. On his way out of the Palacio Real, it was reported, Alfonso saluted her portrait. For 50 years, in her adopted land, Maria Cristina had carried out her duties with patience and great dignity.

Wilhelmina
Queen of the Netherlands, 1890–1948

On August 31, 1880, the 21-year-old queen consort in the Netherlands, the former Princess Emma of Waldeck-Pyrmont, bore her 62-year-old husband, Willem III, a girl they named Wilhelmina. Four years later the last of Willem's three sons by his first wife died. Since none had left children, the little Princess of Orange-Nassau became heiress presumptive. Hers would be a memorable reign.

Like Victoria some 60 years before, she was brought up in comparative solitude. But she had sympathetic nurses of whom she later wrote: "I always enjoyed playing with these companions and never felt the absence of other children to play with—on the contrary, I was happy to be an only child and to have my parents all to myself."

In 1884 an English governess, Miss Winter, came to the palace of Het Loo near Appeldoorn, where Wilhelmina spent her early childhood. Miss Winter was keenly aware of her assigned task to mold the girl's character and to make her into "a bold and noble woman, unflinching, and strong."

When the princess was eight, about the time her father became seriously ill, she received her first lessons in Dutch history. The kingdom she would soon inherit was comparatively new. In 1815 after Napoleon's downfall, the Congress of Vienna had united Belgium and the Netherlands under a Dutch king, Wilhelmina's great-grandfather, Willem I, son of the last stadtholder. He was also named Grand Duke of Luxembourg. In 1830, however, the Belgians seceded and created a separate kingdom, choosing as king Leopold of Saxe-Coburg-Gotha, the uncle of Britain's Princess Victoria. The first Willem was succeeded by his son, Willem II, the "Young Frog," who in turn was followed by his son, Willem III.

The third Willem had ruled almost 50 years when he died in 1890 and was succeeded by his 10-year-old daughter. Until Wilhelmina came of age, Queen Mother Emma served as regent. But citing the Salic law, the Grand Duchy of Luxembourg refused to accept a female ruler.

Life changed markedly for the young queen after her father's death. She was moved to Huis ten Bosch Palace in The Hague with more restrictions on her freedom. Her autobiography, written more than half a century later, pictures the new situation:

> Stories of earlier times have given me the impression that under Father there was a period when a clear distinction was made between official and private life; when one was at liberty to arrange one's private life as one liked. In my time things were different; I could only be an ordinary human being when I was alone with Mother. Court etiquette required us to lead a life that was permanently semiofficial; that is to say, we had to be prepared at any time to step into rigid formality.

To describe her hemmed-in environment, the young princess began using the word "cage." At 10 she finally felt the absence of playmates her own age. The autobiography notes: "Normal companionship with children was unthinkable in the cage. I never knew it and had little or no opportunity to make friends. I have hardly any friends from my childhood, only acquaintances." Those children Queen Mother Emma did invite to the palace "played and romped" in the drawing rooms, which had none of the qualities of a home.

In 1892 mother and daughter went to Saxe-Weimar for the golden wedding of Willem III's sister Sophie and her husband, Grand Duke Karl. During the festivities Wilhelmina first saw her future husband, Duke Heinrich, the strapping, 16-year-old, youngest son of Friedrich Franz II, the Grand Duke of Mecklenburg-Schwerin.

Several tutors came to the palace, but the severe English governess remained. That year Wilhelmina took what was for her a decisive step. She refused to accept Miss Winter's moral authority and turned increasingly to her mother. Miss Winter threatened to leave but agreed to stay until Wilhelmina was confirmed in 1896. From then on the young queen's religious faith grew rapidly, and she would constantly speak of "God's Guidance" in her life.

To further her daughter's education, Queen Dowager Emma took her to London to meet Queen Victoria, and to Vienna, Paris, and Florence. At 18 Wilhelmina was ready to assume her official duties. Because two centuries of republican rule preceded the monarchy, the Dutch have never crowned a monarch, preferring to inaugurate their king or queen. So, with her crown remaining on a table beside her, young Wilhelmina was inaugurated on September 6, 1890, and exuberantly received.

Like Victoria, she was determined to be a role model. "You cannot always be an example, but it is a 'must' that you are much more guilty than anybody else if at any time you are not.... You must [try to] be an example at all times as long as you live. Because I took this seriously, my life has been so different."

The new queen was instrumental in offering Huis ten Bosch Palace in The Hague as the seat of the International Peace Conference, called by the Russian czar, Nicholas II, in 1899. (A second peace conference was held there in 1907.) During the Boer War, when the Dutch openly sympathized with their former countrymen in South Africa, Wilhelmina stood ready to mediate between the Boers and the British but was turned down. Still, when a Dutch warship set out on its homeward journey from the Netherlands East Indies, the queen wired its commander to bring Paul Kruger, the president of Transvaal, safely through the British naval blockade. She was the only monarch in Europe who dared receive him.

In 1900, attending the wedding of her youngest aunt in Germany, Wilhelmina was afraid that somebody would place the bridal wreath on her head to designate her as the next bride. Although the custom was not observed on that occasion, she had a strong premonition she would be the first among the girl guests to marry. From the family gathering she and her mother moved on to Schwarzburg-Rudolstadt in Thuringia to enjoy the mountain air. During their visit Duke Heinrich showed up for a short stay with his grandmother, the Princess of Schwarzburg, at the Schwarzburg castle. It was a fine opportunity to renew an acquaintance begun eight years earlier at Weimar.

After the fresh-faced Dutch queen returned home, Heinrich requested a further meeting in Hesse. There he proposed and was accepted. At 26 Duke Heinrich was a cavalry officer, fond of hardy outdoor life and interested in forestry. Wilhelmina described him as kind and open and always willing to help: "Simplicity was his first characteristic. He was simple in his manner, in his tastes, in his character." She was determined that he should be allowed to lead the life he wanted, which meant a great deal of driving four-in-hands. For their wedding, celebrated in great splendor at The Hague, Duke Heinrich was created a general and named Prince Hendrik of the Netherlands.

During the ceremony, a foreign ambassador remarked: "The Prince Consort is to be pitied. He gets two mothers-in-law. One, Queen-Dowager Emma, is the sweetest mother-in-law one could wish for. But the other is a truly jealous mother-in-law. It is the Dutch people, who will watch him scrupulously and will never forgive him if he does not make [Wilhelmina] happy."

The first years of their marriage passed smoothly, but the young wife felt a certain distance between her husband and her subjects. Then in 1907 Prince Hendrik won the wholehearted respect and admiration of the Dutch people during a maritime disaster. After a ship ran aground on the pier off the Hook of Holland and broke in two, he rushed there to stand as chief inspiration behind the rescue work. When the largely figurehead post of president of the Netherlands Red Cross fell vacant, Wilhelmina appointed him. She herself had taken on extra tasks by helping the families of the workers at Het Loo Palace, which the queen mother had presented to the young couple.

Wilhelmina had suffered three miscarriages since her marriage. Finally in 1909, to national rejoicing, she gave birth to a daughter. Juliana would be her only child, and the ties between mother and daughter became extremely close.

In the years before World War I, the Netherlands was confronted with labor unrest and demands for social reforms, which included a revision of the suffrage law so that all males could have the right to rule. The queen's own inclinations were conservative, but as a constitutional sovereign she remained above politics. She was determined to keep her strong commitment to parliamentary institutions and government. She possessed the power of veto, but during her long reign she never used it.

During the war, the Netherlands remained neutral; nonetheless the royal couple had new duties. In his work with the Red Cross, Prince Hendrik helped to set up a postal service for prisoners of war and to arrange the transport of wounded prisoners through the Netherlands. Usually on horseback, Wilhelmina paid frequent visits to her troops, whose morale was tested by having to stand at arms almost constantly.

Early in 1916, new worries beset her. Heavy storms caused the dikes of the Zuyder Zee to collapse and overflow along the western shores, flooding the province of North Holland. Through the hectic weeks that followed, husband and wife divided their work in the distressed areas.

Severe food shortages triggered demonstrations in Rotterdam, Amsterdam, and other cities, and in 1918 the Social Democratic Workers' Party called for revolution. But its parliamentary leader, Pieter Troelstra, was quickly disavowed by other party members. The Protestant queen also found unexpected support from Dutch Catholics. Nonetheless, the conservative government responded to the radicals' dissatisfaction by legislating universal manhood suffrage, enacting labor relations laws, and providing social security.

In the fateful November of 1918, Wilhelmina learned that Kaiser Wilhelm had crossed the Dutch frontier. The Netherlands government gave him a place of refuge at Doorn but demanded he promise to abstain from all political activity. After his abdication, the Dutch queen invited the German empress to join her husband. Allied governments pressed for the kaiser's extradition, but Wilhelmina and her government refused to release him, causing a sensation in the world press.

After the war, Wilhelmina detected a new spirit of the times and declared that there would be no more ostentation at the stiff and usually unsmiling court. The government emphasized social progress, and she frequently dedicated a new school or hospital. Meanwhile she saw her daughter, a frequent traveling companion, enrolled at the University of Leiden.

As her country plunged into the Great Depression and unemployment rose alarmingly, Wilhelmina also had to face the threat of a Dutch Nazi movement called the NSB. Then in 1934 she suffered two great bereavements. Her beloved mother died, followed some weeks later by Prince Hendrik. Keeping an old promise, she gave him a "white funeral." (All mourners were dressed in white.) Three years later, however, she could rejoice at Juliana's marriage to the charming Prince Bernhard zur Lippe-Biesterfeld.

Wilhelmina. The Embassy of the Netherlands, Washington, D.C.

When World War II erupted in 1939, Wilhelmina kept her country in a state of neutrality, but it leaned toward the British. On May 10, 1940, Nazi troops invaded the Netherlands, and two days later, on the queen's orders, Princess Juliana, Prince Bernhard, and their baby daughters, Beatrix and Irene, escaped to England, carrying the crown jewels. On May 13, Wilhelmina was warned to leave The Hague. At the Hook of Holland she boarded a British destroyer, intending to sail either to Flushing or Zeeland Flanders, where the military situation was not so dangerous. But the English commander told her his ship could sail only for his home country. Within five days of the Nazi invasion, the rugged Dutch resistance collapsed.

Once in London, the Dutch queen issued a proclamation transferring the seat of government. As heavy air raids threatened, she decided that her daughter and grandchildren must be taken to a country far removed from the theater of war. She herself remained in London to stand as the symbol and conscience of Dutch resistance.

As Juliana and her daughters went on to Canada, Wilhelmina and Prince Bernhard settled in at a house in Eaton Square. The German-born Bernhard, so eager to prove his Dutch patriotism, volunteered as liaison officer to the British armed forces. Dutch pilots began to fight in Allied air units, and the Dutch navy and merchant marine soon carried war supplies and food from around the world to England and other Allies. In the Dutch underground, determined men and women continued to carry on their resistance.

Soon the basement of the Eaton Square house had to be converted into an air raid shelter. While the work was being completed, the queen often stayed at the large shelter at Claridge's Hotel. When the air raids worsened, she and Bernhard moved to a country house in Stubbings, an hour's drive from London. She also leased a new London house in Chester Square.

For the most part Wilhelmina lived quietly, but her home was always open to men and women who had escaped from the Netherlands. In her parlor she poured tea for them, offered cigarettes, and listened with deep interest to their stories. Well aware of her continuing symbolic role, she took to wearing a white marguerite, the national flower of the Netherlands. Most important to her were the radio broadcasts over Radio Orange to her people, who listened in secrecy. Her voice, one Dutchman said, was "a light penetrating the darkness."

In 1942, longing to see her daughter and grandchildren, Wilhelmina flew to Canada for a reunion. Later Juliana rented a house in Lee, Massachusetts, to serve as a base while the queen traveled about on the eastern coast to demonstrate Dutch tenacity. A weekend visit at Hyde Park, New York, with President and Mrs. Franklin D. Roosevelt was followed by receptions in New York City, Boston, and Albany. In Washington, D.C., she addressed both houses of Congress, her appearance marking the first time in American history that a sovereign ruler had been invited to speak to a joint session. President Roosevelt took her on a tour of Mount Vernon and presented a destroyer to the Dutch navy. Before returning to London, Wilhelmina also visited the large Dutch colony in Montreal. Then came news that the Japanese had seized the Netherlands East Indies (Indonesia).

From now on there was endless waiting. Wilhelmina knew that her primary duty was to maintain friendly relations with Allied leaders and with different heads of state who lived in exile in London. She recalled in her autobiography: "Needless to say, this life of expectation, of keeping ready, year after year, was not an easy one. Moreover, I was not told any military secrets and therefore could follow the development of the great day only from a distance."

Early in June 1943 Wilhelmina crossed the Atlantic again to be present for the christening of her third granddaughter, Margriet, born in January and named for the marguerite. Once more the queen spent a weekend at Hyde Park with her friends, the Roosevelts.

By the next year she had moved from Stubbings to a little country place near South Mimms. There one February night an aircraft dropped a bomb, which exploded only a yard and a half from the house. Two sentries were killed, and Wilhelmina's entourage suffered from shock. As a sergeant cried "Where is the queen?" a courageous Wilhelmina answered through gas, smoke, and flames: "I am all right."

She was evacuated to Stubbings, which again seemed too close for comfort to the industrial pollution of Slough. Seeking to improve her health in cleaner air, the queen found another house, Laneswood near Reading. After D-Day in June 1944 she knew it was time to make plans for her country following its liberation.

As Allied troops approached the Dutch frontier in the autumn of 1944, Wilhelmina suggested to her minister for general war affairs that the resistance men in the Netherlands be given the status of combatants under their own commander. For that post she selected her son-in-law, Bernhard. Meanwhile she asked Juliana to fly to England from Canada.

On March 14, 1945, Queen Wilhelmina crossed the frontier between Belgium and the Netherlands. Then for ten days she traveled through villages and towns, accompanied only by two officers and a few troops. She was buoyed by her enthusiastic reception but returned to London exhausted.

News came on May 4 of the German capitulation, and the royal family went home. Although their conduct during the war years had gained the monarchy fresh strength and respect, Wilhelmina, Juliana, and Bernhard were heartsick at the war toll. In retreat the Nazis had blown up dikes to flood acres of farmland; they had destroyed thousands of homes and two-fifths of the factories. Thousands of persons, including the teenaged Anne Frank, had died in concentration camps. The challenge of reconstruction was formidable, but Wilhelmina and her government met it head on.

The war had convinced the Dutch to abandon their stance of neutrality, and quickly the Netherlands became a charter member of the United Nations. But the great Dutch colonial empire, source of much Dutch prosperity, had begun to crumble. For the next few years Indonesians fought the Dutch for the independence of the Netherlands East Indies. Wilhelmina, always astute in business affairs, was still described as the world's wealthiest woman with enormous land holdings, costly paintings, family jewels, and stocks in corporations like Royal Dutch Shell.

She had always been a robust figure; now she realized that her health was deteriorating. Juliana had given Wilhelmina a fourth granddaughter, Maria Christina, in February 1947. From October to December that year and again in May 1948 she acted as regent. Then Wilhelmina announced that she would abdicate after the observance of her Golden Jubilee. Her health and age were important factors in her decision; another was her wish to have her daughter gain the throne "at an early age."

The jubilee was celebrated on August 31, 1948, and on September 4 Wilhelmina signed an abdication document transferring her authority to Juliana. Smiling broadly, she stood on the balcony of Dam Palace in Amsterdam and greeted her daughter and her people with a cheer, "Long live the queen!"

Modestly insisting that she be titled only Princess of the Netherlands, she retired to her favorite palace, Het Loo, where she looked for "inner peace" and where later she wrote her autobiography, *Lonely but Not Alone.* Painting, which had long been a relaxing hobby, also occupied her time. In 1953 she emerged from relative seclusion to join Juliana in visiting the victims of a flood disaster.

Royally dignified to the end, much loved, and well satisfied that her daughter's record of strong leadership in many ways matched her own, she died on November 28, 1962. To prove her high international standing, representatives of every European state attended her elaborate "white funeral."

Marie-Adélaïde
Grand Duchess of Luxembourg, 1912–1919

Even before Marie-Adélaïde was born, events of the year 1890 helped determine her destiny. Willem III, King of the Netherlands and Grand Duke of Luxembourg, died and left his throne to his young daughter, Wilhelmina. But Luxembourg, independent since 1867 although tied to the Dutch monarchy since 1815, would not accept a female ruler. Since Willem had been the last male heir of the junior branch of the House of Nassau, the little country turned to the senior branch and the septuagenarian Adolphe, who had reigned over the German duchy of Nassau until Prussia absorbed it in 1866. By the end of 1890 he returned from exile and became Grand Duke.

Adolphe's son, the future William IV, was serving as lieutenant and chief administrator of the grand duchy when his wife, Marie-Anne of Braganza, gave birth to their first child, Marie-Adélaïde, on June 14, 1894, at the castle of Colmar-Berg. The baby's maternal grandfather was the long-deceased Miguel, who had usurped the Portuguese throne of his niece, Maria da Glória, only to be overthrown by her angry father, Dom Pedro.

Within eight years Marie-Adélaïde had five sisters, Charlotte, born 1896; Hilda, 1898; Antonia, 1899; Elizabeth 1901; and Sophia, 1902. By the time of his last daughter's birth, William of Nassau showed signs of the creeping paralysis that shadowed his last ten years, and his condition had worsened when he succeeded his father in 1905.

In 1907, having given up all hope of producing a son, he promulgated a family statute that voided the Salic law and allowed him to proclaim his eldest daughter heiress apparent. After submission to the Luxembourg Chamber of Deputies, the statute became law. By the next year William was so ill that his wife assumed the regency. Marie-Anne, however, showed such exclusive devotion to her husband that she grew increasingly indifferent to affairs of state and largely entrusted her daughters to ladies-in-waiting or governesses at Colmar-Berg and at Hohenburg, the family residence in Upper Bavaria, outside the grand duchy. Generally the pretty girls were secluded from other children.

Their father's long illness hung heavily over their childhood; their world seemed composed entirely of relatives, especially a great bevy of constantly visiting aunts. Still by themselves, they enjoyed such simple pleasures as billiards, charades, hide and seek, pillow fights, and practical jokes. Once in a while, under careful supervision, the girls played with the children of foresters and gardeners on the estates. Each Christmas, dressed in identical suits and round, felt hats, they walked behind a donkey cart heaped with packages and small trees for the poor.

The adolescent Marie-Adélaïde was often timid, sometimes obstinate and even sullen, but she found a welcome outlet in nature, taking long walks by herself to fill her arms with wild flowers. In the park at Hohenburg, she acquired a little hut as her private property, and she spent hours there with her collections of butterflies, moths, lizards, beetles, and snails. One winter she kept a butterfly in her room, feeding it with sugar water. For a time she tended three bears, later donated to the Munich zoo.

In 1911 she accompanied her mother and sister Charlotte to the wedding of Marie-Anne's niece, Zita of Bourbon-Parma, to Franz Joseph's nephew, Karl, who five years later became the last Austro-Hungarian emperor. Her mother subsequently divulged that on the return journey from Schwarzau Castle, Marie-Adélaïde declared she would never marry and had no wish to reign. Heretofore she had never shown any great religious faith, but the wedding festivities made her think of becoming a bride of the church, a nun.

Back at Colmar-Berg she found in place a new lady-in-waiting, a few years her senior. The sprightly Countess Anna Monteglas turned out to be an ideal companion for the shy, young girl, so afraid of bestowing affection.

In February 1912 Grand Duke William IV died, completely paralyzed. His widow continued to hold the regency until June 18, when her 18-year-old daughter took over. Then on June 18 Marie-Adélaïde, willowy and graceful, entered the capital to the sounds of bells and cannons. Her subjects received her enthusiastically; she was clever, dignified, and beautiful, with intense, dark-blue eyes and naturally curly, golden-brown hair. Her most fervent admirers compared her long neck and full-lipped mouth to those of a Botticelli Madonna.

After taking the oath to uphold the constitution, Marie-Adélaïde gave an emotional speech, which ended, "Today the keeping of the flag is entrusted to a young girl. I will hold it high and firmly, and by God's help I will fight for its honor. A daughter of Nassau as well as of my forefathers, I shall be faithful to the motto of our old house, *je maintiendrai!*"

On beginning her reign, she showed increasing piety, going to church on foot early in the morning and returning by afternoon, no matter what the weather. Since family tradition maintained that sons should be brought up in

Marie-Adélaïde. Archives Marcel Schroeder, Luxembourg.

their fathers' religion, daughters in that of their mothers, she honored the Braganza ties to Catholicism.

Marie-Adélaïde also inherited Paul Eyschen, the venerable Minister of State, who had loyally served her father. With the same devotion he now shepherded his young ruler. In the spring of 1913 he encouraged Marie-Adélaïde to take the classic Italian journey. Traveling as the Countess Reinau and accompanied by Countess Anna, a Baron Brandis, and several servants, she visited Venice, Florence, Rome, Sorrento, Naples, and Paestum. At the crater of Vesuvius, Baron Brandis had to pull his adventurous sovereign back by the skirts to keep her from going too close.

Shortly after her return, Marie-Adélaïde paid her first official visit to the

Grand Duchy of Baden, whose Grand Duke Friedrich was married to her Aunt Hilda. Four days after her 19th birthday the grand duchess appeared officially at the Belgian court and six months later at the court of Wilhelmina, Queen of the Netherlands. Abroad or at home in Luxembourg, she surprised onlookers with her mixture of shyness and royal pride. More than ever, in her palely shining gowns (dubbed "moonbeam"), she looked radiantly beautiful. But she remained aloof in matters of love.

For all their delicate appearance, the six sisters were athletic and healthy, and Luxembourgers delighted in watching them take almost daily horseback rides toward Bambusch Forest. Although devoted to her family, Marie-Adélaïde was temperamentally unable to show much open affection for her mother and sisters. Still she often cradled in her arms the children she visited in a crèche under her protection.

Political troubles began almost at once. The so-called Academic Law of 1912, resisted by the ecclesiastical powers, proposed to dilute religious instruction in the schools. Liberals and socialists, first elected to the Chamber of Deputies in 1908, criticized Marie-Adélaïde when she procrastinated in ratifying this law. Even Eyschen told her she had erred. By the time she finally signed the document, she was completely alienated from politicians of the left.

Marie-Adélaïde had ruled for just two years when World War I broke out. She happened to be at the parish church of Colmar-Berg when news arrived that the Germans had invaded Luxembourg. Rising from prayer, she hurried by motorcar to the palace in Luxembourg City to consult her ministers. Later a legend arose that she had stood on a viaduct near the frontier and forbidden the Germans to pass.

In recognizing an independent Luxembourg in 1867, the Treaty of London had imposed an unarmed neutrality on the country. Therefore Marie-Adélaïde and her government could take no military measures. They could only protest the violation of their neutrality and notify the powers which had signed the treaty.

No country rushed to Luxembourg's aid. Kaiser Wilhelm II, his son, Crown Prince Friedrich, and their staff installed themselves in the country for a month, and soon it became a large camp for troops marching into France and Belgium. Turning her attention elsewhere, Marie-Adélaïde directed the Luxembourg Red Cross, and in her long white nurse's smock stood ready for any task. Despite their rank, her mother and sisters joined her in making beds, scrubbing floors, and carrying food to hospital patients.

Eyschen's death in 1915 led to fresh political conflicts. Radicals objected to Marie-Adélaïde's appointment of Hubert Loutsch as prime minister. Always insisting on her royal prerogative, she decided to appeal to the nation, and in the December elections the left lost heavily. But bickering continued, and in February 1916 the Loutsch ministry was replaced by that of Thorn-Walter.

Toward the end of 1916 Marie-Adélaïde left her duchy to go to Königstein near Frankfurt to sit a few days at the bedside of her grandfather's second wife, Adelheid Marie, a beloved figure from her childhood. One month later she returned for the old grand duchess's funeral. The two visits inspired the politicians of the left to plaster her with the catchword "pro-German" and to revive charges that in 1914 she had received Kaiser Wilhelm for tea and supper. Taunts multiplied when she announced the engagement of her sister Antonia to a German prince. The Allies also accused the grand duchess of being partial to Germany.

The winter of 1917-1918 proved particularly distressing. German coal arrived in insufficient amounts, and American grain became scarce; for a time the government ordered rationing. Meanwhile war planes constantly droned overhead, terrifying the hungry Luxembourgers, many of whose sons died fighting with the Allies.

In September 1918 a coalition government was formed under Emil Reuter, the only public official with whom Marie-Adélaïde got along well. By November fighting raged in the Vosges mountains close to the Luxembourg frontier, and the people believed the Armistice came just in time.

As the German defeat precipitated revolution in Berlin and elsewhere, and the thrones of the Hohenzollerns, the Hapsburgs, and other sovereigns collapsed, revolutionary fervor infected Luxembourg too. On November 11 a self-styled Council of Workmen and Peasants unsuccessfully tried to proclaim a Communist republic. The next day when the Chamber of Deputies heard a proposal to depose the grand duchess, Marie-Adélaïde sought to calm political passions by announcing her pleasure "to subject the question of the form of government to the decision of the Luxembourg people freely expressed."

On November 20 General John F. Pershing, commander of the American Expeditionary Forces in Europe, arrived in Luxembourg and stood in the city palace beside a smiling Marie-Adélaïde as khaki-clad troops filed below. Almost on his heels Marshal Foch paraded with his French army.

Despite Foch's presence, Reuter did not achieve his goal of resuming diplomatic ties with France and forming an economic union. Meanwhile the diplomatic representatives of Belgium, France, and Italy delayed returning to Luxembourg. Finally Belgium sent a chargé d'affaires. Increasingly rumors spread of a possible annexation of Luxembourg by either Belgium or France.

After the French minister of foreign affairs refused to receive a Luxembourg minister, radicals again proclaimed a Luxembourg republic on January 9, 1919, but won no popular support. Nonetheless, within the Chamber of Deputies, fresh calls arose for Marie-Adélaïde's abdication. Liberals and Socialists finally voted the deposition and charged a Committee of Public Safety with maintaining public order. To obtain popular approval of the coup d'état, committee members harangued a steadily growing crowd. But the mob, fearful of radicalism, howled back, and within a few hours the committee was dissolved. Still Marie-Adélaïde's position remained precarious.

Now psychologically prepared for her fall, the grand duchess decided to abdicate if the dynastic party of the right would declare her departure necessary for the ultimate good and security of the country. She wrote to the prime minister that in relinquishing her role as grand duchess, she was acting "to save the Luxembourger people from all difficulties liable to hinder negotiations with the one or the other of the neighboring nations in the aim of preparing and organizing the economic future of the country." She designated her sister Charlotte as her successor.

Meanwhile a cousin arrived at the castle of Colmar-Berg on an important mission. Xavier of Bourbon-Parma, brother of Felix, Charlotte's fiancé, had attended the wedding of their sister Zita seven years before and been impressed by Marie-Adélaïde's beauty and reserved manner. In the uniform of an English service captain, Xavier became a last-minute suitor. Since he had served with the Allies, he was assured that by marrying Marie-Adélaïde he could save her throne. Later Xavier revealed that on her refusing his marriage proposal, he had begged her at least to allow the rumor of an engagement to reach the Allies. When she felt secure in her position, he could withdraw. Again Marie-Adélaïde firmly rejected his offer.

On January 13 she appeared before her ministers and presented Charlotte as her successor. Two days later at Colmar-Berg, Marie-Adélaïde stoically watched her sister sworn in as ruler of Luxembourg.

With her mother and three of her sisters, she drove to the border town of Dienhoffen on January 29. There she boarded a train with Countess Anna and the court marshal, who accompanied the two women to Strasbourg.

When he left, Marie-Adélaïde and Countess Anna proceeded directly to Montreux, Switzerland. By March they had temporarily settled in Villeneuve on Lake Geneva. In May they rented a small house at Spiez on Lake Thun so Marie-Adélaïde could escape from hotel life.

Accompanied by her sister Antonia and the devoted Countess Anna, Marie-Adélaïde set out for Italy in October, determined to enter a religious order. Once in Rome she gained her first audience with Pope Benedict XV, who advised her to choose the convent of the Discalced Carmelites in Modena. For Christmas another sister, Hilda, joined her.

With spring Marie-Adélaïde went to visit the Carmelite convent and was told to return in the autumn. To pass the intervening time, she left for Hohenburg to stay with her mother and sisters. She considered Luxembourg out of bounds even though she knew that Charlotte would have received her warmly.

In 1920 she entered the Carmelite convent, deciding on cigarettes as one of her first renunciations. But the strange new life made her melancholy and nostalgic. After the prioress wrote to Marie-Anne that her daughter's health was declining, the Duchess of Parma, Xavier's mother, hurried to Modena and brought her niece to the family estate.

During her convalescence, Marie-Adélaïde still felt drawn to the religious life, and soon the Congregation of the Little Sisters of the Poor caught her attention. By October she moved to Rome to the Little Sister's clinic for the care of aged and infirm men, and for a few months, as Sister Maria de Parma, she washed and fed the sometimes infantile patients. Again she could not handle the stress, and the supervisor advised her to leave.

Humiliation brought on deteriorating health. After Marie-Adélaïde spent some time in a nursing home, the Duchess of Parma reappeared and insisted on taking her to Switzerland, where they stayed at a simple convent pension in Einsedeln. Marie-Anne and some of her daughters visited them there. To feel useful Marie-Adélaïde taught for a while in an elementary school run by the nuns. But she remained pensive and sad. "I have suffered much. Something has snapped," she told her aunt.

Vainly she searched for a religious order that would accept her. At last Marie-Anne told her to come home to Hohenburg. Feeling that her failure had stained the House of Nassau, Marie-Adélaïde returned to Bavaria in April 1922. At Hohenburg she attended the wedding of her sister Elizabeth to Prince Philip of Hesse and Saxe. One week later she left for Germany to work briefly in the hospital of the Franciscans at Cologne and to inspect rather aimlessly the Red Cross institutes on the Rhine.

In 1923 she began to study medicine at the university in Munich with the goal of becoming a nurse. She lived as frugally as possible, going back and forth by tram to her classes and avoiding personal contacts as much as possible.

When she arrived at Hohenburg for her summer vacation, her pallor and lassitude greatly worried her family. She seemed to find pleasure only in leisurely nature walks. She no longer spoke of returning to medical studies in Munich. Staying on at Hohenburg, she grew weaker by the day; one morning she could not rise from her bed. The doctors diagnosed her illness as paratyphus, the return of a malady she had contracted in Rome with the Little Sisters of the Poor.

She had no will to recover. With her mother, her sisters, and the members of her household around her, she died on January 24, 1924. The first Luxembourg ruler since John the Blind (1296) to be born on its soil, she was the first freely to abdicate, and the first to die in self-imposed exile. Sadly, she had not yet reached her 30th birthday.

Charlotte
Grand Duchess of
Luxembourg, 1919–1964

The year 1919 proved quite extraordinary for the young Grand Duchess Charlotte. She succeeded her sister Marie-Adélaïde on the throne, she married, and she saw herself confirmed as sovereign in a national referendum. The women of Luxembourg also obtained suffrage.

Born January 23, 1896, at Hohenburg, the family castle in the Bavarian Alps, Charlotte was the second of six daughters of the future Grand Duke William IV and Marie-Anne of Braganza. On the death of his father, Grand Duke Adolphe, in 1905, William became Luxembourg's ruler. But he was already ill, and over the next seven years his steadily deteriorating health cast a shadow over Hohenburg and the Chateau Colmar-Berg, where the girls grew up in semiseclusion. Although their mother was named regent in 1908, she spent most of her time at her paralyzed husband's bedside.

Charlotte and her sisters, Hilda, Antonia, Elizabeth, and Sophia, developed a close and tender relationship, but the oldest girl, Marie-Adélaïde tended to be aloof. Much less complicated, pretty Charlotte was warm-hearted and engaging, and at 15 she attracted considerable attention when she accompanied her mother and Marie-Adélaïde to the wedding of a cousin, Princess Zita of Bourbon-Parma, to the Archduke Karl, nephew of the Austrian emperor, Franz Joseph. Her gentle charm made a lasting impression on the bride's attractive, 18-year-old brother, Felix, who shared with her an interest in sports.

The next year Grand Duke William died, and Marie-Adélaïde succeeded him. Charlotte watched proudly as her sister took the oath of office, never dreaming that the reign would become very difficult or that within seven years she herself would swear the same oath. Soon Marie-Adélaïde found herself embroiled with the leftists in the Chamber of Deputies.

Then in 1914, on the outbreak of World War I, the Germans invaded a neutral Luxembourg, and Marie-Anne and her daughters promptly offered their services to the Red Cross. Although the war years meant privation and humiliation to Luxembourg, they brought romance into Charlotte's life. Felix turned up as her suitor, and on November 6, 1918, five days before the Armistice, their engagement was announced. But political signs were ominous. As leftist politicians in Luxembourg and even Allied governments accused Marie-Adélaïde of being pro–German, demands for her abdication mounted. To cool passions, the grand duchess announced her decision to seek a referendum on the monarchy.

Even so, the pressures increased, especially after the French refused to restore diplomatic ties. On January 9, 1919, Marie-Adélaïde decided to abdicate in favor of her sister. Imbued with a strong sense of duty, Charlotte did not refuse the challenge. On January 15 she wept as she took the oath of office, but Marie-Adélaïde remained dry-eyed.

The new sovereign faced the same diplomatic problems as her predecessor. The leftists too proved troublesome, raising a clamor over her succession and getting caught up in the Belgian overtures. While in refuge at Le Havre, the Belgian government had been making plans to annex Luxembourg. On its return to Brussels after the Armistice, it sent the Prince of Ligne to Luxembourg to prepare ground for annexation. No sooner had Charlotte begun to reign than Belgian propaganda flooded the country.

Emile Reuter, her prime minister, sent a memorandum to Georges Clemenceau, president of the Peace Conference at Versailles, informing him that the Luxembourg people would be urged to vote on the dynastic question and on the matter of concluding an economic alliance either with France or Belgium. The next day Belgian delegates at Versailles proposed attaching Luxembourg to Belgium, but Reuter had acted opportunely and soon won support for his country; nothing came of the Belgian proposal.

With relief Charlotte watched the Chamber of Deputies unanimously adopt an order of the day proclaiming and reaffirming the independence of the grand duchy. It also voted the first draft of a law which declared that women as well as men would be asked to choose their form of government. Later the Chamber called for a second referendum to decide whether an economic treaty should be concluded with France, or Belgium.

The plebiscite was scheduled for May. Then in mid–April Britain and the U.S. asked the Luxembourg government to postpone voting until after the Allies signed a peace treaty with Germany. The intervention baffled the new ruler, her government, and her people, who by staging a huge patriotic demonstration caught the attention of the Big Four at Versailles. But these leaders insisted that the peace treaty be signed before a vote was held.

Three months after the ink dried on the Treaty of Versailles, the referendum "to settle the Luxembourg question" took place on September 28. For the first time in history the women of Luxembourg participated in an election. Nearly 80 percent of the people pronounced for Charlotte, only 18 percent for a republic. One thousand votes were cast for Marie-Adélaïde. The great majority also declared themselves in favor of an economic union with France. By the following year, however, France rejected any such union.

The plebiscite behind her, Charlotte prepared to wed her cousin Felix. After the ceremony on January 21, 1921, the bridegroom received the title of Prince of Luxembourg. The sweet-faced grand duchess and her prince produced a large family. A son, Jean, was born in 1921, followed by Elizabeth, 1922; Marie-Adélaïde, 1924; Marie-Gabrielle, 1925; Charles, 1927; and Alix Marie, 1929. Their happiness was shadowed only by the death of the ill-fated former Grand Duchess Marie-Adélaïde in 1924.

Charlotte's reign went exceedingly well. The period between the two world wars saw great political and economic stability, which owed much to the passage of highly advanced social legislation and to an amazing expansion of the iron and steel industry in the country. Also, as a member of the League of Nations, Luxembourg worked toward international cooperation.

In 1940 Charlotte's countrymen witnessed a tragic replay. On May 10, the same day the Nazis entered the Netherlands, their tanks crossed the Luxembourg frontier, guns fired, and parachutists dropped in a full-scale invasion. Just ahead of the Germans, the royal family escaped by automobile to France, where a chateau near Paris was put at their disposal. Shortly afterwards they settled in the south of France. But as French fortunes in the war worsened, they traveled through Spain and took refuge in Portugal, homeland of Charlotte's mother. When the British invited the grand duchess to take up residence in London, the Luxembourg government established its seat there. Meanwhile President Franklin D. Roosevelt sent an American warship to Lisbon to bring the grand ducal children and their father to the United States. From there they moved on to Canada.

In London the government-in-exile received an emotional message from Luxembourg:

> Tell the sovereign that we remain steadfast. Tell her we thank God she is safe and guarding the flame of our independence on a national altar across the sea. Tell her we will not allow her feet to touch the ground when she returns with our liberty and happiness. Say that we will carry her on our shoulders from Rodange to Luxembourg.

Charlotte drew fresh courage from such loyalty.

In 1941 she came to the United States for the first time and in Chicago helped launch the National Relief Fund for the Aid and Support of the Luxembourg People. The Roosevelts entertained her, Prince Felix, and Jean, the hereditary grand duke, at the White House. Shortly thereafter Jean and Prince Felix flew to London to enlist in the Allied forces, the father in the British northern command, the son in the Irish Guards.

Meanwhile reports of her people's suffering greatly distressed Charlotte. They detailed attacks on the Jews, seizure of property, intimidation of holders

Charlotte. Information and Press Service, Luxembourg.

of public office, impressment of Luxembourg citizens into the labor force, and their transportation to Germany. The Nazis also tried to outlaw the use of French, the official language, and forbade men to wear the popular Basque beret.

But then came more heartening accounts. Because of the outrages, the Luxembourg people dared sport the monarchical red-lion sign, staged strikes and boycotts, published underground newspapers, smuggled draft resisters to France, forged papers, spread symbols, sabotaged production, and organized at least five clandestine movements.

On a September morning in 1944, Prince Felix crossed the Luxembourg frontier; that afternoon Jean also came home, both arriving as soldiers with the liberating American forces. Appearing together at the Town Hall, a beaming father and son acknowledged wild cheers from Charlotte's subjects. The next April, Grand Duchess Charlotte triumphantly returned.

Like the Netherlands, the small country lay in smoking ruins, particularly its northern half, devastated by the Rundstedt offensive and the Battle of the Bulge. More than a third of the farmland was destroyed. Thousands of homes had disappeared, bridges and tunnels were rubble, miles of railway had been removed, and most of the steel plants had been burned down.

During the period of reconstruction, the dignified Charlotte stood as a beloved and inspiring symbol. Soon she and Prince Felix showed active interest in important political and diplomatic developments. In 1945 Luxembourg became a charter member of the United Nations. In 1948 it joined with the Netherlands and Belgium in a customs union called Benelux, which in 1960 would evolve into an economic union. Membership in the Common Market and the European Atomic Energy Organization in 1958 led to many changes in the economic and social sectors: modernization of the steel industry, reform of agricultural practices, and development of new power and transportation products.

During these years, Charlotte and Prince Felix kept a busy social calendar, paying official visits to other sovereigns and heads of state and in turn receiving them. In 1953 the Hereditary Grand Duke Jean married his mother's goddaughter, Princess Josephine Charlotte, sister of King Baudouin of Belgium. During this same decade Jean's four sisters were also married. In 1967 his brother Charles chose a commoner as his bride. Charlotte and Felix gained 23 grandchildren.

On November 12, 1964, after reigning for 45 years, the grand duchess decided to abdicate in favor of her son, Jean. Through study and service in the Luxembourg City Council he was unusually well prepared to succeed her.

Prince Felix died in 1970, shortly after he and Charlotte had celebrated their 50th wedding anniversary. Quietly the grand duchess lived on, dying in her 89th year on July 9, 1985, at Fischbach Castle.

Her people mourned a ruler who had moved smoothly in her role and brought new stature to Luxembourg. Her sister's reign had been tragic and incomplete; hers, the war aside, had been happy and fulfilling.

Juliana
Queen of the Netherlands, 1948–1980

On April 30, 1909, two mounted trumpeters galloped through the streeets of The Hague to announce the birth of the long awaited child of Queen Wilhelmina and Prince Hendrik; then the cannon boomed. The baby was named for Juliana von Stolberg, the mother of William the Silent, founder of the House of Orange-Nassau. (Almost 50 years later Wilhelmina dedicated her autobiography to her daughter, writing that the two Julianas were "intimately related," both possessed of "higher wisdom and inner strength.") The child was remarkably sturdy, and as she developed, the Dutch people doted on photographs that came from Het Loo Palace showing Juliana playing in her sandbox, riding ponies, or dressing dolls.

Wilhelmina determined to give her daughter the daily company of other children at school and at play. So, after early private lessons, the six-year-old princess began attending a class held at Huis ten Bosch Palace. The teaching followed the methods of Jan Ligthart, recognized as the foremost progressive educator in the country. In 1920 Dr. J.H. Gunning Willemzoom took over most of Juliana's education, and Queen Wilhelmina provided religious instruction. She also arranged for painting, drawing, and violin lessons. Enrollment at various summer youth camps and frequent travel holidays with her mother rounded out the girl's development.

Juliana's 18th birthday opened an eventful year for her. She acquired her own household at Kneuterdijk Palace in The Hague, she entered the Dutch Reformed Church, and as a new member of the Council of State, she attended the first opening of the Estates General, arriving with her mother in the famous Golden Coach.

That same year Juliana became the first member of the Dutch royal family to study at a public university. Under the name Julia van Bueren, she enrolled as a regular student at the University of Leiden, founded by her ancestor William the Silent, and spent her student years living with three friends in a small villa at Katwijk, a seaside resort. This setting inspired the girls to call themselves the "Merry Sea Stars."

Since she had not obtained a certificate for completing secondary education, Juliana could not be admitted to the customary university examinations. But finally administrators agreed that she could take the preliminary examination in international law and pick two other subjects; her choices fell on religion and modern Dutch literature. After passing all three examinations, the princess received an honorary doctorate in literature and philosophy in 1930.

The next few years passed quickly with increasing royal duties which she performed punctiliously. After her father, Prince Hendrik, died in 1934, she succeeded to his post as president of the Netherlands Red Cross.

For all her observance of necessary protocol, she was disarmingly informal and without any fanfare introduced her fiancé to the Dutch court. On a winter sports holiday in Germany in 1936, she had met and fallen in love with 25-year-old Prince Bernhard zur Lippe Biesterfeld, a dapper, bespectacled young businessman, who worked for the Paris branch of I.G. Farben, a giant German dye firm. The day Dutch radio broadcast news of their engagement, the young couple, casually dressed, arrived in Bernhard's two-seater Ford at Noordeinde Palace in The Hague.

Their wedding took place on January 3, 1937, and Bernhard assumed the title of Prince of the Netherlands. Privately Juliana called him Bernilo; to him she was Jula. After their honeymoon he and Juliana moved into the palace at Soestdijk in Baarn, which has remained their home.

That November Bernhard sustained a broken neck and several ribs when his car collided with a truck, but he came home from the hospital in time to celebrate the birth of their first child, a daughter Beatrix, in January 1938. The next year Juliana gave birth to a second daughter, Irene. She chose both princesses's names with particular care, Beatrix meaning "she who brings happiness" and Irene "peace." Thereby she abandoned the family tradition of naming children after relatives.

In May 1940 the Nazis overran the Netherlands, and British warships carried the royal family to England, Juliana preceding her mother. Within a month, because of the blitz, Juliana sailed on the cruiser *Sumatra* with her daughters and a small entourage for Halifax, Nova Scotia. From there she went on to Ottawa to receive a warm welcome from the Earl of Athlone, the new Governor-General, and his wife Princess Alice, Wilhelmina's cousin and one of Beatrix's godmothers. Princess Alice later wrote about Juliana: "She was really magnificent. She never once complained or expressed unhappiness, but threw herself into everything that was being done for the war." Living quietly and simply, the big-boned, pleasant looking Juliana never demanded protocol or special privileges. Sometimes she even did the grocery shopping.

Queen Wilhelmina and Prince Bernhard had remained behind in London with the Dutch government-in-exile. Meanwhile Bernhard, who had to overcome prejudice against his German birth and background, trained as a pilot and served as adviser to the queen and chief liaison officer to the Royal Navy, Army,and Air Force.

In 1941 he joined Juliana for a short tour of the United States, ending with a visit to President and Mrs. Franklin D. Roosevelt at the White House. Wilhelmina and Bernhard came on separate visits the next year, the queen spending the summer with her daughter and granddaughters in the Berkshires.

At the beginning of 1943 Bernhard flew to Ottawa once more to be with his wife for the birth of their third daughter, Margriet. Again the name carried special significance, referring to the characteristically Dutch flower, the marguerite, that Queen Wilhelmina always carried with her as a symbol during the years of exile. The proud grandmother appeared for the christening. Juliana, who had overcome much of her shyness in Canada, also toured Surinam (Dutch Guiana) and the Netherlands Antilles in 1943 and 1944.

In the autumn of 1944 Wilhelmina summoned Juliana to England, but the children stayed behind in Ottawa. Mother and daughter crossed the Dutch frontier in May 1945 and settled at Breda to await developments. On May 4 the Germans capitulated, and quickly the royal family was united. Shocked at the war's devastation, Juliana resumed her presidency of the Netherlands Red Cross and also assumed the presidency of the Council for the Rehabilitation of the People of the Netherlands. Bernhard was proving his mettle as commander-in-chief of Dutch armed forces; he had been head of the home resistance front under General Dwight D. Eisenhower.

Juliana and Bernhard's fourth child, a daughter, Maria Christina (Marikje), was born at Soestdijk Palace early in 1947. During her pregnancy Juliana had caught the German measles, and the baby had cataracts in both eyes; doctors were able to restore some vision to one. Eight months later, on a friend's recommendation, Prince Bernhard brought a graying faith healer, Greet Hofmans, to Soestdijk Palace, where she soon moved in. About the same time Wilhelmina fell ill, and Juliana acted as regent for several weeks. In May 1948 she did so again.

On September 4, following her Golden Jubilee, Wilhelmina abdicated. At the New Church in Amsterdam, in the presence of both parliamentary chambers, 38-year-old Juliana was inaugurated as the constitutional head of state. She showed deep awareness of her responsibilities: "I have been called to a task so difficult that no one who has given it a moment's thought would wish to do it, but also so splendid that I can only say – who am I to be permitted to perform it?" Her new duties were both executive and legislative, but all orders and royal decrees had to be countersigned by her ministers.

By 1948 the war trials had not yet ended. Juliana strongly opposed the death penalty, which had long been abolished in the Netherlands except for war criminals. As the courts issued death warrants, the new queen refused to sign them, and the sentences were commuted to life imprisonment.

Along with continuing the monumental job of postwar reconstruction, Juliana and the Dutch government faced the problem of Indonesian nationalism. After the Japanese occupation of the Netherlands East Indies ended, rebels proclaimed independence in 1945. In the last years of Wilhelmina's reign, full-scale fighting had erupted between Dutch and Indonesian troops. The United Nations secured a cease-fire, which the Dutch broke by a surprise attack at the end of 1948. For Juliana and her ministers, the strong pro–Indonesian sentiment in their country came as an unpleasant surprise. Meanwhile the Indonesians' "scorched earth" policy ruined many valuable Dutch properties. Bowing to the inevitable in 1949, the Netherlands gave up its 300-year-old sovereignty, and Juliana signed a treaty recognizing the United States of Indonesia as a separate and sovereign state. Of all the old Dutch territories in the Indies, only the western half of New Guinea remained. That same year the Dutch became members of the North Atlantic Treaty Organization.

By 1950 Greet Hofmans had not improved Marikje's sight. Bernhard sensed that his wife depended too much on the faith healer, and he ordered her out of the palace. The mystic moved on to Wilhelmina's residence, Het Loo, where she addressed religious gatherings and where Juliana continued to seek her out.

Terrible floods in Zeeland and South Holland in February 1953 cost over 1800 lives and caused millions of dollars of damage. Wearing an old coat, boots, and a headkerchief, the queen spent days in the disaster area, wading through the flood waters. Afterward she worked to set up the Delta Project to close off the estuaries with storm surge barriers. It was a gigantic undertaking; the last barrier would be completed in 1986.

As her mother had proposed during the years of exile, Juliana gave her royal assent in 1954 to a charter proclaiming Surinam and the Netherlands Antilles equal partners with the Netherlands but declaring that the Netherlands would deal with foreign affairs and defense in its two former colonies. Soon afterwards, she and Prince Bernhard paid an official visit to these territories. (Twenty-one years later Surinam would gain complete independence, and the charter would no longer apply to it.)

The Dutch people, who knew little about Greet Hofmans, were highly satisfied with their queen, who exuded such a comfortable housewifely air. Her dislike of pomp and elaborate ceremony even caused her to cut down on the curtseys at court.

From the outset, Juliana built a loving family life. As she wrote, "For a Queen, her duties as a mother are as important as they are to any other Dutch woman." Many of the family pleasures involved sports—skating, skiing, cycling, horseback riding, and swimming.

Unlike their mother and grandmother, who had been educated in the palace, the princesses were sent to progressive public schools. By 1956 the youngest daughter, Maria Christina, who preferred using her second name,

Juliana. The Embassy of the Netherlands, Washington, D.C. (Photo by Max Koot.)

had so profited from expert medical treatment and visual exercises that she was able to ride her bicycle on the street.

Bernhard and Juliana had several fallings-out over the woman who had done nothing for the princess, but who had come to influence the queen politically. Certain officials found Juliana's dependence embarrassing and demanded that she cut ties. Some even feared divorce and a forced abdication if she refused. Wilhelmina loyally stood behind her daughter, but pressure increased and finally Greet Hofmans was refused entrance to Het Loo.

All along Juliana had championed international solidarity and close cooperation with her European neighbors. Thus she gave wholehearted approval for her ministers to start negotiations to establish the European Economic Community or Common Market. The Netherlands became a charter member in 1958. Once consulting with a minister, she told him, "You, of course, carry the political responsibility, but I carry the moral responsibility when I let my name be used anywhere or sign it at the bottom of a document." At the beginning of her reign, the Netherlands, Belgium, and Luxembourg formed a customs union establishing a single external tariff. An economic union, created by the Benelux Treaty of 1958, came into force in 1960.

These economic treaties interested Prince Bernhard, who with easy charm had become a goodwill ambassador for booming Dutch industry. From the beginning of his marriage he had made clear that he wanted to do far more than help his wife at official functions. He also smilingly declared, "In affairs of state, my wife is the boss, but at home I am."

For the royal family, the year 1963 proved most unhappy. Appropriately large headlines heralded the surrender of the last large Dutch colony when, in accordance with a United Nations proposal, the Dutch government turned over West New Guinea (Irian) to Indonesia after five years of controversy and seizure of Dutch property in Indonesia.

That same year Princess Irene's engagement to Prince Carlos Hugo of Bourbon-Parma brought special difficulties for her mother. He was the son of Prince Xavier, the Carlist pretender to the Spanish throne and once the would-be rescuer of Grand Duchess Marie-Adélaïde of Luxembourg. The Dutch linked Carlos Hugo to fascism and suspected him of wanting to use their princess to add luster to the Carlist claim. The Dutch Parliament refused to approve the marriage, but Irene decided to wed her prince anyway. By following her own heart she gave up her right and that of any of her descendants to the Dutch throne. The wedding ceremony was held in Rome, and Carlist shouts and slogans almost turned it into a political rally. Although the couple continued to live abroad, they frequently visited Irene's family. In 1981 they were divorced.

Juliana had been particularly pleased that Princess Beatrix had followed her to the University of Leiden and been an exemplary student. Carefully she trained her for her future role. But in 1966 the heiress presumptive's announcement of her engagement brought a storm of criticism. Her fiancé, Claus von Amsberg, a German diplomat, had been a member of the Hitler Youth and a German soldier during World War II. The Dutch Parliament, however, decided he had never been a Nazi. Nonetheless political and social protesters staged street riots on the wedding day. Fortunately for the royal family, the Dutch people soon accepted Claus.

In 1967 the marriage of Juliana's third daughter, Margriet, to a commoner, Pieter van Vollenhoven, raised little criticism. In 1975 Christina also wed a commoner, Jorge Guillermo from New York City. Eventually Juliana and Bernhard counted 14 grandchildren.

Bernhard had won praise as chairman of various national and international committees and organizations, as founder and chairman of the Prince Bernhard Fund to encourage cultural life in the Netherlands, and as mediator and chairman of the Bilderberg Conferences, which discussed political, economic, and social problems. In the 1970s some of Bernhard's activities suddenly became suspect. In February 1976 a Dutch government commission began investigating allegations that in spite of his wife's vast fortune he had accepted $1.1 million in bribes from Lockheed Aircraft Corporation for promoting the Dutch government's purchase of 138 Lockheed Stratofighter jets. When the commission's report went to Prime Minister Johannes Martin den Uyl, the royal couple cut short an Italian vacation and came home amid talk of abdication. After six months of investigation, the commission found no evidence that Bernhard had accepted any money, but declared that since the 1960s he had "entered much too lightly into trangressions that were bound to create the impression that he was susceptible to favors." To the royal family's relief, den Uyl said there would be no criminal investigation or judicial inquiry. In a letter to Parliament, the prince wrote, "I have not been critical enough of initiatives presented to me. I have written letters I should not have sent. I accept full responsibility for this and thus accept the disapproval expressed by the commission." Parliament then endorsed the cabinet decision and thanked Juliana for not abdicating. During the uproar, through which his wife stood staunchly beside him, he resigned his post as inspector general of the Netherlands Armed Forces and adviser to various defense agencies. He also relinquished his presidency of the World Wildlife Fund, but later he became president of its Dutch section.

Four years later Juliana decided it was finally time to step down. On January 30, 1980, the 42nd birthday of Princess Beatrix, the queen announced on television and radio that on her 71st birthday she would abdicate in favor of her eldest daughter. On April 30, she signed an act of abdication in a solemn ceremony and then, following in her mother's footsteps, declared that from henceforth her title would be that of Princess of the Netherlands.

Like Wilhelmina she made a graceful exit after a historic reign. Since then she and Bernhard have lived in quiet retirement at their well-loved Soestdijk.

Elizabeth II
Queen of the United Kingdom of Great Britain and Northern Ireland, 1952–

At the time of her birth on April 21, 1926, in the Mayfair mansion of her maternal grandparents, Elizabeth, first child of the young Duke and Duchess of York, did not appear destined for the English throne. Her grandfather, George V, was reigning king, and next in line stood her Uncle Edward, the sophisticated and popular Prince of Wales, who was expected to marry and produce heirs. In all likelihood too, Elizabeth's parents would one day have sons. As things turned out, the former Lady Elizabeth Bowes-Lyon bore her husband Albert only one more child, a daughter, Margaret Rose, in 1930.

In January 1927 the duke and duchess embarked on a six-month tour of Australia and New Zealand, and the little princess first stayed with her grandparents, the Earl and Countess of Strathmore, at St. Paul's Walden Bury, their home in Hertfordshire. Then she was brought to King George and Queen Mary at Buckingham Palace. (During the next nine years "Lilibet" became the special favorite of the old king, a strong disciplinarian.)

On the Yorks' return in June, they found a new house waiting for them at 145 Picadilly, just across Green Park from Buckingham Palace. In 1931 the king offered them the Royal Lodge, Windsor, as a weekend retreat. Family life was quiet, loving, close, and conventional. The girls had a governess, Marion Crawford, who found her elder charge both conscientious and excessively neat.

When Elizabeth was 10, her future role changed dramatically. King George had died in January 1936 and had been succeeded by the Prince of Wales. In December Edward abdicated so that he could marry the American-born Wallis Simpson. The royal family, the British government, and the Anglican church all objected to her because once divorced, she was in the process of divorcing her second husband. Some pessimists feared that the crisis might topple the dynasty. In a relatively smooth transition, however, Elizabeth's father and mother became king and queen consort, Albert taking the name of George VI.

The curly-haired young princesses, clad in long robes, sat wide-eyed during the solemn and impressive coronation in Westminster Abbey in June 1937. Later they stood with their parents on the central balcony of Buckingham Palace to almost hysterical applause. It was reported that after being told of her position as heiress presumptive, Elizabeth began praying for a baby brother.

King George VI, shy and afflicted with a pronounced stammer, felt completely untrained for his role and disliked the limelight. Slowly, however, he began to develop a quiet though firm authority. His ever-smiling wife and their pretty, blue-eyed daughters brought unity to a badly rocked throne.

There were few playmates, but many pets—horses, ponies, dogs, and budgerigars. A troop of Girl Guides was organized at Buckingham Palace, and Elizabeth took part eagerly. Miss Crawford continued as governess, her work later supplemented by Sir Henry Marten, the vice-provost of Eton College, who taught the teenage princess constitutional history. Visiting tutors instructed her in music and languages.

The heiress apparent first met Prince Philip of Greece when the royal yacht sailed along the south coast of England in the summer of 1939 and anchored at the Royal Dartmouth Naval College. According to her governess, the Viking good looks and athletic skills of the 18-year-old Philip, a naval cadet, greatly impressed Elizabeth, especially when she saw him fly over a tennis net. The son of Prince Andrew of Greece and Princess Alice, one of Queen Victoria's granddaughters, and the nephew of Lord Louis Mountbatten, he was her third cousin. The princess also impressed the prince. When the royal yacht finally sailed off, he and the rest of the senior cadets followed in a flotilla of small boats. Yet when the others turned back, Philip rowed on. Only his uncle's commanding voice made him return.

Scarcely two months later Britain entered World War II. Practicing the same wartime austerity as their embattled subjects, members of the royal family won even greater popularity. The king and queen regularly visited bombed out areas to show sympathy and concern. When officials suggested to Queen Elizabeth that she take her daughters to safety in Canada, she made an oft-quoted remark: "The Princesses cannot go without me, I cannot go without the King, the King will never go."

While their parents remained at Buckingham Palace during the blitz, the reserved Elizabeth and the roguish and often capricious Margaret moved full time to Windsor Castle. Elizabeth longed to be in service, but was not old enough to qualify until the last months of the war. Finally, in March 1945 the heiress presumptive got into khaki, went into training with the Auxiliary Territorial Services (ATS), and passed as a qualified driver. In a few months she had advanced to junior commander. Although she still slept at Windsor, she was treated like any other girl in the group and enjoyed showing her mother her greasy hands.

After the war, as the Labour government introduced a socialist welfare state, Elizabeth busied herself with royal duties, constantly drilled in etiquette and procedures by the regal Queen Mary. For several years she had corresponded with Philip, who served in the navy, and he had paid several visits to Buckingham Palace. Late in 1946 the couple became secretly engaged, but the court delayed the announcement until Elizabeth and her sister Margaret had accompanied their parents on a ten-week tour of South Africa.

Marriage waited on Philip's naturalization, when he also relinquished his family title. On the eve of the wedding King George conferred on Lieutenant Philip Mountbatten the rank of royal highness and the new title of Duke of Edinburgh, Earl of Marionett, and Baron Greenwich. (In 1957 Philip would be declared a prince of the United Kingdom. Unlike Victoria's Albert, he refused the title of Prince Consort.)

The couple was married on November 20, 1947, in Westminster Abbey at a huge gathering of royalty, regnant and exiled. King George later wrote his daughter: "You were so calm and composed during the service and said your words with such conviction that I know it will be all right." The young pair honeymooned at the Mountbatten home, Broadlands, in the Hampshire village of Romsey. Their first child, Charles, arrived in 1948. The following year Philip took up a naval posting at Malta, and Elizabeth flew out to join him. For a brief period she could be free of official duties, but within a few months she returned to Clarence House, the Edinburgh London residence, to await the birth of a daughter, Anne. After nursing her baby for a few months, Elizabeth flew back to Malta. A short time later she and Philip were called home because the king had lung cancer.

After surgery, however, George VI seemed well enough so that they could travel across Canada and go on to Washington, where President Harry Truman wrote to Buckingham Palace: "We've just had a visit from a lovely young lady and her personable husband."

On January 31, 1952, Elizabeth and Philip set out on an even longer journey to Australia and New Zealand. On the way they stopped at the Forest Lodge in Sagana, a wedding gift from the people of Kenya. There on February 6, following an exhilarating day of snapping pictures of the wildlife, they received the message that King George had died in his sleep. The young queen and her husband flew home immediately. A small, dignified figure in black, she read her accession declaration in a clear voice: "I shall always work, as my father did throughout his reign, to uphold constitutional government and to advance the happiness and prosperity of my people, spread as they are the world over."

Queenship meant a special role as symbolic head of the steadily expanding British Commonwealth, the association of nations and dependencies that had been part of the British Empire. India and Pakistan were its newest members. Before Elizabeth's coronation, the Commonwealth prime ministers held a conference to choose the proper title for the new monarch and came up with "Elizabeth, the second, by the grace of God of the United Kingdom of Great Britain and Northern Ireland and of her other Realms and Territories, Queen, Head of the Commonwealth, Defender of the Faith." In a centuries-old ritual she was crowned on June 2, 1952, and Philip was the first to pay her homage.

During the ceremony reporters closely watched Princess Margaret and Group Captain Peter Townsend, comptroller of the queen mother's household. Their love affair presented problems to the government and the Church; it did not seem proper for a Princess of the Blood to marry a divorced man. According to the Royal Marriages Act of 1772, permission had to be obtained from the sovereign and parliament before a member of the royal family could be married. At the age of 25 the royal person did not need that consent but was required to give a year's notice to the Privy Council. Any such marriage, however, meant relinquishing all royal rights and financial benefits for the Civil List, Parliament's annual grant for upkeep of the royal households. Elizabeth herself felt sympathy for her sister, but great pressure was brought on Margaret, and in the end she and Townsend decided to part. (In 1960 she married photographer Anthony Armstrong-Jones, who was created the Earl of Snowdon. Their marriage ended in divorce in 1978.)

Five months after her coronation, Elizabeth and Philip began touring her widespread dominions. She explained that she was visiting them, not as Queen of Great Britain, but as their own national queen. The itinerary included Bermuda, Jamaica, Fiji, Tonga, New Zealand, Australia, the Cocos Keeling Islands, Ceylon, Aden, and Uganda. At Malta the royal couple enjoyed a happy reunion with their two children, who had been staying with Lord and Lady Mountbatten.

A principal component of the constitutional theory Sir Henry Marten had taught the young princess had been Walter Bagehot's definition (1867) of a monarch's role in relation to a prime minister—to be consulted, to encourage, and on occasion to warn. The routine took the form of daily "doing the boxes" (reading foreign office cables and ministerial documents), a practice instituted by Queen Victoria. Although Elizabeth carefully stayed out of politics, she held weekly private meetings with her prime ministers.

Winston Churchill, her first prime minister, was extravagantly devoted to the pretty young queen, treating her much like a granddaughter. He had never missed an opportunity to praise her. When she was four, he had remarked on her "air of reflectiveness, astonishing in an infant." Succeeding prime ministers, Tory and Labour, were Anthony Eden, Harold Macmillan, Alec Douglas-Home, Harold Wilson, Edward Heath, James Callaghan, and Margaret Thatcher, Britain's first female chief executive of a parliamentary government, who remains in office. Whatever their party, all found the queen well-informed and extremely conscientious. In her devotion to duty ("it must come first") she was like Queen Victoria, the predecessor she most admired.

Early in Elizabeth's reign, the "Suez adventure" shook up the country. When the United States and Great Britain refused to finance the construction of the Aswan Dam across the Nile River, Egyptian President Gamal Nasser seized the Suez Canal. Half the United Kingdom's oil moved down the canal, and British politicians across the spectrum howled in outrage. Israel and France felt threatened, and Eden, the prime minister, made plans to retaliate: Israel would invade Egypt, and France and Britain would "intervene."

That summer Elizabeth had issued a proclamation calling out the army reserve, but she appeared completely surprised when in October, French and British armies did invade Egypt. Later Eden remarked that the queen had understood what the government was doing and had remained impartial. Some of his colleagues believed that he had not given her the full picture of his maneuvering with the French.

Within two weeks the invasion attempt collapsed; the United States had threatened to let the pound drop disastrously unless the invaders turned back. As a result of this crisis, Eden's health deteriorated and he resigned. Next came Macmillan, with whom Elizabeth developed her first working relationship.

Fulfilling her wish to have a good-sized family, Elizabeth gave birth in 1960 to a second son, Andrew, and again in 1963 to another boy, Edward. She and Philip agreed that like Charles and Anne they should be educated outside the palace.

Through the 1960s and 1970s, England faced a color problem as immigrants flooded London. But the riots that filled the streets paled in comparison to the violence in Northern Ireland. There a Catholic civil rights movement began to gather force in 1969, igniting the age-old hatred between Catholics and Protestants, the proponents of English rule. Bombings, assassinations, and fierce brawls between the Irish Republican Army (IRA) and British troops dominated the headlines for the next decade. Meanwhile Britain's African colonies marched steadily toward independence.

In 1973 Princess Anne, a prize-winning equestrienne, was the first of the royal children to marry. Her wedding to Captain Mark Phillips, also a superior rider, took place with the customary pomp, but the bridegroom did not want a royal title. Four years later Elizabeth celebrated her Silver Jubilee as queen. Beacons were lit from the Channel Islands to the Orkneys, and the outpouring of affection was lavish. The empire had been dismantled, violence persisted in Ulster, and nationalists in Scotland and Wales screamed for independence; still the monarchy flourished.

Elizabeth and Philip had begun the Jubilee Year with a six-week tour that took them to Western Samoa, Tonga, Fiji, New Zealand, Australia, and Papua, New Guinea. Later they visited Canada, Scotland, Wales, and Northern Ireland. Elizabeth had long since set a record as the most traveled

Elizabeth II. British Information Service, New York.

monarch in British history. She and Philip had made over 50 tours by plane and the royal yacht *Brittania* to cover more than a hundred countries.

The Irish civil war hit the royal family especially hard in August 1979 when Lord Mountbatten, distinguished soldier-statesman and Philip's beloved uncle, was killed as the IRA blew up his fishing boat off the Irish coast. Helping to blot out that tragic memory was the exuberance attending the wedding in 1981 of Prince Charles to Lady Diana Spencer, possibly the world's most photographed ceremony.

By the next year, however, the queen knew the anxiety of sending a son off to war. Britain had never relinquished its claim to the Falkland Islands off Argentina, and when the Argentinians invaded in 1982, the British fought back vigorously and successfully. Through the brief campaign Prince Andrew served as a Navy helicopter pilot and came home unscathed. Three years later he was married to Sarah Ferguson, and the couple received the titles of Duke and Duchess of York.

Center of many national ceremonies, Elizabeth continues to ride in a glittering coach to the annual opening of Parliament, where she reads a speech written by the prime minister. Royal duties in the midst of television cameras and microphones include visiting many parts of Great Britain to inaugurate scientific, industrial, artistic, and charitable enterprises. She also presides over every Commonwealth conference. Seventeen of these 47 nations still recognize the queen, represented by a governor general; others have their own heads of state.

In spite of the trappings of immense wealth, which includes an extraordinary art collection, Elizabeth has remained a countrywoman at heart. As a girl she once told her riding master that she really would like to live like an ordinary lady in the country with lots of horses and dogs, especially corgis and labradors. Horse racing fascinates her; she has owned the winners of five British classics, but has yet to win the Derby.

Occasionally newspaper photographs show her, relaxed and happy, walking about in an old tweed skirt, sweater, head scarf, and rubber Wellington boots, inspecting the animals on her Norfolk farm at Sandringham or giving her dogs a run at Balmoral, Queen Victoria's favorite Scottish retreat, where Elizabeth is said to do some of the cooking for her family.

Prince Philip, who has sometimes irritated the press with sharp, sarcastic remarks, has carved out his own niche. His interests have concentrated on industry, technology, polo, wildlife, and conservation. His inner sensitivity, friends say, is expressed at the easel.

The days of royal power are long gone. But Elizabeth, now a grandmother of five, has never shirked the duties that remain. Her reward for treading a gracious and dignified path for more than 35 years had been relative freedom from criticism although at least one British peer and several journalists have bewailed the "social lopsidedness" of the court and the expense of maintaining it. Some Englishmen also note that the pomp and ceremony lavished on the monarchy mask pressing social problems. Generally, however, her subjects find that Elizabeth has been eminently suitable for the throne, and they revere her immense prestige. She remains a symbol of continuity, a focus for national spirit.

Margrethe II
Queen of Denmark, 1972–

Margrethe II of Denmark did not have a glittering coronation like England's Elizabeth II. The prime minister simply proclaimed her queen from the balcony of Christiansborg Palace in Copenhagen, where the Danish Folketing meets. Nineteen years earlier, the world's oldest monarchy, which allowed only male rulers, had held a referendum to establish her right of succession.

Margrethe was born at a particularly trying time for the country. Danish schoolchildren are still told that her arrival was "like a light in the darkness." One week before her birth in Copenhagen on April 16, 1940, to Crown Prince Frederik and Crown Princess Ingrid, Denmark had been invaded by Nazi troops and had been powerless to resist. But defiantly the Swedish-born crown princess wheeled her child in a pram along the city's seafront, as a symbol of better days to come.

Meanwhile the reigning king, Christian X, the baby's grandfather, continued to take daily horseback rides through the streets to encourage his countrymen's morale.

From 1943 to 1947 "Princess Sunshine" attended kindergarten and primary classes with other children at the royal family residence, one of the four rococo Amalienborg palaces. Before long she had two sisters, Benedikte, born in 1944, and Anne Marie, born in 1946. Their father ascended the throne as Frederik IX in 1947.

That year Margrethe, known to her family as Daisy, was enrolled at the well-known Zahle School in Copenhagen. At 14 she entered an English girls' academy, North Foreland Lodge in Kent, England, coming home in 1956 for matriculation studies.

By that time a new constitution, signed by King Frederik, approved by the Folketing and ratified by a plebiscite, had established the right of female succession for the first time in Denmark. In 1953 Margrethe assumed the title of "throne heiress." As she later said in an interview:

My first reaction was utter horror because I realized for the first time that it involved the possibility of my father's death. It wasn't terror of the office, though I was dreadfully shy of the idea and of the extra attention taken of me. ... Then my parents, wise people that they are, made me see that there could be no higher service that I could render to my country.

From her 18th birthday on, she regularly participated in meetings of the council of state. At this time Frederik invested her with the Order of the Elephant, Denmark's highest order, which had never before been held by a woman. That same year Margrethe took recruit training in the Danish Women's Air Corps and simultaneously received instruction in military terminology and affairs of the North Atlantic Treaty Organization.

The princess proved a gifted linguist, speaking Swedish, English, and French fluently and learning some German. Well prepared, she studied from 1959 to 1967 at universities in Copenhagen and Århus, Denmark; Cambridge, England; Paris; and London. Her courses covered philosophy, constitutional and administrative law, sociology, political science, history, and archeology.

There was also more practical instruction. In 1965 she and her sister Benedikte enrolled for a *cordon bleu* cooking course at Miss Skov's School of Domestic Science in Copenhagen. One year later Margrethe underwent second lieutenant training, again in the Women's Air Corps.

She had inherited an interest in archeology from her maternal grandfather, King Gustav VI Adolf of Sweden, and enthusiastically accompanied him to several excavations of Etruscan sites north of Rome. Later she helped do rescue work after the temples at Abu Simbel were threatened by the construction of the Aswan Dam. Subsequently Margrethe traveled around the world on still other expeditions and often contributed articles to archeological journals and appeared in television documentaries based on those trips. She once noted:

I would have become an archeologist had I not been a princess. Archeology is not of much importance for a future head of state, but it gave me a sense of having achieved something personal, and in a way, of having a possible profession. I have always had a dread of becoming a passenger in life.

While studying in London in 1965, Margrethe met the handsome Count Henri de Laborde de Monpezat, the third secretary in the Oriental affairs department of the French embassy. Both later declared that it was love at first sight. On their engagement, Count Henri converted from Roman Catholicism to evangelical Lutheranism. Their wedding, on June 10, 1967, coincided with the celebration of the 800th anniversary of the founding of Copenhagen, and the city exploded with parades, concerts, fireworks, and street dancing.

Hundreds of dignitaries had arrived from abroad for the ceremony, but notably absent were Margrethe's younger sister, Queen Anne Marie, and her

Margrethe II. The Royal Danish Embassy, Washington, D.C.

husband, King Constantine of Greece. It was feared that their presence might spark Danish demonstrations against a recent military coup in Athens, which Constantine sanctioned because he had no other option. (Soon, when he failed to rally the army against the usurping colonels, he and his family fled to Italy.)

Speaking to an American journalist after her wedding, the Danish princess said, "I see no reason why, when someday I must officially take first place, I will not be able to take second place in our marriage at the same time." She gave birth to Crown Prince Frederik in 1968 and to a second son, Prince Joachim, in 1969.

On February 4, 1972, the popular, bluff King Frederik died of pneumonia and heart disease. The following day the Social Democratic minister, Jens Otto Krag, proclaimed her queen. Always showing a stylish flair, blond and blue-eyed, six feet tall, she was an elegant young woman, who had long since overcome her adolescent awkwardness.

Adopting an old Danish motto, "God's strength, the people's love, Denmark's strength," she chose to be called Margrethe II even though the 14th century Margrethe had never been crowned Queen of Denmark. That fall when Margrethe II held a press conference, the first ever given by a reigning Danish monarch, she declared, "To be queen is a richer experience than I have ever dreamed of."

Immediately on her accession she relinquished all the titles held by her father and his forebears. Rather than being known as Queen of the Wends and Goths and Duchess of Schleswig-Holstein, Stormarn, Ditmarschen, Lauenburg, and Oldenburg, she wished to be called simply Queen of Denmark.

As with all constitutional monarchs, power was exercised in her name by her ministers. Through the years the routine has been the same. Every two weeks Margrethe presides over the meetings of the council of state, where legislation and other important government matters are brought up for her signature. Like Elizabeth II, Margrethe has been an impartial head of state and has never discussed party problems. Still there is always the possibility that her most critical decision may someday be the selection of a new prime minister in the event of an election stalemate.

The prime minister calls once a week at the Amalienborg Palace to keep her informed of government activities. She receives ministers, holds audiences, attends military reviews, and gives soirees. As with her royal contemporaries, her incredibly busy schedule has also involved much traveling at home and abroad. One of her most interesting and unusual visits occurred in 1985 when she came to northern Greenland to meet the Service Patrol, which enforces Danish sovereignty from a radio sledge.

Count Henri, who by royal decree received the title of Prince Henrik, followed the examples of Prince Bernhard and Prince Philip and widened his own role. Ever since his marriage, he has taken on a heavy and varied work load, giving most attention to agriculture, industry, and the Danish Red Cross. He eventually was named president of that organization. He also became a captain in the Danish army and air force. Danes warmed to him when he quickly mastered their language.

Throughout her reign the lively Margrethe has displayed many talents. She is a skilled writer and communicator, whose annual New Year's speech on television has become traditional. With her husband she collaborated on a well-received translation of Simone de Beauvoir's *Tout les hommes sont mortels*. She is also a keen student of Lutheran evangelical theology and participates in study groups with the best-known Danish religious leaders. But the Danes are proudest of her artistic talents, inherited from her mother's family, the Swedish Bernadottes. For the Danish translation of J.R.R. Tolkien's *The Lord of the Rings*, she made 70 drawings. In 1970 she designed the Danish Christmas seal, and in 1985 the Danish postage stamp for the 40th anniversary of Denmark's liberation from five years of Nazi occupation. She also does beautiful freehand needlework and has made bishop's copes for Danish Lutheran Church ceremonies. In 1987 the queen again delighted her countrymen by sketching the costumes and properties for a television presentation of a ballet based on Hans Christian Andersen's fairy tale, "The Shepherdess and the Chimney Sweep."

Thorkild Hansen, the Danish author, has described Margrethe as a

> long, wonderful woman who just cannot contain herself and cannot remain quiet. Difficult to shock, but easy to hurt, obliging but totally without a trace of coquettishness, soon in conversation with people, and with a direct glance serious and then cheerful again with a quick response. She seems honest, unaffected, direct, very vocal, often self-ironic with a tendency toward sarcasm. She is protective and authoritarian at the same time, anything but familiar but more influenced by family than most. And under that maternal air the stirring of restlessness, a vehemence, an intellect, a searching for answers.

Every August the press has snapped endearing pictures of the royal family at Cahors, the region in southern France where Prince Henrik spent his childhood and where he has restored a small vineyard estate. Often the queen can be seen buying goat's milk cheese in the village.

The French have a special affection for them. Recently in Paris *Le Figaro* declared: "Margrethe can do anything and knows everything. A Viking queen, a prince consort from Gascony, two handsome sons, who are doing their military service. That is the symbol of traditional values and Danish unity." So secure is Margrethe's position on the throne that few Danes ever debate the value of the monarchy.

Beatrix
Queen of the Netherlands, 1980–

"For the sake of the Kingdom of the Netherlands, for the sake of all of us who are Dutch, it is better that my place should be taken by someone new and vigorous." Queen Juliana spoke with a full heart on April 30, 1980, when she formally abdicated in favor of her daughter, Beatrix.

On January 30, 1938, a 51-gun salute, signaling a royal female, had proclaimed the birth of Beatrix to Princess Juliana and Prince Bernhard of Lippe-Biesterfeld at Soestdijk Palace in Baarn. Sixteen months later, the baby had a new sister, Irene.

Beatrix was only two when the Nazis invaded the Netherlands. Within a few days, on Queen Wilhelmina's orders, Juliana, Bernhard, and the tiny princesses fled to England to stay temporarily in Gloucestershire. The queen herself arrived in England three days later. In June Juliana and her daughters boarded a Dutch cruiser for Halifax, Nova Scotia, while Queen Wilhelmina and Prince Bernhard remained behind in London with the Dutch government-in-exile. Juliana headed for Ottawa on the invitation of one of Beatrix's godmothers, Princess Alice, wife of the Earl of Athlone, new governor-general of Canada.

Beginning in 1941, Bernhard joined his family from time to time. Early in 1943, the lively blond Trix, as she was called, welcomed a second sister, Margriet. Trix and Irene went to nursery and primary school in Ottawa and during vacations accompanied their mother on visits to the United States. Finally in April 1945 the entire royal family was reunited in a liberated Netherlands. By autumn their parents sent Trix and Irene to Kees Boeke's highly progressive Werkplaats school in Bilthoven. At 12 precocious Beatrix entered the grammar school in Baarn.

The years ahead prepared her for her role as queen. In 1956 she was confirmed as a member of the Dutch Reformed Church and installed by her mother as a member of the Council of State. From then on she had her own income and could act as regent in case of necessity. To honor her installation, the Dutch people gave the princess, a fine sailor, with a sloop named the *Green Dragon*; Beatrix, showing talent as a painter and sculptor, designed its interior.

Also in 1956, she enrolled at her mother's alma mater, the University of Leiden, to study sociology, parliamentary history, law, economics, and international affairs. Daughter of one of the richest families in the world, Beatrix led as normal a student life as possible, sharing a house with a few girls and bicycling to classes. She passed the final examination in law in 1961. Studies over, she had more leisure for sailing and riding with her father, who had trained her to be an excellent equestrienne.

By this time the heiress apparent had made two official overseas tours, to Surinam and the Netherlands Antilles in 1958, and the following year to the United States, where New York gave her a ticker tape parade. Beatrix entered the United States through the harbor discovered 350 years earlier by the English sea captain, Henry Hudson, sailing for the Dutch East India Company. As she joined in anniversary celebrations, her hosts found the tall, auburn-haired young woman direct, witty, and charming.

In 1962 she set out on a long trip to Iran, Palestine, India, Thailand, the Philippines, and Hong Kong, where she received word that her grandmother, former Queen Wilhelmina, had died. She flew home for the funeral, but resumed her tour in 1963, traveling to Japan and once more to the United States for an official visit to United Nations headquarters.

On returning to the Netherlands, she moved into her own residence, the 17th century Drakensteyn Castle near Baarn. Ceremonial duties crowded in on her, but she found time to sponsor a European equivalent of President John F. Kennedy's Peace Corps.

Soon her striking sister Irene stirred up a political controversy. Irene fell in love with Prince Carlos Hugo de Bourbon Parma, Carlist pretender to the Spanish throne and member of the Falange (fascist party). To prepare for her wedding, she became a Roman Catholic. Members of the Dutch royal house who marry without permission of the Estates General forfeit their right of succession. Knowing that she would not get authorization, Irene did not ask for it. Her family did not attend the wedding in Rome in 1964, but was always happy to welcome the young couple at Soestdijk Palace.

That same year, at another wedding, Beatrix met 37-year-old Claus von Amsberg, a member of the minor German nobility and a diplomat attached to the West German government. The Dutch still carried bitter memories of the Nazi occupation, and when newspapers reported the romance, a storm broke over von Amsberg's war record.

The actual facts proved far from sinister. While in secondary school he had automatically joined the Hitler Youth. For two months he had served in Adolf Hitler's Labor Group and then been allowed to return to school. For nine months in 1944 and 1945 he had been with the Reserve Armored Vehicle Division, and for three months in 1945 with the 90th Panzer Division in Italy. He had not, however, participated in actual combat, and after Americans captured him he had been sent to a prisoner of war camp, where he acted as driver and interpreter. On his release, Claus von Amsberg was cleared by a denazification court established by the Allies.

Although Beatrix and her family considered Claus free of the taint of Nazism, many Dutchmen regarded him with suspicion. At a press conference, Beatrix faced the issue squarely: "We realize there are people who have genuine rights to be unhappy about our engagement. We are not shocked by the fact that there is a controversy. This is a democratic country, and everybody has the right to speak out." After intensive investigation, the Parliament decided that von Amsberg had not been a Nazi sympathizer, and therefore it gave its approval to the marriage.

New wrangling arose when the couple decided to hold the ceremony in Amsterdam rather than in The Hague, the traditional site of royal weddings. Because of the bridegroom's German background, several municipal councillors and Amsterdam's rabbis announced they would boycott the ceremony. But worse was to come. On March 10, 1966, as Beatrix and her bridegroom rode in the Golden Coach, first to a civil ceremony at the town hall and then to religious rites in the cathedral, smoke bombs exploded all around. Soon violent demonstrations took place in various quarters, but the authorities considered them to be protests against political and social conditions.

Bride and bridegroom demonstrated their interest in social welfare by donating their money gift from the country to four national associations of parents of handicapped children and for additional medical facilities for the Dutch Red Cross ship, the *Henri Dunant*. They also gave money to handicapped young people in Surinam and the Netherlands Antilles.

After the couple returned from a Mexican honeymoon, the bridegroom adopted the Dutch spelling of his name and became Prince Claus of the Netherlands, Jonkheer von Amsberg. Quickly he gained respect and loyalty by learning to speak accent-free Dutch and taking a deep interest, like his wife, in Third World problems.

In 1967 the entire nation enthusiastically celebrated the birth of the first male heir to the Dutch throne since 1849. Prince Willem Alexander was followed by two more sons, Prince Johan Friso in 1968 and Prince Constantine in 1969.

During the next decade, her children's upbringing, social welfare, and cultural matters claimed much of Beatrix's attention. With Prince Claus she also made extensive overseas trips in 1970, 1973, 1976, 1977, and 1978. In spite of her busy schedule, rumor ran, she felt somewhat restive when her mother did not abdicate—as expected—on her 65th birthday in 1974. Again in 1976, during the investigation into Prince Bernhard's alleged involvement with Lockheed, talk surfaced that Juliana might be stepping down. But she stayed on. Meanwhile Prince Claus carefully broadened his duties as a member of the Town and Planning Council and the National Advisory Council on Development. From 1970 to 1980 he served as chairman of the National Committee for Development of

Beatrix. The Embassy of the Netherlands, Washington, D.C.

Strategy. He stood behind a national campaign, "Kom over de brug" (Come over the bridge) to raise money for 700 projects in 80 countries.

Juliana finally abdicated in 1980. As in 1948, a mother and daughter appeared on the balcony of Dam Palace in Amsterdam in a shower of orange confetti that honored the house of Orange-Nassau.

Beside Beatrix stood Prince Claus and their lively three sons. Then from the palace the royal party moved on to the Niewe Kirk (New Church), where Beatrix, wearing a velvet, ermine-lined robe, was inaugurated queen before a joint session of the Estates General. From henceforth April 30 was celebrated as her official birthday.

Elsewhere in the city, violent protests against Amsterdam's critical housing situation punctuated the pomp and pageantry. Thus the new monarch and her consort felt compelled to spend part of their first official day at the Amsterdam Clinic visiting those injured in street riots.

In the following weeks, they came to The Hague, Rotterdam, and the provincial capitals and then sailed to the Netherlands Antilles and Surinam. Only the year before, Beatrix had gone there to observe the social and economic changes that had taken place since the 1950s.

Well trained, the new sovereign settled easily into her role. It resembles that of Elizabeth II and Margrethe II. While dutifully signing all legislation, she does not play a direct role in government. She appoints ministers on the recommendation of a *formateur*, usually the person who becomes prime minister in a new government, which is almost always a coalition. The ministers form the Council of Ministers or Cabinet, whose main duty is to coordinate government policy. As head of state, the queen is also president of the Council of State, the highest advisory body in the country. From the beginning, Beatrix has taken a keen interest in parliamentary affairs.

Two years before Beatrix's investiture, a Kingdom Working Party had been appointed to advise on the future constitutional framework for the Netherlands Antilles, which had enjoyed autonomy in internal affairs since the Charter for the Kingdom of the Netherlands was promulgated in 1954. A Round Table Conference was called in 1983, and Aruba expressed its wish to become independent. On January 1, 1986, Beatrix signed documents whereby the island withdrew from the Antilles constitutional union and acquired its own separate status within the Kingdom of the Netherlands.

Adviser, mediator, unifying figure in a government of many parties, Beatrix is determined to be an active ruler like her mother and grandmother. When necessary, her countrymen say, she can show the steel of Wilhelmina. It came to the fore in 1987 when she overcame a severe bout of meningitis. Prince Claus also had health problems.

Understandably, the Netherlands is proud of its succession of mother-daughter queens over almost a century. No other country can boast such a trio.

Selected Bibliography

Juana II, Queen of Navarre

Bard, Rachel. *Navarra. The Durable Kingdom*. Reno: University of Nevada Press, 1982.
Claveria, Carlos. *Historia del Reino de Navarra*. Pamplona: Editorial Gomez, 1971.
Fawtier, Robert. *The Capetian Kings of France* (tr. by Lionel Butler). London, New York: Macmillan, 1960.
Lacarra, D. José Maria. *Historia del Reino de Navarra en la Edad Media*, Pamplona: Caja de Ahorros de Navarra, 1976.
Tuchman, Barbara. *A Distant Mirror*. New York: Knopf, 1978.

Giovanna I, Queen of Naples

Baddeley, W. St. C. *Queen Joanna I of Naples*. London: Heinemann, 1893.
————. *Robert the Wise and His Heirs*. London: Heinemann, 1897.
Hall, Louisa J. *Joanna of Naples*. Boston: Hilliard, Gray & Co., 1838.
Steele, Francesca M. *The Beautiful Queen, Joanna I of Naples*. New York: Dodd, Mead, 1910.
Trease, Geoffrey. *The Condottieri*. New York: Holt, Rinehart & Winston, 1974.
Tuchman, Barbara. *A Distant Mirror*. New York: Knopf, 1978.

Maria, Queen of Hungary

Bodolai, Zoltan. *The Timeless Nation*. Sydney, Australia: Hungaria Publishing Co., 1978.
Fugedi, Erik. *Könyörülj, bánom, könyörülj*. Budapest: Helikon Kiado, 1986.
Janos, Horvath. *A magyarok krónikája*. Budapest: Bibliotheca Historica, 1976.
Kellogg, Charlotte. *Jadwiga, Poland's Great Queen*. New York: Macmillan, 1931.
Sinor, Denis. *History of Hungary*. Westport, Conn.: Greenwood, 1976.
Varga, Domokos. *Hungary in Greatness and Decline*. Stone Mountain, Ga.: Hungarian Cultural Foundation, 1982.

Jadwiga, Queen of Poland

Gardner, Monica Mary. *Queen Jadwiga of Poland*. Dublin: Browne & Nolan, 1944.
Kellogg, Charlotte. "Jadwiga" in *Great Men and Women of Poland*, (ed. by Stephen P. Mizwa.) New York: The Kosciuszko Foundation, 1967.
————. *Jadwiga, Poland's Great Queen*. New York: Macmillan, 1931.

Margrethe, Regent of Denmark, Norway, and Sweden

Erslev, Kristian. *Dronning Margrethe og Kalmarunionens Grundlaeggelse.* Copenhagen: Jacob Erslevs Forlag, 1882.
Etting, Vivian. *Margrete den Første.* Copenhagen: Palle Fogtdal, 1986.
Koht, Halvdan. *Drottning Margarete och Kalmarunionen.* Stockholm: Natur och Kultur, 1956.
Linton, Michael. *Drottning Margareta fuldmäktig fru och rätt husbonde.* Stockholm: Akademiförlagt, 1971.
Lönnroth, Erik. *"Unionsdokumenten i Kalmar 1397."* Scandia. Department of History, University of Lund, Sweden, 1958.
Moberg, Vilhelm. "Nordens största regent" in *Min Sverigeshistoria.* Stockholm: Norstedt & Söner, 1970.
Scott, Franklin D. "A Saint and a Queen: Two Indomitable Figures of the Fourteenth Century" in *Scandinavian Studies.* (ed. by Carl F. Bayerschmidt and Erik J. Friis.) Seattle: University of Washington Press, American Scandinavian Foundation, 1965.

Giovanna II, Queen of Naples

Baddeley, W. St. C. *Queen Joanna I of Naples.* London: Heinemann, 1893.
Hall, Louisa J. *Joanna of Naples.* Boston: Hilliard, Gray & Co., 1838.
Trease, Geoffrey. *The Condottieri.* New York: Holt, Rinehart & Winston, 1974.

Blanca, Queen of Navarre

Bard, Rachel. *Navarra. The Durable Kingdom.* Reno: University of Nevada Press, 1982.
Clavaria, Carlos. *Historia del Reino de Navarra.* Pamplona: Editorial Gomez, 1971.
Lacarra, D. José Maria. *Historia del Reino de Navarra en la Edad Media.* Pamplona: Caja de Ahorros de Navarra, 1976.
Miller, Townsend. *Henry IV of Castile.* Philadelphia: Lippincott, 1972.
Prescott, William H. *History of the Reign of Ferdinand and Isabella.* Philadelphia: Lippincott, 1904 (original copyright 1838), vol. 1. (Abridged version, ed. by C. Harvey Gardner. Carbondale: Southern Illinois University Press, 1962.)

Isabella I, Queen of Castile

Elliott, J.H. *Imperial Spain: 1469–1716.* New York: St. Martin's Press, 1964.
Fernandez-Modesto, Felipe. *Ferdinand and Isabella.* New York: Taplinger, 1975.
Jackson, Gabriel. *The Making of Medieval Spain.* New York: Harcourt Brace Jovanovich, 1972.
McKendrick, Melveena. *The Horizon Concise History of Spain.* New York: American Heritage Publishing Co., 1972.
Mariejal, J.H. *The Spain of Ferdinand and Isabella.* (tr. by Benjamin Keen.) New Brunswick, N.J.: Rutgers University Press, 1961.
Miller, Townsend. *The Castles and the Crown.* New York: Coward-McCann, 1963.
———. *Henry IV of Castile.* Philadelphia: Lippincott, 1972.

Prescott, William F. *History of the Reign of Ferdinand and Isabella*. Philadelphia: Lippincott, 1904 (original copyright, 1838), vols. 1–4. (Abridged version ed. by C. Harvey Gardner. Carbondale: Southern Illinois University Press, 1962.)

Leonor, Queen of Navarre

Bard, Rachel. *Navarra. The Durable Kingdom*. Reno: University of Nevada Press, 1982.

Claveria, Carlos. *Historia del Reino de Navarra*. Pamplona: Editorial Gomez, 1971.

Lacarra, D. José Maria. *Historia del Reino de Navarra en la Edad Media*. Pamplona: Caja de Ahorros de Navarra, 1976.

Prescott, William H. *History of the Reign of Ferdinand and Isabella*. Philadelphia: Lippincott, 1904, vol. 1.

Catalina, Queen of Navarre

Bard, Rachel. *Navarra. The Durable Kingdom*. Reno: University of Nevada Press, 1982.

Claveria, Carlos. *Historia del Reino de Navarra*. Pamplona: Editorial Gomez, 1971.

Lacarra, D. José Maria. *Historia del Reino de Navarra en la Edad Media*. Pamplona: Caja de Ahorros de Navarra, 1976.

Prescott, William H. *History of the Reign of Ferdinand and Isabella*. Philadelphia: Lippincott, 1904 (original copyright, 1838) vols. 1, 4. (Abridged edition ed. by C. Harvey Gardner. Carbondale: Southern Illinois University Press, 1962.)

Juana, Queen of Castile

Altayo, Isabel, and Nogues, Paloma. *Juana I, Reina Cautiva*. Madrid: Silex, 1985.

Miller, Townsend. *The Castles and the Crown*. New York: Coward-McCann, 1963.

Prawdin, Michael, pseud. Charal. *The Mad Queen of Spain* (tr. by Eden and Cedar Paul). Boston: Houghton-Mifflin, 1939.

Prescott, William H. *History of the Reign of Ferdinand and Isabella*. Philadelphia: Lippincott, 1904 (original copyright, 1838), vol. 4.

Schoonover, Lawrence L. *The Prisoner of Tordesillas*. Boston: Little, Brown, 1958.

Mary, Queen of Scotland

Black, J.B. *The Reign of Elizabeth, 1558–1603*. Oxford: Oxford University Press, 1936, rev. 1959.

Cowan, Ian B. *The Enigma of Mary Stuart*. London: Gollancz, 1971.

Donaldson, Gordon. *Mary Queen of Scots*. London: English Universities Press, 1974.

Fraser, Antonia. *Mary Queen of Scots*. London: Weidenfeld & Nicolson, 1969.

Linklater, Eric. *Mary, Queen of Scots* (reprint of 1933 edition). Philadelphia: Century Bookbindery, 1980.

Marshall, Rosalind K. *Queen of Scots*. London: Her Majesty's Stationery Office, 1987.

Spender, Stephen. *Mary Stuart*. New York: Ticknor and Fields, 1980.

Steel, David, and Steel, Judy. *Mary Stuart's Scotland. The Landscapes, Life, and Legends of Mary, Queen of Scots*. New York: Crown, 1987.

Strong, Roy, and Oman, Julia. *Mary Queen of Scots*. London: Seeker & Warburg, 1973.

Mary I, Queen of England and Ireland

Erickson, Carolly. *Bloody Mary*. Garden City, New York: Doubleday, 1978.

Prescott, H.F.M. *A Spanish Tudor. The Life of Bloody Mary*. London: Constable, 1940.

Ridley, Jasper. *The Life and Times of Mary Tudor*. London: Weidenfeld & Nicolson, 1973.

Simms, Eric A. *Mary Tudor and Wyatt the Younger*. London: F. Muller, 1964.

Waldman, Milton. *The Lady Mary*. New York: Collins, 1972.

Jeanne d'Albret, Queen of Navarre

Buisseret, David. *Henry IV*. London: Allen & Unwin, 1984.

Claveria, Carlos. *Historia del Reino de Navarra*. Pamplona: Editorial Gomez, 1971.

Mahoney, Irene. *Royal Cousin*. Garden City, New York: Doubleday, 1970.

Roelker, Nancy Layman. *Queen of Navarre, Jeanne d'Albret*. Cambridge: Belknap Press of Harvard University Press, 1968.

Elizabeth I, Queen of England and Scotland

Black, J.G. *The Reign of Elizabeth, 1558–1603*. Oxford: Oxford University Press, 1936, rev. 1959.

Erickson, Carolly. *The First Elizabeth*. New York: Summit Books, 1984.

Harrison, G.B. *The Letters of Queen Elizabeth I*. London: Cassell, 1935.

Jenkins, Elizabeth. *Elizabeth the Great*. New York: Coward-McCann, 1958.

Johnson, Paul. *Elizabeth: A Study in Power and Intellect*. London: Weidenfeld & Nicolson, 1974.

Luke, Mary M. *A Crown for Elizabeth*. New York: Coward-McCann, 1970.

————. *Gloriana: The Years of Elizabeth I*. New York: Coward, McCann, and Geoghegan, 1973.

MacCaffrey, Wallace. *The Shaping of the Elizabethan Regime*. Princeton: Princeton University Press, 1968.

Neale, J.E. *Queen Elizabeth I*. London: Jonathan Cape, 1934.

Plowden, Alison. *Marriage with My Kingdom*. Briarcliff Manor, New York: Stein and Day, 1978.

Rowse, A.L. and Harrison, G.B. *Queen Elizabeth and Her Subjects*. London: Allen & Unwin, 1935.

Strachey, Lytton. *Elizabeth and Essex*. New York: Harcourt Brace Jovanovich, 1969 (reprinted from 1928 edition).

Williams, Neville. *Elizabeth the First, Queen of England*. New York: E.P. Dutton, 1967.

Catherine de Médicis, Regent of France

Héritier, Jean. *Catherine de Médici* (tr. by Charlotte Haldane). New York: St. Martin's Press, 1963.

Roeder, Ralph. *Catherine de Medici and the Lost Revolution*. Garden City, New York: Garden City Publishing Company, 1939.

Strage, Mark. *Women of Power. The Life and Times of Catherine de Medici*. New York: Harcourt Brace Jovanovich, 1976.

Vance, Marguerite. *Dark Eminence. Catherine de Medici and Her Children*. New York: E.P. Dutton, 1961.

Van Dyke, Paul. *Catherine de Médicis*. New York: Scribner's, 1922. 2 vols.

Waldman, Milton. *Biography of a Family*. Boston: Houghton Mifflin, 1936.

Watson, Francis. *The Life and Times of Catherine de Medici*. New York: D. Appleton-Century, 1935.

Yates, Francis A. *The Valois Tapestries*. London: Warburg Institute of London, 1959.

Young, George. *The Medici*. New York: The Modern Library, 1930.

Kristina, Queen of Sweden

Christina, Queen of Sweden. National Museum Exhibition Catalog. Stockholm: National Museum, 1966.

Goldsmith, Margaret. *Christina of Sweden: A Psychological Biography*. Garden City, New York: Doubleday, 1934.

Lewis, Paul. *Queen of Caprice*. New York: Holt, Rinehart & Winston, 1962.

Masson, Georgina. *Queen Christina*. New York: Farrar, Straus and Giroux, 1968.

Stolpe, Sven. *Christina of Sweden*. (ed. by Sir Alec Randall.) New York: Macmillan, 1966.

Weibull, Curt. *Christina of Sweden*. Stockholm: Svenska Bogförlaget/Bonnier, 1966.

Sophia, Regent of Russia

Almedingen, E.M. *The Romanovs*. London: Bodley Head, 1966.

Bergamini, John D. *The Tragic Dynasty*. New York: G.P. Putnam's Sons, 1969.

Grey, *Peter the Great. Emperor of All Russia*. Philadelphia: Lippincott, 1960.

Kluchevsky, V.O. *Peter the Great* (tr. by Liliana Archibald). New York: St. Martin's Press, 1959.

Koslow, Jules. *The Kremlin*. New York: Thomas Nelson & Sons, 1958.

Mazour, Anatole G. *The Rise and Fall of the Romanovs*. New York: Van Nostrand, 1960.

Mary II, Queen of England, Scotland, and Ireland

Chapman, Hester W. *Mary II, Queen of England*. London: Jonathan Cape, 1953.

Hamilton, Elizabeth. *William's Mary*. New York: Taplinger, 1971.

Van der Zee, Henri and Barbara. *William and Mary*. New York: Knopf, 1973, reprinted 1976.

Anne, Queen of Great Britain and Ireland

Curtis, Gila. *Life and Times of Queen Anne*. London: Weidenfeld & Nicolson, 1972.
Green, David. *Queen Anne*. New York: Scribner's, 1970.
_____. *Sarah, Duchess of Marlborough*. New York: Scribner's, 1967.
Gregg, Edward. *Queen Anne*. Boston: Routledge & Kegan Paul, 1984.
Hodges, Margaret. *Lady Queen Anne*. New York: Farrar, Straus and Giroux, 1969.
Sutherland, James R. *Background for Queen Anne* (reprint of 1939 edition). Folcraft, Pa.: Folcroft, 1986.

Ulrika Eleonora, Queen of Sweden

Hatton, R. M. *Charles XII of Sweden*. London: Weidenfeld & Nicolson; New York: Weybright and Talley, 1968.
Lundh-Eriksson, Nanna. *Den glömda dronningen. Karl XII's söster Ulrika Eleonora D.Y. och hennes tid*. Norrtalje, Sweden: Affärstryckeriet, 1976.

Catherine I, Empress of Russia

Bain, R.W. *Peter the Great. Emperor of Russia*. London: Archibald Constable, 1902.
Graham, Stephen. *Peter the Great*. London: Ernest Benn and New York: Simon and Schuster, 1929.
Grey, Ian. *Peter the Great. Emperor of All Russia*. Philadelphia: Lippincott, 1960.
Kluchevsky, V.O. *Peter the Great* (tr. by Liliana Archibald). New York: St. Martin's Press, 1959.
Longworth, Philip. *The Three Empresses. Catherine I, Anna, and Elizabeth of Russia*. New York: Holt, Rinehart & Winston, 1972.
Onassis, Jacqueline, ed. *In the Russian Style*. New York: Viking, 1976.
Strong, Philip D. *Marta of Muscovy*. Garden City, New York: Doubleday, 1945.

Anna Ivanovna, Empress of Russia

Curtiss, Mina. *A Forgotten Empress, Anna Ivanovna and Her Era*. New York: Ungar, 1974.
Longworth, Philip. *The Three Empresses. Catherine I, Anna, and Elizabeth of Russia*. New York: Holt, Rinehart & Winston, 1972.
Mazour, Anatole J. *The Rise and Fall of the Romanovs*. Princeton: Van Nostrand, 1960.
Onassis, Jacqueline, ed. *In the Russian Style*. New York: Viking, 1976.

Maria Theresa, Archduchess of Austria, Queen of Hungary and Bohemia

Crankshaw, Edward. *Maria Theresa*. London: Longmans, Green, 1969.
Gooch, George P. *Maria Theresa and Other Studies*. Hamden, Conn.: Archon Books, 1951.
Khevenhüller-Metsch, J. J. *Aus der Zeit Maria Theresias*. Wien: Holzhausen, 1907–1925, 7 vols.

Mahan, J. Alexander. *Maria Theresa of Austria*. New York: Crowell, 1932.
Morris, Constance L. *Maria Theresa: The Last Conservative*. London: Eyre and Spottiswoode, 1937.
Pick, Robert. *The Empress Maria Theresa. The Earlier Years, 1717–1757*. New York: Harper & Row, 1966.

Elizabeth, Empress of Russia

Almedingen, E. M. *The Romanovs*. London: Bodley Head, 1966.
Bain, R.N. *The Daughter of Peter the Great*. New York: E.P. Dutton, 1900.
Coughlan, Robert. *Elizabeth and Catherine. Empresses of All the Russias*. New York: G.P. Putnam's Sons, 1974.
Kaplan, Herbert Harold. *Russia and the Outbreak of the Seven Years War*. New York: Praeger, 1970.
Longworth, Philip. *The Three Empresses. Catherine I, Anna, and Elizabeth of Russia*. New York: Holt, Rinehart, & Winston, 1972.
Mazour, Anatole G. *The Rise and Fall of the Romanovs*. Princeton: Van Nostrand, 1960.
Rice, Tamara Talbot. *Elizabeth, Empress of Russia*. London: Weidenfeld & Nicolson, 1970.

Catherine II, Empress of Russia

Almedingen, E.M. *Catherine, Empress of Russia*. New York: Dodd, Mead, 1961.
Anthony, Katherine. *Catherine the Great*. New York: Knopf, 1925.
Catherine II. *Memoirs* (ed. by Dominique Maroger, tr. by Moura Budberg). London: Hamish Hamilton, 1955; New York: Macmillan, 1961.
Coughlan, Robert. *Elizabeth and Catherine. Empresses of All the Russias*. New York: G.P. Putnam's Sons, 1974.
Cronin, Vincent. *Catherine, Empress of All the Russias*. New York: William Morrow, 1978.
Gooch, George P. *Catherine the Great and Other Studies*. London: Longmans, Green, 1954.
Grey, Ian. *Catherine the Great; Autocrat and Empress of All Russia*. Philadelphia: Lippincott, 1962.
Haslip, Joan. *Catherine the Great*. New York: G.P. Putnam's Sons, 1977.
Oldenbourg, Zoe. *Catherine the Great* (tr. by Anne Carter). New York: Random House, 1965.
Thompson, Gladys. *Catherine the Great and the Expansion of Russia*. New York: Macmillan, 1950.

Maria I, Queen of Portugal

Harding, Bertita. *Amazon Throne*. Indianapolis: Bobbs-Merrill, 1941.
Livermore, H.V. *A New History of Portugal*. London: Cambridge University Press, 1976. (2nd ed.).

Maria II, Queen of Portugal

Harding, Bertita. *Amazon Throne.* Indianapolis: Bobbs-Merrill, 1941.
Livermore, H.W. *A New History of Portugal.* London: Cambridge University Press, 1976. (2nd ed.)

Maria Cristina (1), Regent of Spain

Aronson, Theo. *Royal Vendetta.* Indianapolis: Bobbs-Merrill, 1966.
Jones, Parry E. *The Spanish Marriages 1841–1846.* London: Macmillan, 1936.
Petrie, Sir Charles. *The Spanish Royal House.* London: Geoffrey Bles, 1958.
Polnay, Peter de. *A Queen of Spain. Isabella II.* London: Hollis & Carter, 1962.
Sencourt, Robert. *The Spanish Crown, 1808–1931.* New York: Charles Scribner's Sons, 1932.

Isabella II, Queen of Spain

Aronson, Theo. *Royal Vendetta.* Indianapolis: Bobbs-Merrill, 1966.
Boetzkes, Ottilie G. *The Little Queen, Isabella II of Spain.* New York: Exposition Books, 1966.
Gribble, Francis. *The Tragedy of Isabella II.* London: Chapman & Hall, 1913.
Jones, Parry E. *The Spanish Marriages 1841–1846.* London: Macmillan, 1936.
Petrie, Sir Charles. *The Spanish Royal House.* London: Geoffrey Bles, 1958.
Sencourt, Robert. *The Spanish Crown 1808–1931.* New York: Charles Scribner's Sons, 1932.

Victoria, Queen of Great Britain and Ireland, Empress of India

Bolitho, Hector. *The Reign of Queen Victoria.* London: Coldene, 1949.
Hennessy, James. *Queen Victoria at Windsor and Balmoral.* London: Allen & Unwin, 1959.
Hibbert, Christopher. *Queen Victoria in Her Letters.* New York: Viking, 1985.
Longford, Elizabeth. *Victoria R.I.* London: Weidenfeld & Nicolson, 1964. (Published in the United States as *Queen Victoria. Born to Succeed.* New York: Harper & Row, 1964.)
Plowden, Alison. *The Young Victoria.* Briarcliff, New York: Stein and Day, 1981.
Sitwell, Edith. *Victoria of England.* London: Faber & Faber, 1949.
Strachey, Lytton. *Queen Victoria.* London: Chatto & Windus, 1921. (Modern Classic Series, New York: Harcourt Brace, 1949.)
Weintraub, Stanley. *Victoria: An Intimate Biography.* New York: E.P. Dutton, 1987.
Woodham-Smith, Cecil. *Queen Victoria.* London: Hamish Hamilton, 1972.

Maria Cristina (2), Regent of Spain

Aronson, Theo. *Royal Vendetta.* Indianapolis: Bobbs-Merrill, 1966.
Cavanellas, Julian Cortes. *Maria Cristina de Austria.* Madrid: Edicion Aspes, S.A., 1944.
Graham, Evelyn. *The Life Story of Alfonso XII.* London: Herbert Jenkins, Ltd., 1930.
Pelapil, Vicente R. *Alfonso XIII.* New York: Twayne, 1969.
Petrie, Sir Charles. *King Alfonso XIII and His Age.* London: Chapman & Hall, 1963.
————. *The Spanish Royal House.* London: Geoffrey Bles, 1958.
Sencourt, Robert. *King Alfonso.* London: Faber and Faber, 1942.
————. *The Spanish Crown.* New York: Charles Scribner's Sons, 1932.

Wilhelmina, Queen of the Netherlands

Barnouw, Adriaan J. *Holland and Queen Wilhelmina.* New York: Charles Scribner's Sons, 1923.
Hatch, Alden. *Bernhard, Prince of the Netherlands.* New York: Doubleday, 1963.
Hoffman, William. *Queen Juliana.* New York: Harcourt Brace Jovanovich, 1979.
Two Queens. Wilhelmina, Juliana 1890–1948. Netherlands Information Bureau, 1948.
H.R.H. Wilhelmina, Princess of the Netherlands. *Lonely but Not Alone* (tr. by John Peereboom). London: Hutchinson, 1959.

Marie-Adélaïde, Grand Duchess of Luxembourg

Cooper-Prichard, A.H. *History of the Grand Duchy of Luxembourg* (tr. by Arthur Herchen, 5th ed. by N. Margue and J. Meyers). Luxembourg: P. Linden, 1950.
Newcomer, James. *The Grand Duchy of Luxembourg.* Lanham, Md.: University Press of America, 1984.
O'Shaughnessy, Edith. *Marie Adelaide. Grand Duchess of Luxemburg.* New York: Harrison Smith, 1932.
Trausch, Gilbert. *Le Luxembourg à l'époque contemporaire (du partage de 1839 à nos jours),* vol. IV. In *Manuel d'histoire luxembourgeoise.* Luxembourg: Editions Bourg-Bourger, 1973–1977.

Charlotte, Grand Duchess of Luxembourg

Cooper-Prichard, A.H. *History of the Grand Duchy of Luxembourg* (tr. by Arthur Herchen, 5th ed. by N. Margue and J. Meyers). Luxembourg: P. Linden, 1950.
Newcomer, James. *The Grand Duchy of Luxembourg.* Lanham, Md.: University Press of America, 1984.
O'Shaughnessy, Edith. *Marie Adelaide, Grand Duchess of Luxemburg.* New York: Harrison Smith, 1932.
Trausch, Gilbert. *Le Luxembourg à l'époque contemporaire (du partage de 1839 à nos jours).* In Vol. IV of *Manuel d'histoire luxembourgeoise.* Luxembourg: Editions Bourg-Bourger, 1973–1977.

Juliana, Queen of the Netherlands

Hatch, Alden. *Bernhard, Prince of the Netherlands.* New York: Doubleday, 1963.
Hoffman, William. *Queen Juliana.* New York: Harcourt Brace Jovanovich, 1979.
Schenk, Magdalene. *Juliana, Queen of the Netherlands.* Lochem, Holland: Uitgeversmaatschappij De Tijdstroom. n.d.
Two Queens. Wilhelmina, Juliana. Netherlands Information Bureau, 1958.
H.R.H. Wilhelmina, Princess of the Netherlands. *Lonely but Not Alone* (tr. by John Peereboom). London: Hutchinson, 1959.

Elizabeth II, Queen of Great Britain and Northern Ireland

Bocca, Geoffrey. *Elizabeth and Philip.* New York: Holt, 1953.
Crawford, Marion. *Elizabeth the Queen. The Story of Britain's New Sovereign.* Westport, Conn.: Greenwood, 1986 (reprint of 1952 edition).
Lacey, Robert. *Majesty. Elizabeth and the House of Windsor.* London: Hutchinson, 1977.
Laird, Dorothy. *How the Queen Reigns: An Authentic Study of the Queen's Personality and Life Work.* London: Hodder & Stoughton, 1959, New York: World Publishing Co., 1959.
Longford, Elizabeth. *The Queen. The Life of Elizabeth II.* New York: Knopf, 1983.
Morrow, Ann. *The Queen.* New York: William Morrow, 1983.
Plumb, J.H., and Wheldon, H. *The Reign of Elizabeth II.* London: BBC Publications, 1981.

Margrethe II, Queen of Denmark

Hansen, Ernst Fr. *Margrethe af Denmark. Fra tronfølger til dronning* (available in English as *Margrethe of Denmark. From Successor to the Throne to Queen.*) Fredericia: Frimodt, 1973.
Hansen, Thorkild. *Samtale med Dronning Margrethe.* Copenhagen: Forum, 1979.
Palsbo, Susanne. *Princesse Margrethe. Danmarks tronfølger.* Copenhagen: Rasmus Naver, 1958.
Thomas, Viktor. *Dronningens travlt år. Et tilbageblik på 1982.* Copenhagen: Peter la Cour, 1982.
_____. *Ti år på tronen: 1972–1982. En jublilaeumsbog om Dronning Margrethe.* Copenhagen: Peter la Cour, 1982.

Beatrix, Queen of the Netherlands

Hatch, Alden. *Bernhard, Prince of the Netherlands.* New York: Doubleday, 1963.
Hoffman, William. *Queen Juliana.* New York: Harcourt Brace Jovanovich, 1979.

Massie, Robert K., and Finestone, Jeffrey. *The Last Courts of Europe.* New York: Vendome Press, 1982.

Index

271

M